March, 1986

With ~~T~~ of our
time together and warmest
wishes

Jeff

Building Democracy in Ireland

Building Democracy in Ireland

Political Order and Cultural Integration in a Newly Independent Nation

Jeffrey Prager

University of California, Los Angeles

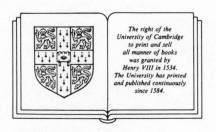

The right of the
University of Cambridge
to print and sell
all manner of books
was granted by
Henry VIII in 1534.
The University has printed
and published continuously
since 1584.

Cambridge University Press

Cambridge
London   New York   New Rochelle
Melbourne   Sydney

Published by the Press Syndicate of the University of Cambridge
The Pitt Building, Trumpington Street, Cambridge CB2 1RP
32 East 57th Street, New York, NY 10022, USA
10 Stamford Road, Oakleigh, Melbourne 3166, Australia

© Cambridge University Press 1986

First published in 1986

Printed in the United States of America

Library of Congress Cataloging-in-Publication Data
Prager, Jeffrey, 1948–
Building democracy in Ireland.
Bibliography: p.
1. Ireland – Politics and government – 1922–1949.
2. Ireland – Constitutional history.   3. Representative
government and representation – Ireland – History – 20th
century.   I. Title.
DA963.P73   1985   306'.2'09415   85–7862
ISBN 0 521 26813 3

British Library Cataloging-in-Publication applied for.

TO THE MEMORY OF MY FATHER, THEODORE PRAGER

Contents

Preface   *page* ix

Part 1   Democracy in Ireland: Theoretical and Empirical Problems

1   Introduction: Theoretical Considerations in the Study
     of Political Stability in New Nations   3
     The Durkheimian Perspective and Democratic Stability   6
     The Case of Ireland   11
     Cultural Analysis and Political Sociology   18

2   Irish Cultural Schisms and the Meaning of Political
     Disorder   27
     Irish-Enlightenment Values and Norms   38
     Gaelic-Romantic Values and Norms   42
     Politics and Culture in the Irish Civil War   50

3   The Free State Constitution and the Institutionalization
     of Value Strains   67
     Introduction: Constitutionalism and Order in New Nations   67
     *The Provisional Government and the Promise of
     the Free State Constitution*   71
     Cultural Polarization and the Drafting Process   77
     Value Dissension and Normative Divergence   80
     The Draft Constitutions and the British Response   83
     *The Free State Constitution: The Juxtaposition of Symbols
     of National Unity and Monarchy*   86

**Part 2   Patterns of Crisis Resolution in the Irish Free State,
            1922–1932**

4   The Army Mutiny and Normative Political Challenges   95
     Introduction: The Political Context of Crisis Politics   95
     Background: The Army and National Politics   100

Contents

The Government's Response to the Mutiny 107
Conclusion 126

5 The Boundary Commission Crisis and the Development of
Strategies of Political Efficacy 131
The Organizational Basis for Political Instability in
the Free State 133
Background of the Crisis: Northern Ireland and Irish Politics 140
The Political Crisis Unfolds: The Collapse of
the Boundary Commission 147
Conclusion 157

6 The Limits of Effective Rule: The Assassination of
Kevin O'Higgins and Its Aftermath 160
Introduction: The Changing Political Context 160
The Government's Response to the Assassination
of Kevin O'Higgins 167
The Response: Fianna Fáil Enters the Dáil 175

Part 3 The Character of Irish Democracy

7 The Democratic Achievement in Ireland:
The Reconciliation of Culture and Politics 185
Introduction: The Irish Public and Its Problems 185
The Persistence of Political Extremism 187
Political Parties and Their Political Isolation 189
Fianna Fáil and the Public: The Reconciliation
of Culture and Politics 194

8 The Uniqueness of Irish Democracy 215

Notes 226

References 246

Index 255

Preface

This book explores the achievement of democratic stability in Ireland during its first decade of independence from Britain, 1922–32. A newly independent nation of the twentieth century, Ireland is among a select few nations that has succeeded in transforming political and cultural divisions into a common base of support for the democratic government. The reasons for this Irish accomplishment are the subject of the following analysis. The purpose is both to better understand the Irish case and to shed new light on the problem of democratic stability (and instability) in newly independent nations of the twentieth century.

In the following chapters, I pose two questions: First, how were deeply divided political cultural traditions coexisting in Ireland transposed into support for democratic institutions? This question explores the problem of political institutionalization when social groups adhere to systems of meaning hostile to the existence of those institutions. The second question considers the same problem from a different angle: How do political institutions, guided by a particular ruling elite, succeed in developing democratic institutions that express and confirm patterns of thought and belief in the political community? This question leads to a consideration of the ways in which social meanings in the political community shape and influence the functioning of a political apparatus. The book examines how new democratic institutions, in their quest for broad-based social support, are constrained and molded by prevailing social understandings. In order to understand the achievement of democratic stability in Ireland, I argue, it is necessary both to study political institutions from the point of view of social meaning and to study social meaning from the perspective of those institutions.

This two-part approach to the study of political order is intended to bring the cultural problem to the study of politics. Institutions both shape and are shaped by the cultural universe or universes that orient social action. The particular forms of political institutions, and their capacity

Preface

to assert authority, are functions, in part, of their correspondence to
ongoing patterns of social meaning. My task in this book, then, is to
capture and interpret the patterns of belief and conviction that framed
Irish men's and women's relation to a changing political environment.
By analyzing available texts – parliamentary debates, public speeches,
political documents – I describe the Irish cultural framework; in so doing,
I evaluate Ireland's political achievement with respect to these systems
of meaning.

But I am also aware of how social meaning is molded, constrained,
and transformed by people's experience within institutional arenas.
Rather than treating culture as standing outside material reality, as
preexisting categories of thought independent of time and space, I define
culture and social understandings on the basis of a vital scholarly tradition that posits culture as a historically constituted system of meanings.
This notion of culture, best articulated by anthropologist Clifford Geertz,
has affected many fields of inquiry and has promoted a new movement
in the social sciences. My book on Irish politics and culture in the 1920s
is part of this new approach, although designed as a contribution to
political sociology. The book seeks to reclaim the problem of meaning
as a legitimate and important domain of macrosociological analysis. By
exploring the interconnections between political structure, social activity, and cultural legacies, its intention is to promote an appreciation of
the meaning-making dimensions of political life and institutions.

In the course of writing this book, I have incurred many debts, both
personal and intellectual. It is one of the real pleasures in seeing this
work to fruition to be able to thank publicly those who were so generous
in their support. This book began several years ago as a Ph.D. dissertation at the University of California, Berkeley. There I was fortunate
enough to come under the intellectual orbits of Neil Smelser, Reinhard
Bendix, Thomas Lacquer, and William Kornhauser. Each played a distinct role in shaping my orientation to Irish politics and, perhaps more
importantly, each revealed his own exacting standards of scholarship to
which I continue to aspire. Through a Dean's and a Regent's Fellowship,
I was able to complete the research necessary for the dissertation.

Many people in Ireland generously gave their time to educate me on
the intricacies and complexities of Irish politics, a gift for which no
amount of reading and research could have substituted. In particular, I
would like to thank Tom Garvin and Maurice Manning of University
College, Dublin, for spending time with me, for reading portions of the
manuscript, and for patiently correcting the misconceptions of an Amer-

ican while, at the same time, encouraging me to proceed. Differences in opinion and interpretation about certain matters remain; nevertheless, they have been extremely gracious in their support of the project. To those many people in academics and politics who granted me interviews and to those who, in chance encounters, continued to impress upon me that an understanding of Irish politics and society was not a simple matter, I am especially appreciative. The staffs at the National Library of Ireland, at the State Records Office in Dublin Castle, and at the University College, Dublin Archives, were all uncommonly cordial, making my several research trips always pleasant and productive.

At UCLA, I have benefited from the excellent work of my research assistants – Michael Hui, Paul Colomy, and Michael Suman. I would especially like to thank Geoffrey Gilbert-Hamerling for his assistance; he familiarized himself not only with the details of the decade but also with my interpretation of it, and therefore proved to be an important intellectual resource during the course of my writing. The Academic Senate Research Committee provided much-needed and much-appreciated financial support to see this project to its completion. Melvin Pollner's and Melvin Oliver's interest in the research, and their always generous personal support, cannot be underestimated, and I am happy to acknowledge their important role. I have been fortunate to have Jeffrey Alexander as a friend and colleague. His contribution to this project is inestimable; a friendly critic and generous intellectual resource, he has provided the consistent support that every scholar seeks.

The final preparation of this manuscript was done while I was a member of the Institute for Advanced Study in Princeton. I am indebted to Clifford Geertz, Albert Hirschman, and Michael Walzer for their hospitality and support. Lucille Allsen and Peggy Clarke aided me greatly in preparing the final draft, and I am appreciative of their efforts. I would also like to thank Stephen Boliver for his assistance in bibliographic work.

There are a few individuals whose importance in my life over the past years makes simple acknowledgment inadequate. To my mother and my father, to Abraham Gottesman, and to David and Tziona Silverman, I am especially grateful for providing the personal support and sustenance that allowed work to progress. My wife, Debora Silverman, has provided the milieu that has given special meaning to my work and for which I will ever be grateful. Her own devotion to the world of ideas and scholarship has been both a challenge and an inspiration.

This book is dedicated to the memory of my father, Theodore Prager, whose own calling in life required that I find my own.

Part I. Democracy in Ireland: Theoretical and Empirical Problems

1. Introduction: Theoretical Considerations in the Study of Stability in Newly Independent Nations

Why have so many of the newly independent nations of the twentieth century been racked by political disorder and social instability? Why have so few been successful in establishing stable, regular patterns of institutional relations that promote the well-being of their citizens and enhance their nation's position among the community of nations? Why has the ordering of their societies according to democratic principles been so elusive an achievement? These problems of instability and disorder have commanded the attention of scholars at least since the 1960s, when many nations emerged from their dependent colonial status and attempted to develop into politically independent, self-sustaining entities.

This book represents another effort to answer these questions. Yet the approach taken here differs from previous ones in at least two ways. First, rather than focusing on those societies in which instability has prevailed, I direct attention to a newly independent nation of the twentieth century – the Republic of Ireland – where a stable political order has, in fact, been successfully established. By appreciating the success of the Irish political elite in creating a stable political order, it is argued, we may gain a greater understanding of the obstacles that have prevented other new nations from following the Irish pattern.[1] Second, and more fundamentally, the theoretical approach used to examine the accomplishment of Irish stability differs substantively from that of the vast body of modernization literature. Explanations of instability and disorder have generally emphasized structural or institutional deficiencies that have prevented the creation of a stable polity or society. Marxist or neo-Marxist accounts, as a rule, have focused on the uneven distribution of economic resources and concomitant class conflict,[2] whereas Weberian treatments have identified the underdeveloped political institutions necessary to incorporate and thereby gain the support of various segments of the population.[3] In both of these approaches, despite their different theoretical emphases, attention is directed to the deficiencies of the modernizing elites or the absence of institutional or material resources necessary to gain popular commitment to the new regime or society. Viewed in this manner, instability and disorder are consequences of organizational underdevelopment and/or material insufficiencies that continue to plague new nations after independence.

There is little question that these factors have all seriously impeded the establishment of political and social order in these nations. Yet, an institutional or structural analysis cannot fully account for the varying degrees of stability among nations with comparable institutional underdevelopment and resource deficiency. These approaches fail to emphasize how these structural variables interact with cultural or normative ones. To attribute instability to insufficient economic resources, underdeveloped institutions, and so on, may not be incorrect, but it is certainly incomplete. We know of poor, institutionally underdeveloped societies that have had more success in achieving stable political orders than wealthier and more institutionalized ones. But we know of no society that achieves stability when the feeling of connectedness and attachment to the nation is absent.

In this analysis, stability is held to depend not only on the development of the nation's institutional capacities but on normative or cultural achievements as well. Modernization theory, in focusing on the problems of underdeveloped institutions and material insufficiencies, tends to ignore the profound challenge that national independence poses for the persistence of traditional cultural orientations and the need to reconstitute them in a new form.

Development and modernity presume the creation of a national community whose members identify with the society and are capable of subordinating their private interests to the demands of national leaders. Although the problem of social solidarity is basically cultural, and not institutional or material, it defines and sets the tone for institutional agendas and social imperatives. In the absence of a unified community, no institution can effectively function or mobilize the available societal resources. Modern solidary relations between individuals in many Third World nations remain fragile or nonexistent, and their absence continually frustrates programs of social, economic, and political development. The critical and fundamental question facing new nations has been, and continues to be, how to create a social community where primary commitment and loyalty are to the nation and not to preexisting religious, regional, ethnic, or familial groups.

This analysis, then, is concerned with the cultural problem of forging modern forms of social solidarity. Yet, to emphasize the normative prob-

4

lem is not to deemphasize institutional concerns. It does not suggest an idealist conception of social change. Rather, we assert that the critical focus of institutional actors – the modernizing elites – and the construction of new institutional structures following independence always stand in relation to the prevailing cultural orientations of the society. The challenge of modernization is to establish complementarity between those orientations and modern institutional forms. Normative commitments set the limits for institutional development and, further, define the institutional agendas for the cultural transformations that must occur. The complementarity problem, it might be added, is all the more acute when the ruling elite and the population both expect that the political order will be organized according to democratic principles, and when political authority depends upon free individual expression and collective action. Democratic modernization creates a more precarious relationship between the institutions and the community; the institutionalization of a democratic morality, when the institutions are weak and the pressures are strong, makes the political challenge even more intense.

The principal problem faced by new nations has been to create a new sense of community corresponding to the new forms of social organization accompanying independence: to create new bonds of solidarity between members of the society consistent with the transreligious, transethnic, transregional, and transfamilial character of the new society. Civil ties, by which individuals acquire a more universalistic perspective toward the nation, must supplant more particularistic, primordial attachments as the primary basis of loyalty and identification. Although this may be viewed as the preliminary problem for new nations to overcome, it is also an enduring one. As Clifford Geertz and others have made clear, primordial ties do not die out simply to be replaced by civil ones.[4] National leaders must continually prevent the resurgence of primordialism. Thus, the achievement of solidarity is an ongoing task of national leaders and, as such, represents a fundamental concern. Without such national loyalties and attachments, economic, political, or social development cannot occur.

It is certainly true that national leaders employ economic, political, and ideological mechanisms to promote the development of the country and thereby enhance popular support, identity, and attachment. It is also true that the resources for such development are often inadequate. But in the final analysis, the failure of a nation to create order and stability cannot be attributed directly to these features; instead, it results from the failure to create a modern national community. It is not the modernizing elites' inability to forge ahead that promotes disorder; disorder occurs because individuals and collectivities in the society remain organized according to different principles and criteria, refusing to accept their leaders' failures.

In sum, instability and disorder are seen here as consequences of a disjuncture between the symbolic sphere – where social legitimation may still focus on traditional patterns of organization and affiliation – and the institutional realm, where new social organizations are constructed according to principles contrary to traditionalism.[5] Some organizational accommodation to traditional understandings must occur, along with a certain degree of cultural transformation that is necessary to legitimate the modern structures. When this does not occur, or occurs insufficiently, the inevitable result is political instability and social disorder.

This linkage of the symbolic and institutional spheres defines the agenda of all institutional elites in new nations. They must construct modern social, political, and economic orders in the face of cultural convictions that oppose these modern imperatives. The need for modern social solidarity, consistent with the values and norms of modern institutional structures, is a preeminent challenge to the modernizing elites. It defines their essential work; the degree of success in this endeavor defines the parameters within which institutional modernization may occur. As Edward Shils writes:

> A modern society is not just a complex of modern institutions. It is a mode of integration of the whole society. It is a mode of relationship between the center and the periphery of the society. Modern society entails the inclusion of the mass of the population into the society in the sense that both elite and mass regard themselves as members of the society and, as such, as of approximately equal dignity. It involves a greater participation by the masses in the values of the society, a more active role in the making of society-wide decisions, and a greater prominence in the consideration of the elite. . . . A widespread moral consensus, reaching into the outermost areas of society, maintained, renewed and revised by strong personalities and effective institutions, is a real need of the states.[6]

The Durkheimian perspective and democratic stability

This focus on solidarity and the emphasis on the interpenetration of the cultural and political institutional realms rely heavily upon a Durkheimian perspective. More than any other major sociological theorist, Durkheim, in his political sociology, emphasizes the moral underpinning of modern society and identifies malintegration as a primary cause of social disorder and political instability. He believes that the primary tasks of the modern state are to reflect upon, articulate, implement, and transform the collective consciousness of its constituency. Stability in modern society, for Durkheim, depends upon this achievement.

In describing the features of the democratic state, in contrast to those of the premodern, monarchical state, Durkheim insists that the problems of legitimacy and order are independent of the state's capacity or effectiveness in incorporating the population within its structures. He argues that the central task of the democratic state is the establishment of a particular relationship between the political elite and the society. Whereas the collective consciousness is the "vaguely diffused sentiments that float about the whole expanse of the society," the state, in contrast, must serve as the organ of social thought.[7] It is the purpose of the state to make conscious and articulate these inarticulate diverse ideas, beliefs, and sentiments, and to act on them consonant with the social values embodied in the state institutions. Political legitimacy depends upon a state structure in which decisions and deliberations are informed by collective sentiments.

The legitimacy problem, then, requires the democratic state to adopt a specific institutional form and adapt norms dictating the operation of state structures. It requires, first, a state that is interactive with the public yet differentiated from it. Durkheim writes, "The state is nothing if it is not an organ distinct from the rest of the society. If the state is everywhere, it is nowhere."[8] In addition to imposing constraints on the institutional features of the democratic state, the legitimacy problem makes demands on the normative operation of the political system. The state must establish procedures through which public sentiment can be expressed, considered, and potentially reflected in state action. Constitutional norms must be established whereby procedural mechanisms are created and political change is routinely effected.

Durkheim's assertion that the symbolic and institutional spheres must converge to achieve political order distinguishes this theoretical perspective from those of both Marxists and Weberians, for in neither of these scholarly traditions does the moral order – the realm of collective consciousness – possess analytic or substantive autonomy. Not granted independent existence, it is subsumed within an institutional analysis. Even when these traditions of thought seek to explain an essentially social psychological phenomenon like political legitimacy, they exclude the independent role of moral attachments and understandings between members of the society and the structures and procedures of the political system.

The dominant strain of Marxist analysis presumes integration and legitimacy, albeit a false one, when the political system articulates with the economic realm.[9] In Weberian thought, solidarity is essentially viewed as a function of a state in successfully incorporating the population within its structures.[10] Neither tradition accords the symbolic world of individuals – their collective consciousness – a role in the construction of a democratic order, in the interpenetration of that order with given social understandings, or in its significance in the maintenance and reproduction of the political system. In short, the Durkheimian perspective, although not ignoring the problem of institution building in forging a democratic order, asserts the need to place institutional problems in their cultural context. It appreciates not only that the collective consciousness is constrained, molded, and transformed to suit the needs of the democratic political institution but also that the institutions themselves are shaped and constrained by given social understandings and patterns of relatedness. Democratic institutions, in sum, reflect the cultural context in which they operate; they embody the peculiarities of their national constituency and its history. In those nations where the political institutions have proven to be ineffective and unstable, it is also a function of the elites' failure to accommodate to the prevailing cultural norms.

This Durkheimian interest in the role that collective meanings hold for modern orders is more closely related to those researchers who identify political culture as a critical independent variable in the construction of political order. Inspired by the rapid explosion of newly independent nations in the late 1950s and 1960s, their focus on political culture became a powerful tool to account for the enormous difficulty new nations face in establishing stable political orders. Appreciating the power of cultural meanings in political processes, political cultural scholars sought to identify and understand "those critical but widely shared beliefs and sentiments that form the 'particular patterns of orientation' that give order and form to the political process."[11] "Political culture," Sidney Verba writes, "regulates who talks to whom and who influences whom. It also regulates what is said in political contacts and the effects of these contacts. It regulates the ways in which formal institutions operate as well."[12]

Stable political orders, in short, were identified as possessing a political culture concordant with the given political forms, whereas unstable systems were unable to forge belief systems compatible with modern political structures. Attention was directed, on the one hand, to the political cultures of Western democracies, demonstrating their successful accommodation of political cultural beliefs to institutional forms and, on the other hand, to non-Western systems less successful in forging political stability.[13] Through this focus on political culture, it became possible to identify several typical crises – the identity crisis, the legitimacy crisis, the participation crisis – seemingly inherent in the process of nation building.[14]

The political culture tradition, however, lost much of its momentum in the ideological maelstrom of the late 1960s and early 1970s. It became strongly identified with the larger body of modernization literature, which assumed an ideal-typical Western model of development as the standard by which to evaluate political processes in newly independent nations. Modernization theory, critics charged, had implicitly adopted an evolutionary schema, in which nations achieving political and social order, like those in the West, were seen as having successfully made the transition from a traditional society to a modern one.[15] Political culture was viewed as a theoretical analogue to research efforts identifying the economic, political, and personality correlates of the development process; the objective was to detail the "cultural" components needed for modernity to occur.[16] In spite of many disclaimers by political cultural theorists insisting on the need for cultural sensitivity, critics of the political culture concept prevailed.[17]

The power of the critique paved the way for a broad challenge to the presumptions of evolutionism expressed in modernization theory. The political culture school, along with modernization theory in general, was overshadowed in the 1970s by Marxist-inspired social science. Attention now shifted to the dependent status of Third World nations and their economic domination by the colonizing centers. Relying heavily on an analysis of class formations in the periphery, this explanation rejected a political-cultural approach to political stability.[18] Expressing a similar distrust of cultural analysis, the 1970s produced, in addition, world systems analysis, a materialist and historical account of the role of capitalist penetration in non-Western nations. This perspective rapidly gained new adherents, and political and historical sociology have been powerfully informed by this theoretical orientation in the study of new nations.[19]

Recently, however, the complex impact of culture on politics has stirred new interest. This research has emerged not from political or historical sociology, but rather from a central school of historical studies.[20] During the last several years, the chief concern of social history has shifted from the quantitative reconstitution of population, food supplies, and social mobility studies to the qualitative question of the role of culture in the political process. Indeed, many historians trained in and influenced by sociology in the 1970s are now probing the linguistic, anthropological, and symbolic bases of meaning and how these shape political action in particular historical moments. This research has typically centered on the interaction of culture and specific sectors of the national community, such as working-class or peasant politics.[21] More recently, historians have begun to explore the interaction of culture and politics at the macrosocial level, analyzing, for example, the way that an anti-industrial and aristocratizing ethos shared by England's governing classes became the central factor in England's inability to remain a primary economic power.[22] Another example is a study tracing the forging of political legitimacy during the first French Republic through debates over the proper allegorical symbol to represent the new nations of French citizens.[23] Still another example is a study of post–World War II Greece in light of the continuities and tensions of the Greek tradition.[24]

Political sociology can benefit from this form of historical scholarship; indeed, a central aim of this book is to reinvigorate cultural analysis as a way of understanding newly independent nations. Yet, a sociological encounter with cultural variables, in comparison to a historical interest, requires a more self-consciously theoretical agenda. Any sociological appreciation of the achievement of modern political order requires that the political accomplishment be understood in relation to the character of the political community – its value and normative commitments, its emergent political structures, the quality of political leadership, and the relationship that is forged between the political order and the broader national community upon which stable politics ultimately depends.[25]

In more concrete terms, an analysis is required that considers the role of the political elite in forging a modern, solidary nation. Careful attention must be paid not only to the work of institution building but, in addition, to the efforts of the political elite in creating a public consensus to sustain the new institutions. Further, an analysis of political order requires an appreciation of the powerful role of collective meanings in the very shaping and functioning of the new institutional order. Political stability results from an emerging correspondence between institutional forms and processes and from what Parsons has referred to as the "system of legitimate order."[26] The researcher, then, must pay careful attention to special meanings that politics and political life hold for citizens as they shape the institutional arrangements that govern their lives.

Stated differently, the aim here is to understand the relationship between collective meanings and what David Easton calls "regime stability."[27] Although it is generally agreed that the existence of a political community depends upon a consensus by its members on, for example, national identity, it is less widely appreciated that political stability also depends upon the emergence of a consensus concerning the political underpinnings of political rule. Without agreement on constitutional principles, for example, a democratic regime could not survive. This problem of the achievement of democratic stability is at the heart of this research enterprise.[28]

The case of Ireland

The Irish Free State, during its first decade of independence (1922–1932), was a nation that successfully forged democratic stability in spite of extreme political, economic, and cultural obstacles. The Irish state has remained firmly democratic in its orientation and succeeded in imparting democratic convictions to the nation. But, as I shall argue throughout this book, that achievement can hardly be viewed as an example of premodern, traditional convictions giving way to modern, universalistic ones; rather, the Irish example of stability demonstrates the accommodations made by political institutions to already existing social understandings. Without such adjustments, stability would not have occurred. In the remainder of this chapter, I will first place this cultural approach to Irish nation building in the extant social scientific analyses of Ireland's political development and will then return to the theoretical question about politics and culture previously raised.

By and large, those who study world politics have largely ignored Ireland. In fact, except for Irish academics' own interest in understanding their society, modern Irish politics has largely been ignored. This is, of course, less true of Northern Ireland. Since the reemergence of religious hostilities well over a decade ago, a considerable body of literature has appeared, attempting to comprehend its sorry history and politics. But the twenty-six-county republic to the south and west of Ulster has remained out of the academic limelight, at least since it gained its independence from Great Britain in 1921.

There are many explanations to account for this obscurity. Ireland is a small country and largely inconsequential in the world order. It has always played a peripheral role in the European community of nations [though less so today, since its entry into the European Economic Community (EEC)], and its politics, when compared to those of other new nations of the twentieth century, have been uncommonly ordinary. Because it has come to resemble other Western democracies, albeit in miniature, the Irish Republic has apparently been seen as unworthy of careful investigation.

Yet there are sound reasons to understand Irish politics better. First, as a twentieth-century nation faced with the problems of decolonization, it is more comparable in character and condition, in many respects, to the new nations of the Third World than to Denmark, Switzerland, or other small Western democracies to which it is more frequently compared. Its economy and social structure bear the strong imprint of its colonially dependent status. It still remains a largely rural, agriculturally oriented nation, unlike most of its Western counterparts. Its nationalist revolution against British authority figured heavily in its postindependence politics, in ways not unlike those of other twentieth-century nations that gained independence through a nationalist revolution. And, like other newly independent nations, Ireland's population was politically mobilized long before the emergence of indigenous institutions capable of expressing their beliefs in moderate politics.[29]

Still, in contrast to most other new nations of this century, Ireland is nearly unique in having successfully established a stable political system wracked by neither violent revolution nor military takeover. The early years of independence posed the most serious challenges to democratic rule; the institutional structures were fragile, and the forces threatening political order were intense. In 1922, the political party Cumann na nGaedheal emerged amid the chaos of civil war to construct the new state apparatus. It maintained itself in power, despite substantial challenges – both parliamentary and extraparliamentary – until 1932, when Fianna Fáil assumed, through popular election, political control of the Free State. The structures of rule – the Constitution, the parliament (the Dáil), and the party system – that were established upon its inception in the early 1920s are still in place. Although there have been substantial constitutional reforms and changes in the party system, they have all been accomplished through the legitimate constitutional process.

By 1932, democratic stability was firmly secure. The political leaders had successfully established a system whereby power was transferred from one set of elites to another by popular elections. Further, they had created a political order in which Irish citizens understood the political structures to be the rightful ones.

Moreover, Ireland had succeeded not only in achieving a stable political order, but also in establishing one that remains soundly democratic in conviction and in function. Since its inception, the Irish government has remained committed to protecting citizens against complete political domination, and has continued to ensure individual expression even when it has opposed the regime. The government has been broadly supportive of both individual and collective actions insofar as they have adhered to constitutional norms. These original democratic commitments, despite conditions that might have recommended their abridgement, have remained firm.

In these respects, the Irish achievement of a stable democratic order has been an exceptional accomplishment. Unlike the precarious fate of democracy in most decolonizing nations, Ireland, nearly alone, has managed, within a few decades, to promote democratic institutions that have endured. It is precisely because Ireland has achieved a stable, democratic political order that it is worthy of study. To understand the Irish success is to better comprehend the problems confronting other new nations in their similar efforts to achieve stable political order.

How does one account for Ireland's democratic stability? What lessons can be derived from the Irish case to better understand why political order has proven so elusive in other newly independent nations of the twentieth century?[30] Irish social science to date, unfortunately, cannot substantially aid us in generalizing the Irish achievement to other nations because, like political science and political sociology more generally, it has largely ignored the manner in which cultural understandings and institutional structures interacted to produce a legitimate political system. Rather, Irish social scientists have tended to treat Irish political development as paradoxical, that is, as contradicting more universal patterns in the process of nation building and, therefore, as largely idiosyncratic. Yet, as I will argue, these paradoxes may prove less puzzling when cultural factors are included in an analysis of the success of the Irish political elite.

An examination of Irish cultural patterns, of course, even further particularizes the Irish achievement; at the same time, it demonstrates how the accommodation between symbolic and institutional spheres enabled Ireland to achieve what other new nations have largely been unable to do. In this way, Ireland, as a domain of social scientific inquiry, might well serve as a lens through which to view other nations' political successes and failures.

The first frequently noted paradox is that Ireland, over the course of a century, successfully forged a nationalist movement characterized by a long history of consensus building; yet, within only a few months, that solidary movement quickly gave way to bloody civil war. Anti-British sentiment had united the nationalist movement with remarkable

13

effectiveness; yet, with the slightest provocations, this unity dissolved into a bitter internecine battle embroiling political actors and the majority of the population. Moreover, these divisions have continued to influence contemporary Irish politics. Indeed, the sustaining impact of the divisions born in the Irish Civil War have led scholars such as John Whyte to characterize contemporary Irish politics as unique; in the words of Whyte, it is a "politics without social bases."[31] The conflicts created during the Civil War, rather than class composition or other socially based affinities, have mobilized Irish political affiliation into our time. And it is the Civil War, rather than the Irish independence movement, that has proven to be the decisive political fact of the twentieth century.

The second paradox of modern Irish politics is that an independent, stable Irish state was created amid the violence of Civil War and as a consequence of a nationalist movement that celebrated the tradition of physical force. That movement introduced, not only to Ireland but to the world as well, modern techniques of guerrilla warfare. Nevertheless, Ireland succeeded in establishing a stable political order committed to democratic processes and structures. Despite the long-standing tradition of romanticizing Ireland's violent resistance to foreign domination, and despite the violence expressed in the Anglo-Irish War and in the Civil War, the Free State, for all practical purposes, dissipated the popular commitment to force. In its place, it forged a parliamentary order no less stable, and in many cases more stable, than that of other Western political systems, distinguishing it from other newly independent nations of this century.

Both of these paradoxes have motivated social scientific inquiry into the nature of Irish politics and society. Yet, ironically, those who focus on the first paradox – who try to explain the Civil War – characterize Ireland differently than those who seek to explain the second. Social scientists – historians, geographers, and political scientists alike – who begin their inquiry with the Civil War divisions focus their attention on the enduring economic, political, and ecological cleavages in the nation. Patterns of structural inequalities, reflecting socioeconomic and geographic gradients, have become the stock-in-trade explanations for the causes of the Civil War, and they serve as the more general characterization of Irish society. To some degree, certain analysts advocating a cleavage perspective have adopted (perhaps predictably) the political-economic categories of Marxist analysis;[32] others employ primordial-national divisions.[33] But ecological analysis, that is, the East-West, urban-rural gradients, has been by far the most pervasive social scientific explanation in Ireland.[34] These deeply rooted cleavages, it is either implied or stated, help account for the rise of oppositional politics with respect to both the nationalist movement and the Civil War. But although structural strains might help explain, in nonhuman terms, how a movement characterized by such solidarity could so quickly dissolve into hardened patterns of intracommunal conflict, it is difficult to understand how this process occurred. A theory of endemic strain – whether economic, political, or ecological – cannot alone account for the Civil War.[35] It cannot help us appreciate why compatriots could so soon turn against each other in mortal combat. More generally, such an explanation cannot explain both the communality of the nationalist movement and the discord of the Civil War. Ironically, these explanations, in attempting to uncover the bases of strain that prefigured the Civil War, have made the solidarity of the nationalist movement essentially a residual category, incapable of direct explanation.

The second paradox – the achievement of democratic stability in the face of a tradition of violence – has similarly attracted social scientific attention, though less than the first. The explanations used to account for this accomplishment are no more complete than those that attempt to explain the causes of the Civil War. To the extent that they exist, they assert that the modern Irish state benefited culturally from a long-standing parliamentary tradition and institutionally from government personnel trained in the British model.[36] Leaving aside the fact that democratic stability (I will argue) was a more precarious achievement than many commentators admit, scholars argue that Irish political culture and the institutional lessons derived from Ireland's colonial status prefigured the democratic structure and commitments of the new state. But to assert this is to claim simultaneously that the Civil War and even the tradition of physical force represented aberrant expressions of the collective will – a will, they would claim, that was solidly democratic and nonviolent. As Ronan Fanning has remarked in reference to those students of Irish history who stress the strength of the democratic tradition in preindependent Ireland, "while the passing of the old myths [Ireland's violent past] must afford them satisfaction, the growing concerns affirming the strength of the democratic tradition in Irish politics must make them ponder whether new myths are not being conjured up in the place of old."[37]

What we see, in short, with respect to both the Civil War and the creation of a stable apparatus is that macrosociological or historical explanations have failed to develop a perspective that can help us understand the sources of solidarity and intracommunal conflict, on the one hand, and the coexistence of a commitment to both violence and parliamentarianism, on the other. An adequate macrosociological understanding of Irish politics ought to produce an explanation of both the breakdown of political order, as in the Civil War, and the remarkable achievement of democratic stability, as produced by leaders of the Free State. A theory of structural strain, which may illuminate certain aspects of the causes of the 1922 Civil War, cannot satisfactorily account for the achievement of democratic stability a decade later. Nor can a stress on the strength of the parliamentary tradition in Ireland, as an explanation for democratic stability, be very helpful in accounting for the breakdown of order in the Civil War.

What is required is a theory explaining the continuities of thought and action of the Irish people. Rather than treating these different periods of Irish history as discrete events capable of only historicized explanations, a theory of Irish culture is required to explain why, at one time, Irish men and women chose to associate communally and to cooperate in the pursuit of a common goal – Irish independence from England – and why, at another time, their interests were opposed to each other. The fact is that the same people who joined together against Britain chose, shortly thereafter, to do battle with each other over the terms of the Anglo-Irish Treaty.

In the following analysis, I will offer such a perspective by focusing on the profound cultural antinomies that had long existed in Irish society. As I will describe in the next chapter, these antinomies coalesced, at certain historical moments, in a common nationalist ideology that, at different periods, crystallized into two distinctive ideological constructs that competed with each other for dominance. As polarizing ideologies, they each possessed a distinct set of values and norms concerning the appropriate objectives of an independent nation and the necessary measures to achieve them. On the one side, there was an Irish-Enlightenment tradition, deriving its original insights from the Anglo-Irish ascendancy and articulating modern secular aspirations for the Irish nation. Here the objective was to construct a social order characterized by autonomous individuals and independent spheres of social life in which the Irish citizen could rationally influence the course of Irish affairs. On the other side, there was a competing Gaelic-Romantic set of thoughts and beliefs. Its aim was to promote a solidary nation without conflict and disharmony, imbued with a vivid sense of the past in the functioning of the present. Neither secular nor individualistic, this orientation expressed a yearning for a social order protective of the values and patterns of interaction putatively characteristic of the ancient Gaelic Ireland.

Irish nationalism forged into one objective, political independence, elements of each tradition. The nationalist ideology, in fact, obscured for a time the inherent conflicts that lay beneath the surface; yet, independence ensured that the accommodations made in the common interest of national independence would give way, during the Civil War, to radically different understandings of Irish modernity. To be sure, the war served to make these cultural differences enduringly powerful, continuing to redound on Irish politics generations later, but those differences predated the Civil War and prefigured its outbreak.

The challenge to the new postindependent, post–Civil War political leaders was how to forge such powerful and antinomic commitments into a single broad-based collectivity, tolerant of different understandings yet supportive of specific political institutions. The task was to transform contending ideological constructs, heretofore immune to debate and discourse, into a single, integrated national set of convictions. When this was achieved, cultural polarities would be articulated by individual members and social groups of the community while, at the same time, collective decisions emerging through discourse would supersede personal preferences.

In sum, attention to the contending value and normative commitments coexisting in Ireland contributes to an understanding of Irish politics in ways that structural strain or ecological analysis cannot. In focusing on the meaning-making process, we become better able to understand how people behave in ways that, at first glance, seem paradoxical and even contradictory. Such attention to cultural forms, however, need not preclude a consideration of the adaptive and transformative power of the existing political institutions. Indeed, the following analysis will not focus on cultural polarities per se; rather, the aim is to discover the particular way in which the symbolic worlds of Irish men and women interacted with institutional structures and political elites.

The Irish achievement constituted far more than a simple victory of Irish-Enlightenment convictions over Gaelic-Romantic ones; nor can it be said that democratic stability was achieved simply through the national ascendance of universalistic principles and the decline of particularistic ones. The first decade of Irish independence was marked by several roughly concurrent developments: the increasing durability and capacity of the political institutions, organized originally to serve Irish-Enlightenment conceptions of political order, to exert their authority, and to resist its Gaelic-Romantic detractors; the increasing ability of those institutions and their leaders to incorporate dissident sectors into the existing political structures; and, finally, alterations in the structure and composition of political elites so as to embody more closely Gaelic-Romantic sentiments and convictions. Irish democracy, in short, neither succumbed to a purely particularistic or romantic conception of politics nor developed into an ideal-typical universalistic democracy. Instead, it forged a distinctively Irish variant of democracy not completely discordant with either Gaelic-Romantic or Irish-Enlightenment conceptions.

In this sense, the Irish achievement is unique. Successful in producing a stable political order, its institutions expressed a peculiar constellation of competing political-cultural understandings held by members of the national community. No other democracy is organized or functions precisely like the Irish one. And yet, the Irish accomplishment, however unique its specific forms, provides greater understanding to those more generally concerned with the challenge of political order in new nations. This study of the first decade of Irish independence may advance our thinking about political developments in newly independent nations in two ways.

First, it will become clear that modern Irish democracy came to express a deeply rooted conception of politics as a system of patronage. Hardly the universalistic democracy that social scientists often hold up as the objective for developing countries, Irish politics resembles far more the kind of politics found in some Southern European countries and in some urban polities in the United States. Although perhaps an affront to the political aesthetics of social researchers, the Irish achievement nonetheless demonstrates that the standard by which social scientists measure political achievements needs to be situated more precisely within the national cultural matrix in which politics operates.

Second, Ireland illustrates the centrality of culture in the construction of political stability. Stability depends not only on building strong political institutions, not only on political elites responsive to contending visions of political life, and not only on institutions capable of embracing an amalgam of cultural inputs. Political stability has proven to be precarious in the twentieth century precisely because all of these aims have to be achieved roughly in tandem. A malintegrated national community, a poorly responsive political elite, or institutions too rigid to accommodate countervailing understandings are each sufficient to ensure instability and disorder.

Cultural analysis and political sociology

This approach to political development in Ireland, it should be clear, differs significantly from those large-scale, quantitative, and comparative studies concerned with the economic, political, and other institutional requisites for stable political orders. It is less clear how the perspective outlined above differs from the political culture tradition of political science and political sociology. This book builds upon the political culture tradition while, at the same time, being guided by the critiques of social scientists and by the more recent historical research on culture and politics. In this concluding section, I will make explicit how this study of Ireland points to new research directions in the social scientific study of political order in new nations.

Democratic stability, as political culture theorists have argued, is dependent upon the presence of a civic culture in which members of the community grant legitimacy to modern, national interests and ultimately subordinate private interests and beliefs to a transcendent commitment to the public good.[38] A universally held conception of citizenship, with its attendant understanding of rights due and obligations owed, is critical for state institutions to function.[39] As Almond and Verba make clear, no democratic order is possible without the presence of a cultural conception that the state is responsive to the individual – even the passive one – and to organized social interests. When political participation is known to be possible, citizens are freed from the need to be always mobilized in order to protect their interests.[40]

The solidary community, in short, must be preeminently civil if modern democratic order is to be created and sustained. Stability depends upon the absence of *fundamental* social cleavages like class, region, religion, and ethnicity, to which citizens attach primary loyalty. Civil ties must stand above these now secondary bases of attachment and loyalty. The strength of the community, and its capacity to promote modern order, are inversely related to the strength of such divisions, to the extent that the latter continue to command principal fidelity. Political order is contingent upon a substantial degree of value consensus and normative agreement shared by all members of the nation. It stands regardless of contending interests that various members, situated differently in the society, may hold and regardless of the diverse loyalties and commitments that different statuses may produce.[41] Without such a political culture and without an integrated community, democracy cannot long survive.

Yet this picture of the democratic political culture and civility, although identifying perhaps the minimum requirements for political modernity and order, too sharply abstracts political understandings from the broader constellation of cultural orientations, the larger system of legitimate order that itself depends on the successful functioning of the political system. In any nation, modern universalism can quickly give way to premodern particularism; legitimacy granted can all too quickly result in legitimacy retracted. Identifying at any one moment the strength of certain cultural orientations blinds the researcher to the forces challenging such orientations. Political culture and its relation to institution building, in short, cannot be understood abstractly or ahistorically as political culture theorists have been wont to do, but only, to paraphrase Clifford Geertz, through "thick cultural analysis."[42] It is not sufficient to specify the dominant cultural expressions in any one nation without appreciating the oppositional, antinomic forces that challenge those conceptions and, in an important sense, imbue the former with particular meaning and conviction.

There is a further weakness to the prevailing concept of civic culture. Theorists working in this tradition presume that the presence of a civic culture – inspired largely by the political institutions – promotes a solidary national community without considering the ways in which this community itself helps to forge specific cultural meanings that only sometimes support modern political structures. When political modernity occurs, these theorists assert, the new "modern" individual, forswearing old identities and loyalties, becomes a national citizen with a universalist political orientation. The result is the creation of a solidary community sustaining a modern political order. Those who adopt this perspective consider many factors in attempting to explain the simultaneous transformation of political culture and political institutions, but they do not examine particular communal structures and processes as independent sources of change. Once again, it is not enough to identify the cultural convictions needed for political order; we must also attempt to understand, in this thick way, the interactive and situated processes by which they are forged.

To study thick cultural patterns appropriately and to understand their relation to political institutions require a heftier conceptual apparatus than that provided by civic culture. Specifically, a conception of the civil, solidary community must be detailed and elaborated so as to clarify the processes within the community by which specific meanings are forged, gain ascendance over competing meanings, and influence the institutional structures. It is necessary to look at formal structures, like the mass media, as well as informal "interaction nets" connecting all citizens into a single meaning-making universe.[43] Only with this more dynamic conception of the shaping and forging of meanings is it possible to ask how institutions themselves are constrained and even transformed, in structure and function, by the national community.

In the following discussion, I offer the concept of the public as a structural feature of the national community.[44] I am asserting that the solidary realm of interaction, that is, the national community, has certain structural properties that constrain its members in ways not dissimilar to those of other areas of social life. The public, as I shall describe, shapes thought much as the economy shapes the character of work or the family determines the nature of emotional expression. The public realm is the place where individual beliefs, ideas, values, sentiments, and interests concerning the nation and its policies converge and, over time, emerge as collective expression.

The public is presented here as a kind of "meta-concept"[45] in an attempt to capture and assess systematically the importance of patterns of solidary interaction in the creation of political order. The presence of a public realm where individuals communicate and agree to listen to, to be influenced by, and even to be persuaded by other members of the public is essential if a democratic order is to be created and maintained. And yet, despite the concept's importance, it is difficult to measure directly the strength or weakness of the public. For example, a functioning public requires an infrastructure, for example, mass media, through which discourse can occur. But the public sphere might be weak regardless of the necessary mechanisms. If it is believed, for example, that the media represent only narrow, sectarian interests and are untrustworthy, then the presence of many newspapers, radio, and television networks need not indicate a functioning public. Rather, the proliferation of news media may reveal a deeply divided community, with different factors insisting on news media that present their version of the social world. In the same way, the absence of national political debate and controversy cannot be taken to indicate the presence of a strong democratic public characterized by the achievement of political consensus. Nor does it necessarily indicate such deep division that there is an absence of communication. Without interpreting the meaning of political action, it is impossible to determine whether political apathy reveals broad-based public support or simply popular disengagement from the political process and a weak public sector.

In the course of this analysis of Ireland, I will argue that the public sphere became stronger as the 1920s progressed; indeed, the increasing solidarity of the Irish community is identified as the key to the success of the new government. Stated differently, early in the decade a large sector of the Irish population denied legitimacy to any other political position. It offered an alternative explanation for all social facts and, further, questioned the motivation and actions of all those who did not share the same ideological commitments. This polarization sharply impeded democratic discourse and kept the adherents of that position from being influenced by alternative ones; only over time did the political significance of that polarization diminish. Yet, the increasing strength of the Irish public sphere cannot be measured directly. As the reader will discover, evidence for this shift is derived by examining changing voting patterns. Increased voting is believed to indicate the growing strength of the public. But it should be apparent that participation itself need not reflect – in the same way that the presence of many news media need not reflect – a strong democratic public. The public, as a metaconcept, helps define the questions that need to be asked about political activity, but it does not lend itself to direct and easy measurement. To understand the public's role in politics requires an immersion in the political life of the community and an interpretation of the meaning of political activity as it unfolds.

In a functioning public realm, certain understandings emerge as dominant or manifest, whereas others remain beneath the surface or latent. The public produces through its members an independent, though often inarticulate, notion of what it believes in, ways in which it would like to see society develop, and ways in which it expects the state, other institutions, and elites to function. Those understandings, it should be clear, are a result of influences from many different sectors and represent a blend of traditional and modern beliefs. They derive, in part, from the strength and vitality of long-standing, deeply felt cultural traditions passed on from generation to generation and, in part, from contact and experience with specific institutions like the family, the economy, and the church. Through this meaning-making process, whereby individuals make sense of the world in which they live, the systems of legitimate order are created. The particular understandings and orientations that emerge determine the extent to which various institutions, like the political one, benefit from popular legitimacy and help determine whether given institutions will survive or be reconstituted in different forms.

The public, as the arena where meaning is forged, stands above the individual and determines his or her relation to society in terms of this emergent, transcendent order of meanings. These commitments transcend the individual and emerge as cognitive, affective, and normative standards, that is, structures, by which individuals gauge their own relationship to this integrated community – the extent of their own alienation from or commitment to publicly accepted views – and collectively through which the public evaluates social institutions.

The characterization of the public as the central feature of the modern solidary community breaks with the political culture tradition. In contrast to the civic culture concept, the concept of the public makes more vivid the achieved status of cultural understandings, in which emergent views represent a unique amalgamation of modern and traditional constructs, a blend of influences from various sectors of the nation. Further, it clarifies the precarious nature of social understandings, in which one set of convictions may readily give way when a substantial public sector feels too estranged from the dominant convictions.

The public, in short, represents the arena of discourse where meanings are debated and specific understandings forged. Although the public is a necessary feature of democratic order, it is also the mechanism through which legitimacy may be withheld from a given political structure. Non-democratic convictions may become popular, undermining democratic structures. In this solidary national community, citizenship implies the right to discuss; public discourse, therefore, is commonly viewed as a right of every citizen. The discussion of social meaning is the most significant right that members have. Through organized discord and public discourse, individuals and collectivities help to forge social meaning. The fluidity of this process ensures that no understanding is permanent and, therefore, that no institutional legitimacy is eternally secure. As the intellectual historian Keith Michael Baker writes:

> A community exists only to the extent that there is some common discourse by which its members can constitute themselves as different groups within the social order and make claims upon one another that are regarded as intelligible and binding. The interaction involved in the framing of such claims is constrained within that discourse, which it in turn sustains, extends and on occasion transforms. Political authority is in this view a matter of linguistic authority: both in the sense that public functions are defined and allocated within the framework of a given political discourse; and in the sense that their exercise takes the form of maintaining that discourse by upholding authoritative definitions of (and within) it.[46]

Through this realm of discourse, the formulation of collective goals or purposes, although historically conditioned, is constantly subject to redefinition and respecification through both debate and social contest. These new definitions emerge from changes in social organization, new patterns of social interaction within institutional settings, and the development of new status groups, some of whom succeed in redefining or respecifying the character of societal commitments and orientations. In American society, for example, the commitment to equality has been an enduring social objective, but its precise meaning, the legitimate mechanisms for its implementation, and the intensity with which it is pursued have changed dramatically from its original conception and have waxed and waned over the centuries.[47]

Without a solidary national community, there is no discourse; cultural differences become crystallized into political and ideological divisions in which the possibilities of persuasion and accommodation are non-existent. But the presence of the public ensures the emergence of "negotiated" understandings in which new conceptions embrace old and new understandings mediate between contending positions. Newer notions are continuous, in some manner, with those that preceded them, even on those rare occasions when the former represent radical rejections of the latter. To appreciate the role of the public is to understand the continuities of social life through the forging of social meanings, even in the face of dramatic changes in institutional life. In contrast to a political cultural orientation based on a radical split between a traditional past and a modern present, the perspective offered here considers the public as an expression of a continuous process of negotiation between the old and the new. The result, in each national setting, is the production of a culturally specific set of meanings and understandings about the nature of legitimate order.

This conception raises an additional issue for inquiry not frequently considered by political culture theorists. Because the political culture tradition sees modern political institutions and modern political culture as all of one piece, there is little interest in investigating how the institutions themselves are shaped to conform to given social meanings. In addition to being interested in the way the solidary community functions and the process by which social understandings are forged, one must consider the public in terms of how these understandings influence other institutional spheres. In this study of Irish nation building, that question looms large.

The constant production of new status groups articulating new conceptions of old commitments makes continued, albeit changing, demands upon the various institutional elites – including political elites – to embrace, deflect, or respond in some manner to popular inputs. When public understandings diverge markedly from institutional practices, institutional elites must control, contain, and/or mold popular sentiment consistent with the institutional constraints with which they identify. Failure to do so, of course, often proves fatal; in that failure, new contending conceptions of political authority and responsibility gain increasing popularity. Political strategies rejected in the past become part of the vocabulary. As Keith Baker puts it, "A revolution can be defined as a transformation of the discursive practice of the community, a movement in which social relations are reconstituted and the discourse defining the political relations between individuals and groups is radically recast."[48]

An important requisite for political stability is the ability of political elites to organize popular sentiment and interests. It is also clear, of course, that institutional elites do not merely react to given cultural orientations prevalent at the time. A significant part of their work consists of attempts to influence and shape public understanding. Clifford Geertz notes this when he speaks of the need of political leaders in new nations to foster an "integrative ideology" supportive of the given institutions. He writes:

> The function of ideology is to make an autonomous politics possible by providing the authoritative concepts that render it meaningful, the suasive images by means of which it can be sensibly grasped ... the differentiation of an autonomous polity implies the differentiation, too, of a separate and distinct cultural model of political action, for the older, unspecialized models are either too comprehensive or too concrete to provide the sort of guidance such a political system demands. Either they trammel political behavior by encumbering it with transcendent significance, or they stifle political imagination by binding it to the blank realism of habitual judgment. It is when neither a society's most general cultural orientations nor its most down-to-earth "pragmatic" ones suffice any longer to provide an adequate image of political process that ideologies begin to become crucial sources of sociopolitical meaning and attitudes.[49]

Although political elites are actively engaged in seeking to transform the public – to ensure that basic patterns of civility prevail and thereby enable the institutions to function – it is also true that, within these parameters of a civic culture, the state must adopt forms and processes that are culturally meaningful. The challenge is as Geertz describes it, partly ideological, but it is more than that. Cultural meaningfulness is more than a cognitive problem: Support and identity for new political structures also require that the structures, organizations, and political processes, that is, the institutional forms, conform to the deeply felt, more unconscious conceptions of legitimacy. A new ideology helps to make that link, but it is not sufficient for consolidating a new state. A more delicate and profound challenge confronts the political elite of a new nation: the shaping of a resonance between external political structures and the internal wellsprings of legitimacy.

Theoretical and Empirical Problems

Political legitimacy and social order in modern democratic societies, I have suggested, depend upon a public realm capable of supporting a national political apparatus independent of civil society and committed to constitutional principles. Although the public realm and the state are analytically independent domains of social life, they are empirically interdependent. Unlike any other institution in the nation, the democratic state depends entirely upon the public to legitimate its rule. Simultaneously, the public, as the realm of open and free discourse, cannot function without the protection of its members offered by the state. Thus, any effort to appreciate the achievement of stability and order, or their absence, must look to this interpenetration of the normative or symbolic sphere with the institutional one.

The following chapters analyze the ways in which emergent cultural understandings and institutional and elite adaptability to those conceptions coalesced to produce in Ireland a stable, democratic order. Throughout the book, I will argue that the Irish public was weakest – indeed, practically nonexistent – during the Civil War. This weakness lessened the government's capacity to create legitimate political institutions. As the public became stronger – partly as a function of the demonstrated strength of the political institutions – democratic stability became more secure. In the next chapter, I examine the challenges faced by the new institutions and the elite as a result of the absence of a public at the time of independence and the presence of dichotomous ideological convictions undermining political legitimacy. Chapter 3 addresses how, in the interest of incorporating contending cultural values – expressed through opposing ideological positions – the political institutions of the Free State came to embrace contradictory cultural impulses, thereby inhibiting their capacity both to generate a more solidary community and to promote a more integrated public ideology. Part 2 (Chapters 4 to 6) examines three political crises that confronted the Free State in its first decade. I argue that the political elite, unable to develop a strong public capable of securing broad-based political legitimacy for the state apparatus, opted instead for strong institutional structures, thereby protecting the political system from the divisions among the population. In Part 3 (Chapters 7 and 8), I describe the process by which a newly strengthened party system, emerging only in the last part of the decade, was able to promote greater symbolic integration, ensuring finally and for the first time in postindependent Ireland a reconciliation of cultural convictions and political forms.

2. Irish Cultural Schisms and the Meaning of Political Disorder

Civil war, in any nation and at any time, represents the breakdown of fundamental common agreements universally shared by members of the society. It is the undoing of civility. The process may occur slowly or with alarming rapidity, but civil war is the culmination of a process whereby traditional mechanisms employed to forge agreement among diverse and, perhaps, competing sectors of the community are no longer available or viable. Differences become so hardened that neither power nor political authority can achieve agreement. In their place polarized ideologies emerge and crystallize, contesting the given arrangements of the society. A public order in which members "agree to disagree" does not exist. Civil war, in short, reveals, by their very absence, those conditions necessary for political and social order to prevail.

Because of the centrality of the Civil War to modern Irish politics and its obstruction to the initial establishment of a modern democratic order, it is important to understand the causes and character of the war. In this chapter, the question to be addressed is, why, despite the substantial consensus that characterized the nationalist struggle for political independence, did the factors surrounding the Civil War so rapidly and decisively produce major political schisms? The objective is to understand why the Irish public was incapable of resisting the dissolution of political order.

Most immediately, the Civil War was a dispute over the Articles of Agreement for a Treaty between Great Britain and Ireland, that is, the Anglo-Irish Treaty of 1921. The war pitted those who were willing to accept the Treaty, which granted Ireland limited political independence (i.e., dominion status in the British Empire), against those who were unwilling to give up a revolutionary struggle for a complete break with Britain.

The Anglo-Irish Treaty accorded the Irish Free State a status in the British Commonwealth similar in most ways to that of Canada. Ireland assumed a portion of the United Kingdom's national debt and agreed not to raise a defense force greater, in proportion to its population, than that of the United Kingdom. The British were guaranteed the use of certain Irish ports in peacetime, with the use of additional facilities during war. After five years, sole possession of the ports would be granted to Ireland, subject to an agreement by a joint conference. By signing the Treaty, Ireland further accepted the appointment by the British of a governor general to formally oversee politics in the dominion. The representatives to the Irish Parliament were called upon to swear faith and allegiance to the Constitution of the Irish Free State, and to pledge their faithfulness to the king and his successors "in virtue of the common citizenship of Ireland with Great Britain and her adherence to and membership of the group of nations forming the British Commonwealth of Nations."[1]

The Treaty was clearly a compromise document. Although it is not possible to detail the circumstances in which it was signed, suffice it to say that Britain had conceded a form of independence to the Irish because of the intensity of their opposition to British rule. Yet at the same time, it sought to preserve dominion status for Ireland and, in so doing, to protect the integrity of the British Empire.

Toward this end, Britain had gone further with Ireland than it had with any other colony. First, in other dominions of the Commonwealth, representatives to Parliament were called upon to swear direct allegiance to the king. In Ireland, parliamentary representatives swore faith and allegiance to the Constitution while only pledging "faithfulness" to the king. "Paradoxical as it might seem," Leo Kohn has written, "it was the expression of the Free State's adherence to the British Commonwealth in the feudal rite of an oath of fidelity to a sovereign liege which symbolized the full measure of its freedom in the new bond of association."[2]

In addition, the Treaty was one between "Great Britain and Ireland," implicitly recognizing a sovereign Ireland independent of Britain – a treaty between two nations – and also acknowledging the right of the Irish Parliament (Dáil Éireann) to speak for a united Ireland. Although in practice provision was made to maintain the territorial independence of Northern Ireland, the Treaty formally recognized a unified thirty-two-county nation.

The Treaty satisfied a sizable segment of the Irish population. For this sector, this form of compromise independence was superior to the prevailing political relationship between Ireland and Britain, in which there was virtually no Irish autonomy, and certainly preferable to the state of military conflict between the two territories that had begun anew with the Easter Rising of 1916 and had continued nearly unabated since 1918. For all practical purposes, they asserted, with the Treaty Irish independence was achieved. Piérás Beaslái, a parliamentary member, well articulated the pro-Treaty position in the acrimonious Treaty debates held in the Dáil. He said:

> The plain blunt man in the street, fighting man or civilian, sees that point more clearly than the formalist of Dáil Éireann. He sees in this Treaty the solid fact – our country cleared of the English armed forces, and the land in complete control of our own people to do what we like with. We can make our own Constitution, control our own finances, have our own schools and colleges, our own courts and our own flag, our own coinage and stamps, our own police, aye, and last but not least, our own army, not in flying columns, but in possession of the strong places of Ireland and the fortresses of Ireland, with artillery, aeroplanes, and all the resources of modern warfare. Why, for what else has been the national struggle in all generations but for that?[3]

Although recognizing the limitations on their independence, the pro-Treatyites were satisfied that they had acquired from Britain all that they could have obtained and, further, that an Irish nation could flourish in spite of these formal political constraints. Willing to accept continued association with Britain as its dominion, they were intent on getting on with the business of nation building.

Despite these concessions made by the British to the Irish interpretation of Irish history – a nationalist commitment to a free and independent Ireland without British control – a substantial and vocal minority of the Irish population rejected any treaty that did not provide for an Ireland completely independent from Britain. Opposed to dominion status and to the Treaty, this group saw in the Irish negotiators' willingness to accept a qualified form of political independence an abdication of nationalist principles. For them, it marked the abandonment of national goals and the capitulation to British interests.

Several features of the Treaty fueled the anti-Treatyites' conviction that the agreement represented a British victory. First, they objected to the fact that the independence of Ireland was to be ruled upon by an act of the British Parliament. The Treaty was to be submitted for approval not to the Dáil Éireann but to a meeting of members elected to sit in the House of Commons of Southern Ireland, that is, a deliberative body created by the British government. In addition, the Treaty made no mention of Dáil Éireann as the legally constituted authority of Ireland. Finally, members of the Irish Parliament, as indicated, were required to take an oath of allegiance to the king of England. No single clause of the Treaty raised more hackles to the Irish nationalists than this one. For these reasons, the Treaty was rejected by this faction. For them, the new leaders of the Provisional Government – once compatriots in the nationalist struggle and now supporters of the Treaty – were now seen as agents of British interests, not protectors of Irish values.

The outbreak of the Civil War reflected the absence of a public realm capable of mediating between conflicting opinions concerning the Anglo-Irish Treaty. The Treaty caused a fundamental cleavage in Irish society. There was some initial hope, as I will describe, that certain terms for reconciliation might be found. But between the time that the Anglo-Irish Treaty was signed by members of the Provisional Government and the outbreak of the Civil War, the possibility of moderation quickly eroded. Despite some efforts to forge a compromise, the pro-Treaty and anti-Treaty advocates could find no common ground. The search for compromise was usurped by two sectors of the national community fundamentally at odds with each other – a cleavage so deep that civil discourse was no longer possible. Trust, shared interests, and common commitments and outlooks could not prevail.[4]

The formation of the national government in 1922 was predicated, first, on the ability of the pro-Treaty leaders to successfully suppress their previous allies in the nationalist struggle. The stability of the new political order depended upon that suppression. Consequently, within a few short months, many of the heroes of the nationalist movement became the enemies of the state. How can one explain this breathtakingly rapid turn of events? How could a strong nationalist consensus so quickly give way to civil war?

It will be argued that the collapse of the public sector during the Civil War demonstrated the presence of sharply divergent conceptions of the meaning of the Irish nation and distinct understandings of who were the rightful members of that nation and of the social relations that ought to prevail among its members. The Civil War, in short, revealed the strength of what developed into contending ideologies that endorsed radically different values and norms. Although both groups rejected the British presence in Irish affairs and therefore joined in a strong nationalist movement, the consensus could not survive the withdrawal of the "British problem" from Irish affairs.

When, for the first time, a new Irish order was seen to be within reach, the community divided according to these different meanings, purposes, and patterns of social interaction held by different groups. In the absence of a public realm capable of mediating between them, these ideological alternatives grouped these sectors into different political camps. In a word, the Civil War produced, for the first time, explicit formulations – encased in two polarized ideologies – of contending values and norms that coexisted in Irish society.[5] In this sense, the Civil War meant more than two sides disagreeing over the terms of the Anglo-Irish Treaty. Broadly speaking, the Civil War emerged as an arena where contending cultural antinomies within Irish society were expressed and over which battle was waged. These ideologies, reflecting different cultural commitments shared by diverse broad-based sectors of the population, defined the agenda for the new political elite in postindependent Ireland. The success of the new Irish leaders depended upon their capacity to develop political structures capable of sustaining this cultural diversity and, further, to inhibit its expression in any extremist form. The following chapters document the success of the first Irish government in accomplishing these two tasks.

In the remainder of this chapter, I suggest, as F. S. L. Lyons has done before me, that there existed in Ireland two distinct cultural traditions – what I will refer to as the Irish-Enlightenment and Gaelic-Romantic traditions – each with significantly different values and norms.[6] These traditions long antedated the Civil War; in fact, their roots can be traced back at least to the eighteenth century. As Tom Garvin has persuasively argued, these traditions had long been expressed as tensions *within* the various political movements of the eighteenth and nineteenth centuries, producing a long-standing history of fractious debate and political division.[7] But it was in the nineteenth century, especially in the postfamine period, that these contending world views emerged on a national level and actively vied with each other for the hearts and minds of the Irish people.

Postfamine Ireland was characterized by the creation, for the first time, of a national community sharing a common identity and loyalty to Irish territory. It was a community, moreover, that was in the throes of modernization and was suffering from the destabilizing forces that modernity produces. The Irish-Enlightenment and Gaelic-Romantic traditions represented two responses to the crisis of Irish modernity, each offering its own understanding of the proper course of affairs for the nation and the appropriate relations among its members. It would be incorrect to surmise that one tradition, the Irish-Enlightenment, was the tradition of modernity and universalism, whereas the other, the Gaelic-Romantic, was premodern and primordial. Rather, each drew its inspiration from different aspects of Ireland's troubled past, each presented its own set of symbols to depict Irish nationhood, each offered an orientation explaining the uncertainties of postfamine Irish life, and, in time, each offered a distinctive conception of what a modern Ireland ought to be.

The potato famine of 1848 had produced a new order in Ireland enabling an Irish national self-concept to emerge. With as many as half a million people dead from starvation and another million who had emigrated, the landscape of rural Ireland was irretrievably transformed. Those who were worst off – the landless laborers and small tenants – no longer figured prominently in Irish life and society. With these smallest farmers and farms largely eliminated and with the concomitant movement toward pasture rather than tillage agriculture, the famine helped speed the trend toward a more secure and less destitute Irish peasantry. This transformation, however, produced its own unique set of pathologies. Emigration, postponed marriage, and permanent celibacy became enduring features of Irish society in the second half of the nineteenth century – particularly in rural society. These phenomena produced an unparalleled pattern of population decline: The population of Ireland decreased at every census except one between 1841 and 1961. The population of Ireland in 1926 – the first postindependent Irish census – was half of that in 1841.[8] Emigration came to develop a momentum of its own, whereby the pull of industrial employment and family networks abroad encouraged people to leave Ireland, often irrespective of the economic opportunities on the land. In the process of emigration, an Irish identity became more sharply fixed, better able to compete with the still powerful local identities of various counties. To be from Donegal or Clare, for example, remained of central importance to various Irish men and women, but the Irish presence in Scotland, England, Canada, and the United States made the Irish experience a common one.

In addition to the population decline and the creation of a less destitute nation, the second half of the nineteenth century ushered in a less traditional, more modern Irish society. What had been an island of relatively isolated, discrete regional and economic sectors increasingly gave way to a national society with more interdependent units. Although never as strong as in other parts of Europe, commercialization and industrialization were occurring. The result was increasing economic and regional cooperation.[9] Increased rates of literacy and new technology allowed the press to penetrate the countryside, further ensuring the nationalization of the Irish community.[10] As a further indication of Ireland's movement toward modernity, various institutions – the family, the school, the church, and the economy – were becoming more differentiated, each operating according to unique standards and each with specific, delimited social functions.[11] Most dramatically, with the "devotional revolution" of the mid-nineteenth century, secular life was now more sharply independent of sacred life, loosening the religious hold on mass political activity.[12] Finally, the extension of the franchise and other processes of democratization brought active political participation to the bulk of the Irish population.

These national traditions, crystallizing as a response to these transformations, were part of the Irish cultural cosmology through which average men and women made sense of their private universes. They were transcendent of and distinct from any one political position. Unlike the fractious nature of politics, cultural traditions were neither instrumentally focused nor circumscribed by specific issues. More durable and binding than political purposes, the two Irish traditions were powerful resources through which political positions were defined and legitimated.

Seen in this way, political expression in Ireland was informed and shaped by these two competing cultural traditions. They helped to shape popular perceptions of the nature of life for Irish men and women. In the pre-Treaty era, they promoted a widespread conviction that British colonialism was unjust; after the signing of the Treaty, they provided the language necessary to express contending political attitudes toward that document. Through these sets of understandings, political belief and action were understood, crystallized, and defended. And as politics was framed by this rhetoric, the course of postindependent Ireland was shaped.

This analysis of the relationship between Irish politics and cultural traditions serves only to complicate and further illuminate, not eliminate, those efforts to understand the relationship of political actions to specific social and economic conditions with which different Irish subgroups were confronted and, further, that correlate, in some measure, with different responses to nationalist politics and Civil War divisions. In an important book, *Internal Colonialism: The Celtic Fringe in British National Development*, Michael Hechter explains Irish nationalism and political secession from Britain with reference to social structural factors.[13] In attempting to explain why Ireland became independent from Britain, in contrast to Scotland and Wales, he argues that for a series of material reasons Ireland did not develop an urban, industrial enclave separate and distinct from the rural hinterlands. The especially low level of industrialization in Ireland enabled its unique political development in the British Isles. The result was a more solidary nation able to foster a broad-based political party intent on national independence.[14] Hechter writes that "the lack of enclave–hinterland differences in southern Ireland permitted the development of a solidary and broad-based political party capable of effecting independence."[15]

Hechter's aims, of course, are different from mine; his book attempts to explain British political development and the relationship between social structural factors and the conduciveness for solidary political movements. Nonetheless, his is a compelling statement of those structural conditions necessary for the growth of solidary political action. Yet, although Irish nationalism may be understood through reference to those necessary conditions, these factors surely are not sufficient to explain the particular nature of that movement, that is, its language, strategy, or imagery that propelled it forward. Nor can they explain the movement's ultimate success vis-à-vis the British. As Hechter writes, these conditions "permitted" the development of the movement.[16] But, in themselves, they cannot explain the movement's actual shape or its political content. Nor does such an explanation prepare us for the breakdown of solidary bonds that occurred immediately after the signing of the Treaty. My treatment differs from Hechter's, not in rejecting his theory of structural conduciveness but in clarifying our understanding of the Irish case. This is accomplished by attending to the cultural convictions that fueled nationalist sentiment and that, after the signing of the Treaty, produced civil war.

The work of E. Rumpf and A. C. Hepburn, like that of Hechter, explores the relationship between social structural factors and political action.[17] But in this case, differences *within* Ireland are identified to explain differential responses to political events. In what still stands as the most comprehensive analysis of "socio-geographical" correlates of political action in Ireland, these authors demonstrate social structural variations in both support for the nationalist movement and the positions taken during the Civil War. They argue that in the 1919–21 period, the younger and poorer sectors of both urban and rural society most strongly supported the national independence movement.[18] Further, the war against the British was concentrated in southern counties, "where a strong national tradition coincided with a modicum of prosperity among the farmers."[19] Because of the ferocity of the British military response in the Black and Tan campaign and because of the electoral successes of the Irish Republican Army (IRA) and the Dáil, they argue, more prosperous sectors of the Irish population became politically active in the nationalist cause just prior to the signing of the Treaty.[20]

Rumpf and Hepburn further note that the Treaty signing produced new geopolitical constellations; the political impetus for opposing the Treaty emerged in the West, not the South.[21] They argue that the strongest adherents to the anti-Treaty position came from the West; the farmers of the South apparently were satisfied. "The small farmers of the West," Rumpf and Hepburn write, "with their more primitive subsistence economy and traditional Irish culture, were less open to practical economic considerations, and adhered rigidly to the ideal of a republic."[22]

It is clear that, even in Rumpf and Hepburn's analysis concerned principally with the relationship of geography and social structure to political action, the "interpretive" process, that is, the mechanisms by which the Irish made sense of the political situation, played an important role. The most ardent nationalists – the southern farmers – rallied around the Treaty; the small farmers of the West reacted against it, despite, as Rumpf and Hepburn suggest, the economic irrationality of their position. Their support was based, in part, on their rigid adherence "to the ideal of a republic." More prosperous groups supported the independence movement, not for self-interested reasons but because of the extremist military action of the British and the political victories of the IRA and Sinn Féin. Upon the signing of the Treaty, they divided between the various factions.

An explanation of these events and an understanding of the shifting political alliances require an examination of the ideologies that facilitated different responses to the same political reality. Politics can hardly be viewed as a direct, unmediated response to social structural conditions; rather, it is an outcome of individuals sharing the same national cultural universe, although situated differently in the social structure, who developed specific understandings about political events. Although these responses are not completely random, they cannot be predicted solely by reference to a person's social position and geographic location. Equally as important, the political course that the Irish nation followed cannot be adequately comprehended without paying attention to the language and imagery that informed political action.

The challenge is to describe the cultural universe of Irish men and women that illuminates and explains their responses to a shifting political reality. I do this by positing the presence of these two competing cultural traditions that served to orient the population, helping to determine particular responses to political events.

Before detailing these traditions, I must note that these cultural orientations are presented and discussed as ideal types in the sense that Max Weber developed the method of sociological analysis. Weber writes, "An ideal-type is formed by the one-sided *accentuation* of one or more points-of-view and by the synthesis of a great many diffuse, discrete, more or less present and occasionally absent *concrete individual* phenomena, which are arranged according to those one-sidedly emphasized viewpoints into a unified *analytical* construct. In its conceptual purity, this mental construct cannot be found empirically anywhere in reality. It is a *utopia*."[23] The Irish-Enlightenment and Gaelic-Romantic traditions, as ideal types, are not meant to express as historical reality only two dichotomous cultural orientations available to the Irish population. Rather, as I argue, they represent a way of conceiving these two poles of cultural understanding – each at one end of a continuum – through which social meaning was forged. They stand as expressions of the parameters of national understanding that served to shape and constrain interpretations of specific political, economic, and social developments. As cultural resources, these ideal typical constructs provide us with a heuristic tool to evaluate the course of social action in Ireland.

These ideal types are offered to facilitate *verstehen*, an understanding of the shifting patterns of association and action (e.g., nationalist solidarity to fratricide, fratricide to democratic stability) from the perspective of the participants. This objective militates against a purely historicist account of Irish politics and thought. Further, it distinguishes this enterprise of historical sociology from simple historical accounts, unselfconsciously chronicling the course of events in Irish history. These cultural constellations are presented abstractly, and largely without specific reference to given historical figures as "carriers" or articulators of the various positions. They are presented as utopia. Although these traditions were forged as consequences of real political struggles by real individuals – articulating specific versions of the meaning of the Irish nation – I assert that they ultimately stood as transsituational, transindividual social constructs. Individuals existed in relation to these constellations. These positions provided the language and imagery necessary to understand specific events. These traditions assembled in a particular way the available ideas through which individuals filtered their own understanding. And in articulating their personal views through these frames, individuals carried the traditions forward.

If the process is understood in this way, one should not expect that those individuals powerfully swayed by Irish-Enlightenment or Gaelic-Romantic ideas would possess complete unanimity on all dimensions of the tradition. Each individual draws different interpretations from the same stock of ideas. Yet, for analytic and heuristic purposes, political actors may profitably be understood as being guided by these different traditions. As Weber writes, "Those 'ideas' which govern the behavior of the population of a certain epoch, i.e. which are concretely influential in determining their conduct, can, if a somewhat complicated construct is involved, be formulated precisely only in the form of an ideal-type, since empirically it exists in the minds of an indefinite and constantly changing mass of individuals and assumes in their minds the most multifarious nuances of form and content, clarity and meaning."[24]

For example, later in this chapter, I state that the actions of both W. B. Yeats and Arthur Griffith were strongly influenced by an Irish-Enlightenment conception of the Irish nation; yet, as Lyons argues, there was substantial disagreement and controversy between them.[25] On the one hand, Griffith rejected the cosmopolitan outlook inherent in the Irish-Enlightenment world view; but that world view, as it became sharpened and strengthened in opposition to Gaelic-Romanticism during the years preceding independence, sufficiently constrained Griffith's thinking that he abandoned his original desire for a dual monarchy and came to strive actively for political independence. Independence, of course, was a pivotal component of the Irish-Enlightenment tradition. Yeats, on the other hand, became disenchanted with the actual form of Irish independence, what he identified as its parochialism, during the 1920s. Nevertheless, he was sufficiently constrained by Irish-Enlightenmentarianism to hold a seat in the Senate and seek political reforms leading to greater cosmopolitanism.

This ideal typical approach to Irish history, in short, restricts our vision by its tendency to obscure political strain and contest between specific individuals. But it provides an opportunity to understand the more general orientations to social life that historicism overlooks. Weber writes, "Nothing should be more sharply emphasized than the proposition that the knowledge of the *cultural significance of concrete historical events and patterns* is exclusively and solely the final end which, among other means, concept-construction and the criticism of constructs also seeks to serve."[26] In the interest of understanding the cultural significance of specific events, these ideal types are developed.

According to Tom Garvin, nationalist political action in Ireland throughout the nineteenth century represented a cultural amalgam of both traditions.[27] The Irish nationalist movement was successful because it forged from both an anti-British sentiment strong enough to defeat British colonialism. Yet, as an amalgam, it was not resilient enough to sustain the different interpretations that each tradition would give to Lloyd George's offer of a limited form of independence. It was the challenge of the new Provisional Government, in the midst of the Civil War and afterward, to forge a politics of independence that successfully drew upon the prevailing cultural constellations that had been expressed in a broad-based movement for national independence. As I will show, this was not easy to accomplish and the first Free State government was not entirely successful in this synthesis.

Irish-Enlightenment values and norms

The Irish-Enlightenment tradition – articulated first by the Protestant Ascendancy, which helped shape many of the institutions of Irish society – was the dominant cultural orientation, influencing the thinking of a broad sector of the Irish population. Its influence extended beyond the Anglo-Irish who were its chief contributors. It offered a conception of Ireland as a modern urbane nation, like other European nations, committed to nonsectarianism and parliamentarianism.

No member of the Protestant Ascendancy was more important in ensuring a permanent place for the Irish-Enlightenment tradition in Irish life than Wolfe Tone. In 1791, Tone, a Protestant Dubliner educated at elite Trinity College, founded a secret society known as the United Irishmen. Its purpose was to seek a "brotherhood of affection and a communion of rights and a union of power among Irishmen of every religious persuasion."[28] Deeply inspired by the French Revolution, Tone was committed to the creation of an independent Irish Republic governed by the precepts that had successfully overthrown the old order in France. In particular, Tone's movement embodied the conviction that individuals need to be protected from coercive authority and that people possess inalienable rights over and above the state. In addition, Tone adopted the radical idea that all material resources are vested in the hands of the people. English control over Irish land and labor was seen as a denial of this basic democratic right. Tone's radicalism extended beyond his conception of individual rights. He further sought to create an independent nation through a union between Protestants and Roman Catholics, who, in common battle as Irishmen, would defeat the English. The aspiration for an independent, nonsectarian, democratic nation was accompanied by a belief in the natural aristocracy of Anglo-Irish leadership, in which those most able to lead would direct the course of the nation. In the late nineteenth century, Tone's was a vision of radical egalitarianism, but clearly it was sharply constrained by a belief in a natural hierarchy of leadership and authority.[29]

Wolfe Tone led an abortive uprising in 1798 for Irish independence in which he sought the "establishment of the Rights of Man in Ireland."[30] Despite its failure, it and the Irish-Enlightenment cultural ethos that motivated it formed a legacy by which succeeding generations came to define distinctive values and norms for an independent Irish nation. It is important to note that this tradition was stronger in the northern half of Ireland, above the Dublin–Galway divide, and apparently was expressed by both elite and mass political organizations.[31] As Tom Garvin has recently written, Ribbonism of the nineteenth century – predominant in the northern half of the country – was suffused with United Irish ideas and was, therefore, substantially different in orientation and outlook from the agrarian-based secret societies of the southern half.[32]

But the assertion of uniquely Enlightenment values can be more readily seen, and more easily studied, in their elite expression. With the independent Irish Parliament of 1782 and Wolfe Tone's rebellion as its backdrop, members of the Anglo-Irish elite during the late nineteenth and early twentieth centuries sought a revitalized Irish language and literature. Members of the Anglo-Irish elite were at the center of this cultural revival, although not exclusively, most notably in the movement to revive the Irish language, but also in the rediscovery (or creation) and celebration of traditional Irish legends and folklore. This assertion of Irish cultural distinctiveness was hardly a rejection of modern cultural expression. The challenge, as they saw it, was to discover and incorporate in a modern Western culture what was peculiarly Irish. It was an effort to integrate Irish cultural motifs into a modern cultural context.

The language movement, for example, was not an effort to replace English with Irish. Rather, it was an assertion that only by possessing a living language and literature could Ireland hope to maintain a separate national identity and be recognized as one nation among equals. Similarly, the nineteenth-century Irish literary revival – sparked most notably by W. B. Yeats but also producing a whole new generation of poets, dramatists, and novelists – consisted of a romantic re-creation of traditional Irish myths. For those who identified themselves with this cultural renaissance, the objective was not to reestablish an ancient Ireland but, instead, to demonstrate the vitality and dynamism of the modern Irish nation. With particular zeal, Yeats sought to distinguish his literary efforts from those of cultural nationalists like Thomas Davis of the Young Ireland movement. Yeats saw their interest in traditional Irish culture as a tool to mobilize the Irish politically against British rule, and he rejected the conception of cultural revitalization used only for ulterior political ends.[33]

This cultural movement demonstrated the vitality of the Irish-Enlightenment tradition. Consistent with these values, the literary movement helped to define for a large segment of the population the meaning of Irishness and to articulate one view of the nation's proper place in the world community. It was this Irish intelligentsia who grappled with the changing nature of Irish society in the second half of the nineteenth century and gave it meaning in the context of the long-standing Irish-Enlightenment tradition.

The belief in Irish independence was preeminent. It meant that Ireland should be subordinate to no external force or control. It ought to be self-determining, capable of directing the affairs of the population, with the Irish people together determining the course of their history. Seen from this vantage point, the belief was that Ireland was capable of making its own unique contribution to world or Western culture by being cognizant of its own history and tradition. In this sense, the commitment to Irish independence implied no particular transcendent "calling" for the Irish nation except the freedom to determine its own direction.

At the same time, the belief in Irish independence implied a break with what was viewed as the provinciality and sectarianism of Irish society, identified as a product of Ireland's colonial and dependent relationship with Britain. Independence would promote the replacement of traditional orientations with a new dedication to culture and learning. Although the anti-British animus was explicit, there was also an implicit critique of the provinciality of the Catholic bourgeoisie, who were still wedded to a provincial church. Befitting its Anglo-Irish sources, the Irish-Enlightenment cultural tradition envisioned the new Ireland as being led by an elite committed to nonsectarianism and urbane values, that is, Irish-Enlightenment ones. The proud Irish race, shorn of its English shackles and its prosaic sectarian rulers – the Catholic middle class – would now follow the leadership, it was believed, of this new Irish intelligentsia. It was believed that the Irish-Enlightenment commitment to revitalizing a distinctive Irish history and making it live again would ensure that the Irish peasantry, responding positively to this nationalist call, would give their loyalty and affection to those Irish leaders, perhaps Catholic, but dedicated not to Catholicism or a return to a provincial Irish state, but instead to the pursuit of "the golden heresy of truth."[34]

These distinctive values and aspirations were accompanied by a specific set of norms consistent with and derived from these commitments. In brief, what has been defined as the strength of the "parliamentary tradition" in Ireland might be recast as the presence of a strong commitment to political and social forms best designed to promote these Irish-Enlightenment values.[35] Parliamentarianism implies more than the acceptance of parliamentary political forms, reform, and gradualism as the modus operandi for social change in modern life. It means more than the adoption of specified procedures by which law and policy are made and to which all citizens agree to abide. Parliamentarianism further represents a deeper normative commitment. It implies an acceptance of hierarchical arrangements whereby certain individuals, occupying particular social roles and meriting their status because of demonstrated ability, legitimately possess greater authority than others in determining the course of events.

Irish-Enlightenment norms, in this elaborated understanding of the parliamentary tradition, constituted a firm commitment to democratic individualism. First, it was an understanding of the Irish national community as nonsectarian, composed of both Protestants and Catholics. Ireland was viewed as a moral community in which all men and women, as members, possessed inalienable rights but also responsibilities to other members, irrespective of status. It was an understanding of Ireland as a community composed of citizens equal in their rights and responsibilities under the law. This view promoted an acceptance of hierarchy and authority relations only when those who held positions of power, wealth, and prestige did so as a result of common consent. Such consent would be forged within the society, not imposed by alien powers. The antipathy by those who held such convictions toward the British came not from a rejection of modern social and political order, hierarchically arranged and institutionally differentiated, but rather from a view that the British illegitimately controlled the affairs of the Irish nation. It was expected that in an independent Ireland, positions of power and authority would be held by members of the Irish nation, who would legitimately guide and direct its affairs.

Related to this commitment to nonsectarianism and legitimate structures of authority was the expectation that the rule of law and proceduralism would govern and constrain the moral community. Through codified procedures like popular elections, the right to dissent was celebrated and the will of the majority was held to be sacrosanct. Proceduralism, in short, represented not an abdication of moral purpose but rather a belief that the purposes of the community would be served only when each individual agreed to abide by the rules of conflict resolution. The rules, forged through collective interactions, would promote the will of the majority; no transcendent purpose was entrusted to those structures other than promoting individuals' interests, as they themselves came to understand them. Thus, the Irish-Enlightenment commitment to parliamentarianism represented a belief that the values of the Irish national community could be realized only when individuals were free – both from British political control and from Catholic primordiality – to express their will, and when they would agree to abide by the procedures of collective decision making.

Gaelic-Romantic values and norms

The Gaelic-Romantic tradition never had the same influence as its Irish-Enlightenment counterpart. Nevertheless, it emerged in the nineteenth century as a significant system of national meaning. And in certain regions of Ireland and at certain times, this "subterranean" value and normative belief system exerted considerable influence. Its subordination to the Irish-Enlightenment tradition is not altogether surprising, given the inordinate power and prestige held by the Anglo-Irish in the eighteenth and nineteenth centuries who were the principal formulators of this cultural doctrine – and who, as a consequence, had substantially more resources to promote their ideas. But as modernization unfolded in the nineteenth century, the better-educated, more fully enfranchised, and wealthier Catholics developed a countervailing system of thought. With significant assistance from the Catholic Church, this distinctive view of the Irish nation came to vie successfully for popular acceptance.

The Gaelic-Irish conception of Ireland, as forged in response to the modernization process, was that the nation ought to strive to re-create its past and resist those changes that seemed to challenge the basic meaning of Ireland as embodied in its traditions. Modern Ireland was to be celebrated as a preindustrial nation; its identity was to be found in its rural character. The sanctity of the family was to be preserved, the Church was to remain a central social institution second only to the family, and the farm was to serve as the backbone for a healthy, thriving society.

The Catholic Church, more than any other institution, promoted these beliefs even before they became politicized in the Irish nationalist movement. Benefiting in the mid-nineteenth century from a remarkable "devotional revolution," the church took seriously its role as minister to a largely traditional, socially conservative, rural congregation.[36] As Emmet Larkin writes:

> The growing awareness of a sense of sin already apparent in the 1840's was certainly deepened as God's wrath was made manifest in a great national disaster that destroyed and scattered his people. Psychologically and socially, therefore, the Irish people were ready for a great evangelical revival, while economically and organiza-

tionally, the Church was now correspondingly ready after the famine to meet their religious and emotional needs.[37]

The church's traditionalism did not involve a turning away from political and social reform, but its involvement in change extended only
to preserving or, where possible, re-creating presumed earlier patterns
of social relations. By seeking the disestablishment of the Church of
Ireland, it sought the creation of a national system of Catholic education
and land reform – to rid the nation of its contemporary pathology and
to reconstruct a new Ireland that would mirror the mythology of its
distant past.[38] Ireland was to become a harmonious nation, communal
and free from "modern" urban, British, and Anglican influences, from
which it was currently suffering.

It is easy to understand how disestablishment of the Church of Ireland
and national Catholic education would be supported by the hierarchy
of the Catholic Church, and how both reforms would ensure the continued importance of the church for the Irish population. Further, it is
understandable how such measures would promote an identity of Irishness with a primordial sense of Catholicity. Yet land reform, at first
glance, seemed a less likely cause for the church to support in its desire
to re-create an "old Ireland." But as Barbara Solow has argued, the kind
of land reform that the rural population and their elected representatives
to Westminster sought was one intended to resist the modernization of
the land system.[39] The objective was to reinstitutionalize traditional patterns of land tenure and organization. The ideas of fixity of tenure, fair
rent, and free sale for the tenant – the rallying cries of the reform movement – represented a traditionalist challenge to the increasing strength
of the modern conception of land as a commodity. The Gaelic-Romantic
belief that the peasant or, at least, the small farmer represented the
quintessence of Irishness and that his claim to land was sacrosanct challenged this ascendant understanding of property as a commodity. It was
asserted, instead, that no individual or group should restrict others from
the use of land; economic rationality should not prevail over the protection of tenants' rights.

It is not inconsistent, then, that the Catholic Church, in seeking to
preserve traditional social relations, resisted efforts to have property
relations redefined to conform with capitalist interests and supported
instead a precommercial conception of land. Moreover, this long-standing, broad-based social movement came to accept the view that it was
British involvement in Ireland – in particular, the role of the absentee
landlord – that was distorting Irish national development. The land
movement represented more than a policy to defend indigenous land

interests. Like the movement for disestablishment and Catholic education, it promoted the Irish "race" over and against the British assault upon it.

In short, the nineteenth-century understanding and expression of the Gaelic-Romantic cultural tradition articulated a primordial conception of Irishness in which British, Anglican modernity became the symbol of what the Irish were not. As a symbol, it became the definition of the insidious forces in Irish society that needed to be exorcised. The Irish national community was conceived as its antithesis: rural, agricultural, and Catholic. The motivation for Irishmen ought to be the resurrection of the putative values that governed Gaelic life, expressed now in the aspiration for an independent Irish Republic.[40]

In contrast to the Irish-Enlightenment desire for independence, the Republic symbolized a millennial belief that a new age could be ushered in, erasing centuries of foreign penetration. Republicanism invested in Ireland a vision of the new Irish nation that was far more detailed than any commitment to the free rule of individuals in an independent Irish community. In place of a commitment to a moral order of free individuals, a belief was expressed in the power of the Irish people to create a self-sufficient, agricultural, and autonomous nation unlike any other modern nation, and one where Gaelic principles would become preeminent despite centuries of suppression. The "true" character of the Irish people – as distinct from any other people – would be allowed to flourish and would result in a community free of the evils of modern society.

If Irish-Enlightenmentarian sentiments emphasized the power of culture and learning to move the independent Irish nation ever closer to a transcendent ideal of truth, Gaelic-Romantic republicanism embodied a belief in the immanence of the Republican ideal. The ideal order, in this view, was indeed possible, contingent upon the abolition of the evils of cosmopolitanism from the Irish landscape. When the Irish Republican Brotherhood (IRB) in 1867 unilaterally declared that the Irish Republic was "virtually established" and its Supreme Council would serve as the "sole government of the Irish Republic until Ireland secures absolute national independence and a permanent Republican government is established," they expressed a belief in the immediate possibility of a new Irish age and, further, that the specific characteristics of that new order were commonly shared by fellow Irish patriots.[41] The Supreme Council of the IRB proclaimed itself the vanguard representative of the true wishes of the Irish people, assuming the responsibility for implementing this conception of the Irish nation. Their task was not to secure Ireland's place in the world community but, rather, to resurrect an Ireland whose history had been transmuted because of a series of foreign invasions, of which British colonialism was only the most recent.

Irish Republicanism, as an immanent belief that the ideal could be made real, promoted distinctive norms accompanying this central value. First, the Irish Republic was seen to be composed solely of Irish "republicans," that is, those who were primordially related to the ancient Gaels. "Irishness" was not a civil designation but a community of brethren connected by a common ancient ancestry. The meaning of the national community was derived from its Catholicism – which distinguished the true Gael from the British and Anglican interloper. Further, the quintessence of Irishness could be found in the poor countrysiders who had been pushed beyond the pale by the forces of British oppression. With the Irish national community identified as the antithesis of British urbanity, it was the Irish peasant, committed to anti-industrial values, who was celebrated as occupying the symbolic center of the Irish Republic. Moreover, because the community was primordially defined as Catholic, the artifice of boundaries, like the one that divided Northern Ireland from the South, held little meaning. To the extent that boundaries interfered with the realization of the blood-based confraternity, they would not be tolerated.

Second, spokesmen for the Gaelic-Romantic tradition, in proposing a Gaelic Republic, deemed hierarchy and authority illegitimate in the organization of social relations. They came to understand agrarian violence in the Irish countryside as part of an enduring contest of the peasant with his landlord, and they identified themselves as part of this tradition of a never-ending struggle of the weak with the powerful. In the early nineteenth century, it was the landlord – not the British or the economic system per se – who for the Gaelic-Romantics became the central object of opprobrium. But in postfamine Ireland, as the struggle for a Republic became central, the British came to be identified as the rightful object of Irish opposition. Again, the British were more than a political enemy preventing independence; they represented the most recent expression of the forces perverting the "natural" and egalitarian Gaelic community. As I suggested earlier, the movement for land reform in the second half of the nineteenth century was more than a movement for change: It was animated by a dislike of any imposed structure inhibiting the realization of the solidary Gaelic community. As Nicholas Mansergh argues with respect to the peasants and Irish politicians active in land reform, they "were concerned to end the system over and above the evils in it and that being so, their objections and denunciations were ultimately on a matter of principle, not practice. They did not want good landlords in place of bad ones; they wanted no landlords."[42]

The Gaelic-Romantic millennial commitment to the Republic also promoted an unshakable conviction that force and violence were necessary to purge the Irish of British influence. Toward the end of the nineteenth century, the Gaelic-Romantic tradition had become inextricably entwined with the nationalist struggle for complete independence. Within the nationalist movement, however, those who shared Gaelic-Romantic principles imbued violence with a meaning that transcended a tactical assessment of the measures necessary to achieve an independent Ireland. Physical force came to be understood, first, as an Irish rejection of parliamentary negotiation and constitutionalism and, second, as a visible expression of the different commitments of the Irish people compared to either the Enlightenmentarians or the English moderates. The legacy of Irish resistance to various forms of oppression came to be viewed as an attribute of the Irish people and, therefore, celebrated in itself. Violence was the means by which the repression imposed by the modern British order could at last be purged from the Irish soul. Violence, in itself, was an act of collective liberation. Political concessions, however small, were rejected as an abdication of the absolutist conviction in the realization of the Gaelic Republic. To engage in moral appeal, political suasion, and the like, in an effort to achieve the Republic, would be tantamount to a concession that the ideal would always remain unattainable.

But this embrace of violence and its centrality in demarcating the Irish from others also served to define the relationship among members of the nation. The willingness to engage in illegal activities in promoting the Republic was emblematic of one's Irishness, of one's primordial connection to the Irish nation. Further, one's illegal status in the eyes of the British and the Irish constitutionalists helped promote the egalitarianism – equal in their illegality – of all members of the community. Violence, in short, was an essential component of the Gaelic-Romantic normative commitment precisely because it created a moral bond demarcating Republicans from those attempting to uphold the social order. In so doing, it realized the goal of solidarity and common purpose that was at the heart of the Republican dream.

The commitment to violence, as a contemporary expression of traditional Gaelic resistance to oppression, eclipsed the direct influence of the Catholic Church in the Gaelic-Romantic tradition. Long opposed to secret societies and committed to moderation, the church hierarchy opposed the linkage of traditional Irish values with a violent defense of the Republic. As a result, the church came to occupy a no-man's land, supporting Gaelic-Romantic aspirations for a return to the rural and pastoral Ireland of old while opposing those means widely believed necessary to achieve them.[43]

This characterization of the Gaelic-Romantic tradition – which was wedded to the idea of the Republic and embraced a distinctive set of normative understandings – suggests that the common understanding currently held of the physical force tradition in Ireland, like that of the parliamentary tradition, needs to be reexamined. As it is now generally used, the term "physical force tradition" refers to the readiness with which some Irish have been willing to engage in violent acts to achieve given ends. Secret societies, extraparliamentary in nature, and the commitment to violence have been identified as the central features of this tradition. For this reason, the United Irishmen and the IRB, for example, both secret societies, have been characterized as being cut from the same cloth, and Tone's abortive revolution of 1798 and the Fenian rising of 1867, both violent in nature, have been identified as part of the same tradition of violence.[44] Yet these events, I would argue, share only in their later contribution to a unified nationalist response opposed to British rule. To assume that the participants in these events shared similar cultural commitments, other than a common opposition to England, would be to seriously misunderstand both Irish cultural terrain and the antinomies that existed in Irish cultural thought.

This becomes particularly clear when one examines the Sinn Féin organization, the political arm of the nationalist movement, which grew ever stronger in the years preceding political independence. While its membership grew, the strains within the organization became increasingly intense. These strains reflect the fact that the nationalist movement obscured the very real differences among the nationalists concerning the meaning of Irish independence. The Sinn Féin Constitution of 1917, of which Éamon de Valéra was the chief architect, revealed these conflicts. In its preamble, it was stated that "Sinn Féin aims at securing the international recognition of Ireland as an independent Irish Republic. Having achieved that status the Irish people may by Referendum freely choose their own form of government." The preamble also stated that "in the name of the Sovereign Irish People, Sinn Féin would (a) deny the right and oppose the will of the British Parliament and British Crown or any other foreign government to legislate for Ireland and (b) make use of any and every means available to render impotent the power of England to hold Ireland in subjugation by military force or otherwise."[45]

This Constitution is commonly seen as representing in 1917 the victory of the extremists within the Sinn Féin Party.[46] Yet, as I discuss later in the chapter, de Valéra refers to this document as a compromise, important in holding together the fractious Sinn Féin organization. The compromise, as the preamble illustrates, represented an ambiguous construction of the two distinct ideologies that I have described. Each was committed to independence, but it was to be achieved differently and for different purposes. The preamble referred specifically to the Irish Republic, evoking the imagery of both the IRB and those involved in the Easter Rising of 1916, and it legitimated those wedded to the physical force tradition. Simultaneously, it embraced the concept of parliamentarianism, for example, the use of the referendum so that the Irish people could determine their own form of government, and it endorsed nonviolent measures to "deny the right and oppose the will" of the British to legislate on behalf of Ireland. Seen in this way, the document seems hardly the work of extremists, although it shows the increasing stridency of demands for independence. Rather, it is evidence of the delicate and skillfully accomplished task of holding together in one movement persons with substantially different beliefs.

The impressive victory of Sinn Féin in the December 1918 general election further increased the party's strength and membership. But the meaning of that electoral victory and Sinn Féin's mandate were interpreted differently by various Irish nationalist groups. To those who believed in Irish-Enlightenment tenets, the nationalist victory was a popular expression of the desire to achieve independence through any means necessary; it was seen as a popular repudiation of parliamentarianism as the strategy to effect independence. As a result, these constitutionalists reluctantly came to support nonparliamentary strategies while maintaining their commitments to the parliamentary process after independence. They participated in convening the first Dáil Éireann in 1919. The Dáil, of course, was an illegal assembly in the eyes of the British, but its convening demonstrated the Irish resolve for self-government.

The Gaelic-Romantic interpretation was that the election was a mandate by the Irish people to the Republican leaders to do whatever was necessary to realize the Republican dream. The election served as but an affirmation, one that had been stated at least since 1867, that the nation was unequivocally committed to the Republic. Republican leaders, it was believed, now possessed complete license to realize it. As F. S. L. Lyons suggests, the first Dáil Éireann was effectively controlled by those who were more enthusiastic in their understanding of independence; the more moderate leaders, like de Valéra and Griffith, were in prison and unable to participate.[47] The presiding chairman was Cathal Brugha, "an enragé if there ever was one."[48] The immediate work of the Dáil was to begin to decide how the Irish Republic would be organized after the successful wresting of power from the British.

A Democratic Program was quickly passed without much debate or controversy. That program suggested that Irish nationalism was more than a political revolution; it was one in which fundamental social relations would be altered in accordance with Gaelic-Romantic convictions. In one clause it was stated:

> We declare in the words of the Irish Republic proclamation [of 1916] the right of the people of Ireland to the ownership of Ireland and to the unfettered control of Irish destinies to be indefeasible, and in the language of our First President, Padraig Pearse, we declare that the nation's sovereignty extends not only to all men and women of the nation, but to all its material possessions; the nation's soil and all its resources, all the wealth and all the wealth-producing processes within the nation, and with him we re-affirm that all rights to private property must be subordinated to the public right and welfare.

In another clause it was asserted:

> It should be the first duty of the Government of the Republic to make provision for the physical, mental and spiritual well-being of the children, to secure that no child shall suffer hunger or cold from lack of food or clothing or shelter, but that all shall be provided with the means and facilities requisite for their proper education and training as citizens of a free and Gaelic Ireland.[49]

In offering such a substantive vision of the meaning of independence, in contrast to the more limited aspiration of political independence per se held out by the Irish-Enlightenment view, Sinn Féin, in the ensuing years, became the cauldron of those contending conceptions.[50] Yet because of the overriding interest in ridding the nation of continued abuses by the British, these divisions were placed in the background. De Valéra, along with others, succeeded in mollifying both sides sufficiently so that the battle with England could move forward. Both sides, in effect, agreed on this as the central objective of the nationalist movement, despite the grave differences in thought that characterized Sinn Féin's membership.

The physical force tradition, then, cannot be accurately characterized, or its importance in Irish society and politics properly assessed, without understanding the meaning of violence with respect to other normative understandings and appreciating its relationship to the Republican ideal.

There is no denying, of course, Wolfe Tone's belief in the need for violence and the necessity for secret organizations. But in both respects, they represented tactical responses to political exigencies rather than a principled endorsement of secrecy or violence. In contrast, for the IRB and those who shared a Gaelic-Romantic conception, secret societies committed to violence, far from being strategic responses to achieve specific ends, constituted the realization of the Republic in spite of the continued British presence. They expressed in microcosm the egalitarian solidarity to be forged in the Republican macrocosm. Thus, the physical force tradition, rather than being simply a tolerance of violence when necessary, embodied a set of normative commitments – primordial, communal, and expunged of civil and moderate sensibilities. By using physical force and by acting as if the Republic had already been achieved, the Irish were creating the utopian Gaelic community.

Through these two distinct cultural traditions, Irishmen came to understand the problem of Irish modernity in decisively different ways. Each formulation was national in scope, each identified strongly with the Irish nation, and each offered a view of the appropriate features of the national community. Both condemned the British rule of Ireland. But as competing cultural responses to a modern nation, their coexistence after independence proved no longer possible. As I will describe shortly, these traditions came to represent the cultural poles between which political debate occurred in the months preceding the Civil War. The outbreak of the Civil War occurred when political discourse, no longer able to mediate between them, was irresistibly drawn to one extreme or the other. These cultural strands, then, gave meaning to, animated, and intensified the political conflict of civil war.

Politics and culture in the Irish Civil War

If it is true, as I have suggested, that the Irish Civil War represented the breakdown of a public sphere capable of mediating between contending ideologies, then we should be able to identify in the opposing political factions the different cultural commitments that inspired them. By the time of the Civil War, the Gaelic-Romantic and Irish-Enlightenment traditions had become distinct national symbolic systems, both deeply connected to essential features of Irish history and experience and both confronting, in their own way, the same set of troubles besetting the nation. Each offered a system of perception and meaning by which the

Anglo-Irish Treaty could be viewed; in favoring one system or the other, one's stance toward the Civil War became largely determined.

It would be historically inaccurate, however, to suggest that those who supported the Treaty adopted lock, stock, and barrel one system of cultural thinking, whereas the Treaty's opponents embraced its opposite. Social reality was far too chaotic in those months prior to the outbreak of the Civil War to expect that the meaning-making process in which every Irishman was engaged would conform neatly to the ideal typical cultural categories that I have described. Further, the nationalist consensus that had emerged prior to the Treaty had sufficiently confused those distinctions. Individuals were forced to sift through the various collective representations in order to arrive at their own understanding. It is much more reasonable to assume, as the historical record confirms, that the process by which many individuals and political collectivities chose sides was far from an easy one. The Treaty created a moral conflict of a kind that few citizens anywhere ever have to confront. Even for those who were strongly committed to honoring the Treaty and for those who immediately rejected it, it was clear that in opting for one of these positions, they were choosing sides in an immanent war with their previous compatriots in the nationalist struggle. In short, no Irish citizen could rest easy with his or her decision, for its consequence could not be escaped.

Perhaps because of the profound moral issues and the devastating consequence involved, both pro- and anti-Treaty positions were forged and legitimated with reference to these ennobling cultural traditions. The moral ambiguity posed by the Treaty led citizens to understand and defend their position by adopting some amalgam of Irish-Enlightenment and Gaelic-Romantic principles. In fact, by distinguishing between Irish-Enlightenment and Gaelic-Romantic values and norms, the four major political positions on the Treaty can be understood. In time, however, the society divided in two, with each accepting one of the two main positions.

In the remainder of this chapter, I will suggest that the political positions toward the Civil War can be comprehended by understanding them in relation to these conflicting cultural categories. Further, the cultural analysis of values and norms, seen as meaning-making resources available to the Irish population, is necessary to explain why persons occupying similar positions in Irish society would come to adopt different positions on the Civil War. I will examine four different political groups that played central roles in the war; more specifically, I will examine four leaders who were key actors in the political turmoil and who epitomized the political posture of these four groups.

	PRO-TREATY *Irish-Enlightenment Values*	ANTI-TREATY *Gaelic-Romantic Values*
Irish-Enlightenment Norms	Arthur Griffith and the Provisional government	Éamon De Valéra and the Republican Dáil
Gaelic-Romantic Norms	Michael Collins and the IRB	Cathal Brugha and the IRA

Arthur Griffith, president of the Provisional Government, and Cathal Brugha, minister for defense in the pre-Treaty Irish Government and representative of the IRA position, both closely conform in their commitments to the ideal typical categories of thought I have described. Griffith endorsed both the ideal of an independent Ireland and the normative procedures of parliamentarianism required to achieve it. Brugha, in contrast, typifies the commitment to Gaelic-Romantic principles – the desire for an Irish Republic and the celebration of violence as evidence of the Republic's immanent realization. Griffith and Brugha, as symbols of the two endpoints on a continuum of thought, never saw eye to eye even prior to the signing of the Treaty. Each saw in the nationalist movement's aims and aspirations for the Irish national community something fundamentally different. As de Valéra noted in an address to the Dáil in 1921:

> After my imprisonment . . . I came out and found here on the one hand the old chief of the Sinn Féin Organisation . . . our present Minister for Foreign Affairs, Mr. Arthur Griffith – and I found at the head of the Irish Volunteers the Minister for Defense, Mr. Cathal Brugha. I found that they differed then as fundamentally as they differ to-day. I found that I was a sort of connecting link between the two, and at the first Convention of Sinn Féin, or a night or two before it, we devised a basis on which we have worked so successfully for the past four years: the basis of the Sinn Féin Constitution. Since then I have been the link between the two.[51]

The differences that de Valéra had noted between Brugha and Griffith since their entry into nationalist politics reveal, in almost pure form, the different understanding of politics that the Irish-Enlightenment and Gaelic-Romantic traditions brought to the Civil War period. For Griffith and for members of the Provisional Government, Irish independence was the ultimate aspiration. For Griffith, it was the single most important and unalterable conviction, and it explains his devotion to the Irish national cause. During the debates on the Treaty, Griffith declared:

> The principle that I have stood on all my life is the principle of Ireland for the Irish people. If I cannot get that with a Republic I will have a monarchy. I will not sacrifice my country for a form of government. . . . I do not care whether the King of England or the symbol of the Crown be in Ireland so long as the people of Ireland are free to shape their own destinies.[52]

Griffith further iterated his commitment to an Ireland independent of and unencumbered by extraneous ideas concerning the specific shape of the nation, when he asked rhetorically:

> Is there to be no living Irish nation? Is the Irish nation to be the dead past or the prophetic future? Have we any duty to the present generation? I say we have a duty. . . . We have a duty to our country, and our country are the living people of Ireland; we have a duty to our people.[53]

Consistent with this commitment to an independent Irish nation, Griffith believed that the ultimate determinants of political life were the Irish people. "If the Irish people were to say 'We have got everything else but the name Republic, and we will fight for it,' " Griffith insisted that although he would consider them "fools," he would "follow in their ranks."[54] Democratic individualism and the right of the Irish people – Catholic and Protestant, Republicans and Unionists alike – to determine their destiny as they saw fit was the cornerstone of the Provisional Government's commitment to the Treaty. The sense of national purpose was not to be imposed on the people by the political leaders' preconceived notion of what it ought to be. Rather, the political elite should listen to, articulate, and implement the collective wisdom of the Irish population.

This understanding of the meaning and purpose of the Irish national community led to a spirited defense of the Treaty by Griffith and fellow members of the Provisional Government. Referring back to the long-standing Irish-Enlightenment tradition, they asserted that the authority of the people was supreme. Griffith chastised the anti-Treatyites for failing to take the case to the people:

> You are trying to reject the Treaty without allowing the Irish people to say whether they want it or not – the people whose lives and fortune are involved. You will kill Dáil Éireann when you do that. You will remove from Dáil Éireann every vestige of moral authority, and they will no longer represent the people of Ireland. It will be

a junta dictating to the people of Ireland and the people of Ireland will deal with it.[55]

Griffith and others who shared his perspective defended parliamentarianism as an expression and manifestation of the collective will. The structures of rule required defense, by any means necessary, against their detractors. For these proponents of the Treaty, such conviction necessitated the suppression of those forces unwilling to stand by the will of the majority. Only in this instance, where the institutions of public expression were jeopardized, did violence emerge as a legitimate mechanism of social control. Such a belief fully legitimized, in these pro-Treatyites' eyes, the use of force to suppress the army irregulars who refused to recognize the Provisional Government as the rightful political authority. It fully justified the Civil War. But there were additional aspects of the Provisional Government's role in Irish politics that demonstrated its preeminent Irish-Enlightenment commitment to the parliamentary process.

First, the Provisional Government was firmly and decisively committed to the subordination of the army to parliamentary control.[56] This issue was hardly an easy one in nationalist-minded Ireland. Given the central role the army had played in securing Irish independence and, even more importantly, because the army organization had existed prior to the creation of the Irish political apparatus, the status of the army was an ambiguous one. Nevertheless, parliamentarianism demanded civilian control of army life, and to this end, the new government never wavered. Second, the erosion of British authority, especially in the West of Ireland since at least 1919, resulted in increasingly frequent and strident land seizure actions by rural Irishmen. Perhaps imbued with Republican idealism and certainly inspired by the devolution of British political authority, these peasants believed that their actions were consistent with Irish control of Ireland. As Peadar O'Donnell comments, "Loyalty to the Republic was, somehow, involved in the repudiation of landlordism. The rent itself was not a great hardship on the people, for it bore lightly on their economy, but the decision to abolish it interpreted the Republican struggle to them and gave them an active part in it. Within the Republic they created their own landlordless Republic, and they were proud of it."[57] Members of the Republican Dáil, then, and the Provisional Government later, rejected such an understanding of Irish rule. The minister for agriculture in 1920 remarked of this land agitation that the "mind of the people was being diverted from the struggle for freedom by a class war."[58] That sentiment, like the later actions forcefully discouraging rural "lawlessness," reflected an assertion of the preeminence of parliamentary process in dispute settlement and, moreover, a rejection of the idea that Irish peasants held some sacrosanct status in the Irish national community.

The contrast between these understandings was particularly striking when compared with those held by members of the IRA. Whereas the Provisional Government was committed to values and norms decisively within the Irish-Enlightenment tradition, the IRA just as consistently espoused Gaelic-Romantic cultural sentiments. Whereas Griffith and others in the Provisional Government deferred articulating their own conception of the ideal society and instead believed that Irish people, once independence was achieved, would collectively specify that ideal and take steps to achieve it, Cathal Brugha and the IRA saw in the symbol of the Irish Republic something that was immanently real and possible. Therefore, all detractors from their Republican ideal were ir-retrievably enemies of the state. In defending and accepting the terms of the Anglo-Irish Treaty, in agreeing to compromise with Britain, mem-bers of the Provisional Government, in the eyes of the IRA, were fla-grantly rejecting the realization of the Irish Republic. Brugha and others wedded to this tradition of thought saw themselves as representing the forces of history, entrusted, by their very actions and against extreme odds, with the task of bringing heaven to earth. There could be no wavering from this path. Brugha proudly and vividly characterized him-self as just such an extremist during the Treaty debates:

> Why, if instead of being so strong, our last shilling had been spent, and our last man were lying on the ground and his enemies howling around him and their bayonets raised, ready to plunge them into his body, that man should say – true to the traditions handed down – If they said to him: "Now, will you come into our Empire?" – he should say, and he would say, "No! I will not!" That is the spirit that has lasted all through the centuries. . . . [59]

Members of the IRA, like Brugha, were men of faith. They were in-fused with the Catholic conviction of the union of spirit and flesh. This imperative was transposed into an absolutist political commitment. Con-ceived as a fixed ideal, the national tradition was open to a single inter-pretation and demanded absolute realization. Doctrines were either correct or incorrect, and compromise for the sake of expediency could not be tolerated. Deputy Etchingham floridly articulated this political conception in the Treaty debates in the Dáil:

> (D)on't let any of you young men or old men get away with the idea that, if you sign the Treaty and give up the position, that you are standing for an ideal. You were elected here because you fought

and suffered for that ideal but if you vote for that Treaty, you, that vote for it, will have forsaken that ideal. Don't forget that. Once you wander off the straight road and go down the sideways of expediency you will find leafy bowers and sycamore trees and mossy banks and happiness and luxury – the flesh pots of Egypt – but don't forget you, that are committing yourself to this tragedy, that you are going to come out again and fight.[60]

Extending the metaphor beyond the danger of wandering off the straight and narrow Republican path, and reflecting the puritanical variant that typified Irish Catholicism, this pure expression of the Gaelic-Romantic tradition saw an ever-present danger of corrupting influences undermining the pursuit of the ideal. Mary MacSwiney, a member of the Dáil who lost her brother during the Black and Tan campaign, raised the issue of remaining pure of heart and serving the cause of the Republic:

Search your soul tonight and in the face of every martyr that ever died for Ireland take an oath in your own hearts now that you will do what is right no matter what *influences* have been brought to bear on you. I do not speak of my right any more than I do of others to allude to those who have gone but I ask those here tonight who are putting expedience before principle to kindly leave the names of the dead out of their speeches.[61]

Because men could be so easily influenced by corruption, there were those, like Brugha, who opposed even sending a delegation to England to negotiate for the Republic. As Brugha put it:

A lot of you . . . already know that I was against ever sending men across to England; not that I considered that we were giving the Republic away by doing so, but that I knew the terrible influences that would be brought to bear upon them there – influences that I thought might be too much for them – but I hoped, especially where there were certain instructions drawn up, that the influences would not be too strong to get the better of them. . . .[62]

If membership in the Irish nation was contingent on support for the Republic, a true consciousness of one's link with the Gaelic-Catholic-Irish past, it was also understood by the Republican leaders that they would have to lead that sector of the population graced with a primordial connection to the past, yet consciously reluctant to identify with it, in order to secure the Republican state. In other words, Brugha and the IRA lived with a basic mistrust of the collective wisdom of the people, as presently constituted, because of the perverting influence of British colonialism. Miss MacSwiney, responding to the demand by the pro-Treatyites to put the Treaty to an election test, commented:

If we put it to the people to-morrow a lot, perhaps the majority, would accept. Cannot you remember what we were told about the slave mind? Can you not realise the slave mind it took a 100 years to create, it will require a few years of freedom to bring us back. Our people are still of the slave mind, but they will do what we ask them to do.[63]

In this view, the Irish Gaels, in this transition to the Republic, were to be celebrated as the rightful members of the national community, entitled to the protection and support of the Republican leaders; yet, to the extent that the community embraced non-Republican ideals, they were to be controlled in their long-term best interest. When confronted with the sticky problem of the IRA's relationship to political authority, members of the IRA proposed the formation of a government to "preserve the continuity of the Republic." Liam Lynch, a member of the Army Executive of the IRA, revealing the IRA's only qualified support for political institutions, wrote that "we pledge this Government our wholehearted support and allegiance *while it functions as the Government of the Republic* and we empower it to make an arrangement with the Free State Government, or with the British Government provided such an arrangement does not bring the country into the British Empire."[64]

The army's role was envisioned to be much like that of a hierarchy of priests, delegating authority to proper administrants but always capable of retracting support when and if that authority promoted policies inimical to the Republic's interest, as the army determined it. In serving its priestly function, the IRA aimed to create a community of believers equal in their shared commitment to the Republic. With the Gaelic Republic as its ideal, violence was fully legitimated. Both as the symbol of Republican virtue and as the means to ensure the harmonious order, terror directed at recalcitrant Irishmen and violence toward the Protestant and British enemies of the Republic was deemed both necessary and appropriate. Cathal Brugha, when surrounded by Free State forces and given the opportunity to surrender, instead chose death, emerging from his position with his guns firing. What better illustration of the central role of violence in the symbolic world of Republican ideals than Brugha's decision to die a martyr's death?

Brugha's and Griffith's positions toward the Civil War both epitomize the appeal of a pure Gaelic-Romantic or Irish-Enlightenment understanding in lining up support for the opposing Civil War positions. A pro-Treaty stance, like Griffith's, meant that the values and norms of the Irish-Enlightenment tradition were employed and were sharply opposed to those of men like Brugha and his fellow anti-Treatyites, who stood at the other end of the cultural field. In contrast, Michael Collins of the IRB and Éamon de Valéra, as president of the Irish Republic, when confronted with the Anglo-Irish Treaty, took no such pure, absolutist position. Both, unlike either Brugha or Griffith, made heroic efforts to prevent war. Each sought to construct a middle political position and acted for a time as a mediator in attempting to ward off civil war. This middle position represented their efforts to borrow from the rich imagery offered by both traditions; it was an attempt to offer an amalgamation of argument that would resonate with the Irish population, resulting in a more moderate course. Yet both Collins and de Valéra were unsuccessful in stemming the tide toward cultural polarization, the collapse of the public, and civil war. What from a different vantage point might look like two cases of political opportunism, when seen in this light, turns out to be an example of two men of conscience, identifying strongly with the Irish nation and in their effort to prevent fratricide, articulating a political position that employed the full linguistic range of the available cultural symbols. What they offered the Irish nation was two distinct hybrid political positions. In supporting the Treaty, Collins came to accept, roughly speaking, Irish-Enlightenment values while still holding to Gaelic-Romantic norms. De Valéra, for his part, opted to fight against the Treaty by fashioning a position that broadly combined Gaelic-Romantic values and Irish-Enlightenment norms.

Yet despite their political acuity and charismatic qualities, Collins and de Valéra were both unsuccessful in preventing the outbreak of civil war. Although both had a sizable personal following, they were incapable of resisting the powerful drift toward either of the two polarized positions. Understandably, their efforts to amalgamate elements of both failed in the end because, as political mutants, the positions they offered failed to resonate with the population. Amid the politically charged atmosphere prior to the outbreak of war, Irishmen tried to find political understanding in the long-standing and well-articulated systems of cultural thought that were already available and meaningful.

Collins's and de Valéra's attempts to combine essentially irreconcilable aspects of two cultural traditions could not compete effectively with the more powerful and persuasive Irish-Enlightenment and Gaelic-Romantic systems of meaning articulated by the Provisional Government on the one hand and the IRA on the other. Subtle political arguments and fine distinctions were insufficient responses to political crises when compared with the ability of these traditions to galvanize diverse groups within the two cultural traditions. In calmer times, when political authority itself was not at issue, de Valéra and Collins might have forged a politics of cultural convergence; indeed, years later, de Valéra would be instrumental in doing this. But in this 1921–2 period, both became the victims of cultural opposites. The strength of cultural antinomies and value dissension preempted the arena of political discourse and the forging of a new political understanding; instead, Collins and de Valéra, like all others in the society, were ultimately forced to choose one of two sides in the impending Civil War.

The efforts by Collins and de Valéra to avert war are well known. Both rightfully perceived themselves as occupying political terrain that could not be easily understood and, except for their interest in preventing war irrespective of principle, was hardly explicable. Their actions, seen from the vantage point of the anti- and pro-Treatyites, were patently contradictory. Each caught between Scylla and Charybdis, they singlehandedly attempted to forge a political position that would mitigate this process of rapid polarization.

Collins's dilemma was apparent even as one of the original negotiators, appointed by de Valéra, of the Anglo-Irish Treaty. He accepted the appointment "in the spirit of a soldier who acts against his judgment at the order of a superior officer."[65] His decision to sign the Treaty was no less in conflict. As Winston Churchill commented of Collins just prior to signing the document, "Michael Collins rose looking as though he was going to shoot someone, preferably himself. In all my life, I have never seen such pain and suffering in restraint."[66] Collins, in the end, chose to sign the Treaty, support the Free State, and press for an Irish accommodation to the document and to the new government. In this way, and despite his ambivalence, he came to espouse the values of the Irish-Enlightenment tradition. He helped convince the IRB to break with their revolutionary tradition and their Republican idealism, and to support those forces defending the Treaty. In the Treaty debates, he was a vocal spokesman on behalf of the Treaty, seeking to justify his own decision to break with his previous Republican commitments. In a fundamental political shift, Collins argued that the Irish Republic was an ideal, distinct from the real world. In order to achieve the Republic, political independence first had to be secured. In distinguishing means from ends, Collins embraced a fundamental feature of the Irish-Enlightenment perspective on politics. He justified his participation in the treaty negotiation conference with the English when he said:

> The communication . . . from Lloyd George made it clear that they were going into a conference not on the recognition of the Irish Republic, and I say if we all stood on the recognition of the Irish

Republic as a prelude to any conference we could very easily have said so, and there would be no conference.[67]

Collins continued by saying:

Now as one of the signatories of the document I naturally recommend its acceptance. I do not recommend it for more than it is. Equally, I do not recommend it for less than it is. In my opinion, it gives us freedom, not the ultimate freedom that all nations desire . . . but the freedom to achieve it. . . . The history of the nation has not been, as is so often said, the history of a military struggle of 750 years; it has been much more of a history of peaceful penetration of 750 years. It has not been a struggle for the ideal of freedom for 750 years symbolized in the name Republic. It has been a story of slow, steady economic encroach by England.[68]

Through a remarkable recasting of the nature of Irish history, and by revealing his break with Brugha and other Republicans, Collins was formally and publicly giving up on the immanence of the Republic, replacing it with the rhetoric of independence. He suggested instead that the Irish Republic remained as a desirable end that could be achieved only after independence. Irish independence and the abolition of English influence were necessary stepping stones to the Republic.

The IRB, in the main, supported their president, Collins, and endorsed the Treaty. At the same time, they remained as an organized and vigilant military force awaiting the subsequent Constitution before determining the extent to which they would support the new Provisional Government. Collins, in retaining his leadership role in the IRB, continued to be the servant of these two contending commitments. He moved between a belief that the new government would be that stepping stone and a suspicion that efforts might be made through the constitutional drafting process to sabotage the Republic. In still aligning himself with the IRB, Collins vividly embodied the ambivalence of a substantial sector of the population, torn between a commitment to an independent nation but disbelieving that such independence would produce the Republican ideal.

Collins's positions during this period reflected these different culturally derived understandings of the political order. On the Gaelic-Romantic side, he came to perceive the Treaty debate as a battle between the forces of good and evil, not unlike perceptions expressed by Brugha, Etchingham, and MacSwiney. Yet for him, to oppose the Treaty was now tantamount to false consciousness and evidence of the slave mentality. In writing to his close friend Harry Boland, for example, who split with him in the IRB and opposed the Treaty, he demonstrated the passion of his conviction:

> Harry, it has come to this! It is in my power to arrest you and destroy you. This I cannot do. . . . If you will think over the *influence* which has dominated you, it should change your ideas. You are walking under false colours. If no words of mine will change your attitude, then you are beyond all hope – My hope.[69]

Here Collins transposed the imagery of evil influences leading people astray to a defense of the central political value of Irish-Enlightenment thinking: Irish independence. Those, like his friend Harry Boland, who failed to endorse the Treaty, were wrongfully swayed from the path of reason. At the same time, and befitting his Gaelic-Romantic normative commitments, Collins appeared to lend support to those IRA forces, both pro- and anti-Treaty, that were continuing to wage war in the Northern counties against the Ulster Special Constabulary. Although he publicly decried those acts of lawlessness, there is substantial, albeit inconclusive, evidence that Collins, if not directly involved, privately gave his support and consent. It has even been speculated that Collins ordered the assassination of Field Marshall Sir Henry Wilson in London, the event leading to the British demand that the Provisional Government crack down on army irregulars.[70] Even if Collins was not directly involved, the continuing hostilities in the North by both pro- and anti-Treatyites is indicative of the conflicting convictions that existed among those Republicans, like Collins, who came to support the Anglo-Irish Treaty.

Collins also embraced political positions reflecting Irish-Enlightenment normative sentiments. Despite having the power to do so, he was extremely reluctant to suppress with force his previous nationalist allies who were now threatening the Provisional Government. The great terrorist against British rule now insisted that the Provisional Government organize a national army and police force, and combat terror not with terror but through law. Collins agreed to order the attack on the Four Courts in Dublin, held by the army irregulars, only after the most extreme pressure was brought by the British government. The national army, it is certainly true, was no less brutal than its opponents, but it clearly operated under the political authority of the Provisional Government. This distinction between legality and illegality deeply impressed Collins.

Finally, Collins's reluctance to commit himself to the Civil War was further revealed when he made an agreement with de Valéra in the months preceding the outbreak of war. At the Sinn Féin Ard-Feis (Convention), convened in February 1922 to nominate candidates for the upcoming general election, Collins and de Valéra agreed to postpone the election and to instruct the candidates not to discuss the Treaty. The aim was to ensure that the national elections would take place, that the Free State government would be duly empowered, and that the Treaty would not interfere with the normal functioning of parliamentary government. At the last minute, Collins failed to support the pact that had been formalized in May 1922 – for reasons that will become clearer in the next chapter – but, nevertheless, his actions revealed the lengths to which he was willing to go to attempt a reconciliation between opposing political factions. Indeed, they demonstrated Collins's hope of reconciling contending value commitments. In retrospect, of course, Collins's failure is not surprising, and in the end, he was forced to support and fully defend the Provisional Government's position in opposition to the anti-Treatyites. The capacity to forge a purely pragmatic response to events that had already become interpreted as possessing great cultural significance was simply not available.

De Valéra's efforts at reconciliation were no more successful than Collins's, and his failures stemmed from the same source. Although de Valéra attempted to create a position on the Treaty more sympathetic to the Gaelic-Romantic tradition, he too failed in the attempt to resist value polarization. As president of the Republican Dáil, de Valéra had long perceived his role as that of mediator between factions of the Sinn Féin party.[71] De Valéra, reflecting on his political role since assuming leadership of Sinn Féin, commented in the Treaty debates:

> I felt that if I was to be of any use to the country and if there was to be any unity in the country, it was to try and harmonize these two voices as far as possible. I had a difficult task to play for four years, to try, so to speak, to hold the balance even in public discussion, no matter what my own personal views might be, and privately, and certainly in public never did I do anything which tended to lead to the disruption of these forces. I felt that the unity of these forces was absolutely essential for national success; and until the sixth of December I succeeded in my task. On the sixth December a document [the Anglo-Irish Treaty] was signed which irrevocably sundered that connection.[72]

In his role as president, de Valéra embraced many of the norms that I have characterized as Irish-Enlightenment. He was devoted to parliamentary process and compromise, rejecting secret societies as inimical to the Irish spirit. He was long committed to the subordination of the army to parliamentary control and was critical of the terrorist campaigns, when politically unmediated, of both the IRA and the IRB. As Carlton Younger states, "Collins' tactics did not belong to de Valéra's ethical code . . . he [de Valéra] was ruthlessly committed to a cause but critical of the methods adopted by his side to further it."[73]

De Valéra apparently believed that, through the parliamentary process, an autochthonous Irish Republic could be achieved. At the same time that he remained committed to a politics of gradualism and compromise, he was convinced of the immanent realization of "a frugal, Gaelic Ireland, as little despoiled as possible by the forces of civilization, especially English civilization; a state in which there would be no rich and no poor, but rather a countryside scattered with small farmers and small industries."[74] This combination of commitments could be sustained in the spirit of nationalism but, as events quickly demonstrated, once Irishmen and women confronted themselves, Irish-Enlightenment and Gaelic-Romantic sentiments were incompatible.

De Valéra sought, first, to replace the Treaty with his Document No. 2. Rather than have Ireland assume a place within the British Commonwealth of Nations, de Valéra sought, through this document, to have Ireland "externally associated" with the Commonwealth. The difference for de Valéra, although technical, better represented Ireland's desire for autonomy from Britain, whereby the nation could better secure its Republican ideal. In addition, the extra concessions that the document could gain from the British government were, in his mind, perhaps sufficient to ensure the agreement of reluctant Republicans to this political compromise.[75] In the same spirit, and with the same ever-present hope of avoiding divisions among the ranks of nationalists, de Valéra entered into the election pact with Collins previously described. In both cases, then, de Valéra sought to embrace, within one political stance, positions that at the time were perceived as irreconcilable.

De Valéra ultimately failed to mobilize the nation behind a political position combining two cultural orientations. With each effort failing, de Valéra was pushed ever more securely into the ranks of the Gaelic-Romantic opposition to the Treaty. Upon tendering his resignation as president of the Dáil following the Treaty's approval by that body, he concluded his statement by expressing his solidarity with the Irish people. He said, "I know what I am talking about; and whenever I want to know what the Irish people wanted I had only to examine my own heart and it told me straight off what the Irish people wanted."[76] Now at one with that mystical Irish Republican sentiment, de Valéra left public office and became a private in the IRA.

The fate of Collins and de Valéra revealed the strength of the two cultural poles, serving to attract individuals to both extremes, and the untenability of any moderate political positions capable of resisting such value polarization.

The purposes of the foregoing analysis are twofold. First, it suggests the necessity – in order to understand Irish politics – of comprehending the cultural schisms that prevailed in Irish society prior to the Civil War. The presence of contending value and normative commitments produced two distinct political stances toward the Treaty, preempting reasoned discourse and compromise. The effort to forge hybrid politics, given the intensity of these schisms and shown by the inability of Collins and de Valéra to lead, was doomed to fail. The strength of these cultural convictions, then, largely prefigured the civil war conflict. The antinomies of cultural thought, although not determining who embraced which side, did determine the contours of political argumentation and the issues on which political allegiance were divided.

It bears restating that this cultural treatment of the failure of de Valéra and Collins to ward off civil war is not intended to explain the Civil War through a cultural variable standing independent of (or opposed to) political and geostructural factors. The Treaty created a discordant social reality because of the antinomic readings of its meaning by the Irish population. Had there not been a Gaelic-Romantic tradition, complete with an understanding of the nature and purposes of the Irish Republic, reality would not have been so chaotic and the increasing polarization of the community would not have occurred. This attention to the competing cultural traditions demonstrates the interplay between cultural understandings and political reality. The rhetoric of support for and opposition to the Treaty revealed the important influence of the meaning-making process in political developments.

But of even greater importance for subsequent chapters, this analysis demonstrates the considerable obstacles faced by the new political elite in attempting to establish a modern democratic order. The challenge for the new leaders would be to create a postindependent political system capable of incorporating, in culturally meaningful terms, all sectors of the national community. Because each tradition embraced divergent understandings and because the Gaelic-Romantic tradition, in particular, possessed strong primordial and precivil convictions, the task of finding commonality in diversity and forging a democratic civic consciousness was a formidable one.

There is little question that such a cultural challenge posed a less intense problem than those faced by new nations where racial, religious, and/or regional heterogeneity almost precludes the possibility of national civic cooperation. Ireland, in contrast, was populated, for the most part, by an ethnically homogeneous people. Although the various invaders of Ireland over the centuries – the Danish Vikings, the Normans, the English – had all made unique contributions to the principally Celtic gene pool, they quickly became absorbed into an Irish hybrid that was largely unaware of its various contributors. In addition to its ethnic uniformity, Ireland had benefited from an extraordinary degree of religious homogeneity. At the time of independence, 93 percent of the Free State population were Roman Catholics and probably in no other country were the dictates of Catholicism so religiously obeyed.[77] The Catholic Church was omnipresent in the lives of nearly all Irishmen. As Horace Plunkett wrote in 1904, "In no other country in the world, probably is religion so dominant an element in the daily life of the people in Ireland and certainly nowhere else has the minister of religion so wide and undisputed an authority."[78] The church has less firm a hold today on the Irish citizenry, but Plunkett's characterization of the place of the church at the turn of the century remained largely accurate during the first decade of Irish independence.

It is also true, as I have described, that the Irish, irrespective of their cultural and political differences, by the time of independence had long held a conception of an Irish national community that was autonomous and self-governing. The nearly century-long struggle against British rule had surely strengthened this shared desire for a nation independent of foreign control. Again, when compared to other new nations, this national consciousness facilitated the achievement of parliamentary democracy because the idea of a national political authority was not in question. Nevertheless, even with respect to this factor, Ireland resembled other newly independent nations: The institutionalization of civility was hardly an easy process. As the Civil War dramatically showed, although the consciousness necessary for a modern civic order was widely shared when Britain was perceived as preventing its realization, the Republicans continued to adhere to an ideology concerning the character of the new Irish community that undermined the possibility of a national political authority. And as in other new nations of the twentieth century, the political mobilization of the Irish countryside, where Republican sentiments were particularly strong, occurred long before the creation of political structures capable of containing and shaping political expression into a more moderate, universalistic, and civic form.

The tasks of the new leaders, then, were two. First, they had to develop political institutions that would produce a more moderate civil politics: Their task was to reconstruct a functioning public realm. And they had to begin this effort while the Civil War was being waged. But simultaneously, they had to attempt to rechannel the nationalist consensus – the common elements of civic consciousness held by all – into support for the new independent Irish political order. The institutional problem could not be solved independently of the symbolic one. Therefore, the immediate tasks of the new government were to defeat its political opponents on the battlefield while turning itself into the true inheritor of the Irish nationalist legacy. As the only force capable of producing a convergence of national sentiment, the government had to attempt to wrap the state apparatus around the symbols of nationalist struggle. The drafting of the Free State Constitution represented for the new government the first challenge, and opportunity, to demonstrate its ability to transcend the cultural cleavages and to assert the presence of an Irish national community characterized by common civic and democratic convictions. Yet even here, as the next chapter will demonstrate, the Constitution itself became the victim of polarities, incapable of transcending them. The cause of cultural integration would have to wait until after the Civil War.

3. The Free State Constitution and the Institutionalization of Value Strains

Introduction: constitutionalism and order in new nations

I have argued that an understanding of the causes of the Civil War requires an appreciation of the competing cultural orientations that existed among the Irish population. Although ostensibly a political dispute, the Civil War expressed the resurfacing of cultural differences that had been previously subordinated to the nationalist aspirations of much of the Irish community. In order to understand the challenges faced by the leaders of the Provisional Government, it is necessary to appreciate the depth of these divisions in the political community. The government's aspiration for a civil, democratic order could be fulfilled only after these divisions had somehow been resolved. Democracy depended upon widespread agreement concerning the nature and appropriate course of the independent Irish nation. Yet this account of the cultural antinomies in the nation presents only in broad outline the political challenges faced by the new leaders.

In this chapter, I will focus on the drafting of the Free State Constitution to demonstrate more contextually and concretely how these splits impeded the ability of the Provisional Government, and later the Free State Government, to produce a united political community. An examination of the drafting process, and the content of the Constitution itself, shows the impact of competing symbolic systems and value strains on the political order. I will argue that the Provisional Government's task of defeating the anti-Treaty forces on the battlefield was, in the long run, less challenging than its creation of a symbolic order that all members of the community – pro-Treaty and anti-Treaty alike – could, in conscience, support. As I will demonstrate, the Constitution proved incapable of standing above fractious political divisions and, instead, became identified with a partisan political position. As a result, it, and the government along with it, lost the capacity to transcend the cultural and political divisions besetting Ireland. Symbolic integration and constitutionalism would have to be achieved not with the aid of the Constitution but in spite of it.

In the industrialized nations of the West, constitutionalism historically has played a key role in mobilizing and integrating members of the political community in opposition to autocratic, absolutist rule. The constitution has typically been used to assert the existence of the nation, one united in its conviction that political authority derives from the people (originally, only a small proportion of the whole population) to the political elite, not vice versa.[1] It is the expression of those underlying values and norms that all members of the community share and is the ultimate referent by which discourse and interaction between members are regulated. In the last instance, it successfully subordinates political interests to a higher, more integrative order in which partisan division, however intense, presumes the presence of the national community and accepts the ultimate authority of the political institution to resolve conflict. It stands as the symbol of national unity, as an expression of common political destiny, and as a rejection of any absolute, predetermined authority.

Most abstractly and fundamentally, constitutionalism represents the claim that the people possess the authority to regulate the relations among all members of the political community, including those who rule. As beliefs and sentiments shift and as membership in the community expands, so too does the meaning of the constitution. Either through new readings and interpretations of the abstract assertions or through specific amendments, the constitution remains the central document of a modern political community. The belief in this mandate of the people, whereby behavior is regulated in accordance with certain basic principles, is, as Carl Friedrich has argued, a common conviction shared by all those in constitutional orders. Further, the meaning of justice is neither divinely defined nor handed down from above, but constitutes the central responsibility of the community. In linking the rise of constitutionalism to a specifically Christian conception of the moral order, Friedrich writes, "constitutionalism presupposes the true faith. Upon the unanimity which such faith provides by determining fundamental values, but more particularly those values which the idea of a Christian man's vocation involves, rests the authority of government."[2]

The assertion of consensus within a constitutional order should not be misunderstood. It claims only that there is widespread agreement on the right of the people to govern, on the appropriateness of the document that represents the collective will and regulates behavior, and on a shared belief that justice is an abstract and elusive goal. Through the constitutional order, justice, as understood by the community members, although never fully realized, becomes ever more closely approximated. By specifying the mechanisms and procedures governing interaction within the community, and by rooting all law in the constitution, constitutionalism reflects the modern commitment to justice as realized through reason and rationality. To characterize the constitution as a procedural document, implying an absence of substantive purpose – as many critics on both the political right and the political left do – is to divorce the procedures from a commitment to certain kinds of justice.

Moreover, constitutionalism is not synonymous with universal membership in the political community. "Voice," as Albert Hirschman characterizes it, is granted only to those who are deemed legitimate members of that community; agreement about constitutional principles can be presumed only among those who share in the rights of citizenship.[3] Constitutionalism means that members of the political community share a common cultural universe that includes popular legitimation of government and that identifies a particular constitutional document as the expression of the collective will of the community. The constitution comes to hold a deep meaning that only members of the community can fully appreciate.

Although constitutionalism embraces an abstract and transcendent notion of the political community, it is also a more concrete expression of a specific national identity. Through that identity, the constitution makes explicit certain national symbols. Symbolic integration is most often achieved by incorporating in the constitution, at a concrete level, specific references to the community's shared memories and traditions as well as explicit references to common unifying values. Where religious, regional, or other cleavages are significant, the constitution often embraces those differences and celebrates diversity. When a nation has faced either mythic or actual adversity, the constitution frequently emphasizes those conditions in order to create a sense of common historical experience and common destiny. The constitutional preamble, in particular, is often the most explicit self-characterization of a political community, with references to a stressful national past, a sense of common purpose, and a statement of the ultimate aspirations of the nation. The preamble attempts to capture and express the values and commitments of a people, thereby demonstrating its right to speak for and symbolically represent the collective voice of the community. Those same values become embodied in the constitution itself, but specific, concrete references to the people and common experiences are seldom made. More than any other section of the document, the preamble is intended to resonate with the population, to evoke a deep cultural understanding, and consequently to promote a commitment to the constitution.

Through a common, perhaps even primordial, conviction that the constitution embraces in a sacred manner the mundane and taken-for-granted understanding of the national will, the constitution itself becomes sacred. It becomes part of the national lore and the collective self-understanding. As Max Lerner writes when discussing the American Constitution, "A constitutional legend was built as values which the document embodied were preached, exhorted and praised from all corners. It became a symbol for the moral foundations of the Republic."[4]

Most commonly, then, a constitutional document makes itself culturally important first by embodying a national tradition. In so doing, constitutional safeguards, provisions, protections, and so on themselves emerge as sacred. As Friedrich argues, "The constitution tends to become a symbol, and its provisions become so many symbols in turn."[5] One need only think of the sanctity in American society of the concept of equal protection, first expressed in the Fourteenth Amendment of the U.S. Constitution; it has become part of the American self-concept despite the fact that it is a comparatively new addition.

The rise of constitutionalism in the West, however, represents a very different process from its emergence in the new nations of the twentieth century. First, in the older states, the constitution typically was drafted by a group of revolutionaries united in their opposition to political autocracy. Alternatively, in some cases, it represented a cooptive mechanism from above in response to an increasingly restive sector of the nation. In either case, the constitution was a revolutionary manifesto expressing the new and widely held conviction that political authority ought to be constrained by the "mandate of the people."[6] It was an expression of the unity of the political community, a unity that preceded the constitutional doctrine. Although the constitution served to strengthen that unity further, it was not forged first through the document. Second, constitutionalism arose in the West when the political community was composed of a relatively small, privileged group. It enhanced their privilege; only in time did the constitution become the vehicle to promote universal citizenship among less fortunate groups.

In new nations of the twentieth century, the rise of a constitutional order is a very different matter. Although often intended as an assertion of national sovereignty against colonial authority, constitutionalism is also an effort to integrate a diverse, already mobilized national population hardly unified in their sentiments and convictions. Not so much a revolutionary document of liberation, it is typically an effort by the ruling elite to contain and constrain populist challenges to the new political order. The twentieth-century movement toward universal democracy has caused the constitution to emerge as a document of unity, transcendence, and integration where very little unity, in fact, may exist among members of the political community.[7]

In this case, rather than expressing a value consensus among elites of the political community or of substantive integration among various sectors of the society, the constitution is one of many weapons used by the political elite to forge political order. As a result, given the intensity of religious, ethnic, regional, and economic cleavages in most new nations of the twentieth century, constitutionalism has met with only occasional success.

The Provisional Government and the promise of the Free State Constitution

Ireland did not escape these problems at the time of its independence. The challenges faced in drafting the Free State Constitution in the early months of 1922 could not have been greater. At the same time that they were appointing a Constitutional Draft Committee in January of 1922, the leaders of the Provisional Government were gearing up to wage civil war.

At first, these leaders saw in the drafting of the Constitution an opportunity to shore up the national consensus that the signing of the Anglo-Irish Treaty was so quickly undermining. In the first months of 1922, the Constitution was being identified as precisely the means of avoiding Civil War. Michael Collins, now president of the Provisional Government and chairman of the Constitutional Drafting Committee, hoped through the Constitution to bring de Valéra and his supporters into the Free State, thereby isolating the extreme Republicans.[8] To this end, Collins traveled to London to gain British agreement that they would ratify the Treaty before approving the Constitution. Only after Collins suggested to Lloyd George the possibility of the fall of the Irish government by anti-Treaty forces did George agree to push for the immediate ratification of the Treaty. It was agreed that the Draft Constitution would be shown to the British cabinet for approval before its publication by the Provisional Government.[9] Having gained room to maneuver from the British, Collins sought some freedom of action from the Republican flank. Promised a Constitution reflecting the principles of Irish nationalism without reference to the Treaty or the British connection, de Valéra pledged his cooperation. The Collins–de Valéra pact was formed. As I described in the last chapter, this pact symbolized the effort by these two major moderates to avert civil war.

Collins's successful efforts provided some reason for optimism. The hope was that a Constitution might be drafted that could successfully subordinate the Anglo-Irish Treaty to Irish national consciousness. The goal, in effect, was to present the Constitution to the Irish nation as the highest expression of moral aspirations and commitments; the Treaty, in contrast, would merely represent the ability to act expediently and pragmatically to achieve more noble purposes. The strategy reflected Collins's philosophy of using the office of the state as a stepping stone to achieve the Irish Republic. And in the initial stages of this process, it almost looked as though Collins would singlehandedly achieve his goal.

Collins selected a Constitutional Committee made up of individuals who stood above the political fray. He appointed to the committee several members who were active in the Irish White Cross, a charitable organization whose members were motivated by moral rather than political concerns. In addition, he selected others who were constitutional experts – either barristers or university professors. In short, Collins sought individuals whose credentials were unimpeachable, standing above politics. They would form a committee, Collins hoped, that might resist political pressures and not succumb to the polarization occurring throughout the country.

Yet, even in this early phase of the process, Collins came under strong political pressure from Arthur Griffith to appoint Darrell Figgis, a journalist and poet, as chairman of the Constitutional Committee. Figgis, like Griffith, held strong Irish-Enlightenment convictions. Although active in nationalist politics prior to the Treaty, he saw no objections to placing the Treaty squarely in the center of the new constitutional document.

Collins was reluctant to appoint Figgis, disliking him personally and suspicious of his Anglo-Irish connections. However, responding to Griffith's insistence, Collins appointed Figgis as deputy chairman, taking the chairmanship for himself – probably only to prevent Figgis from assuming the position. Griffith's extremism again proved to be a decisive factor in the ultimate failure of the Constitutional Committee to produce a Constitution able to bridge the widening gulf between members of the Irish political community. In insisting on the appointment of Figgis and, unlike Collins, in being insensitive to the need for a Constitution as a compromise between Irish-Enlightenment and Gaelic-Romantic principles, Griffith helped ensure that the Constitution would fail as a mechanism of reconciliation.

It should be said that Griffith did support cooperation with the anti-Treaty wing of Sinn Féin in the interest of preventing civil war. In fact, acting with Collins's approval, Griffith arranged with de Valéra and the Sinn Féin Ard-Feis in February 1922 to prevent the split of the party prior to presenting the Constitution to the electorate.[10] Yet, as Akenson and Fallin point out, the Constitution, in "standing election," became essentially a party and political document to be voted up or down by the electorate.[11] The cost was high; national polarization meant that the Constitution would not be perceived as being above politics. Despite Griffith's participation in this maneuver to give the Constitutional Committee room to operate, his subsequent actions, such as his insistence that Figgis be appointed, revealed that he was far more interested in a Constitution acceptable to the British than to Gaelic-Romantics.

Collins, in contrast, recognizing that any reference to the Anglo-Irish Treaty and any provisions requiring an expression of Irish subservience to the British crown would ensure civil war, directed the committee not to duplicate in the Constitution any provisions already covered in the Anglo-Irish Treaty. He insisted that no reference to the Treaty and no inclusion of the British role in Irish governance be made. Collins instructed the committee: "You are not to be bound up by legal formalities but to put up a constitution of a Free State and then bring it to the Provisional Government, who will fight for carrying it through. It is a question of status and we want definitely to define and produce a true democratic constitution. You are to bear in mind not the legalities of the past but the practicalities of the future."[12]

For a time, all members of the committee, including Figgis, attempted to implement Collins's directive and achieve what would prove to be impossible: to embody in one document nationalist convictions that expressed both Irish-Enlightenment and Gaelic-Romantic sentiments. They sought to do this most apparently in the Draft Preamble. Here, they attempted to express Irish nationalist sentiment – distinct from British control and authority – by combining in one document two distinct, and not necessarily compatible, cultural understandings. Although in the drafting process more than one preamble was written, the first working draft illustrates this effort:

(We the people of Ireland in our resolve) to renew and establish our state, and to found it upon principles of freedom and justice,

Theoretical and Empirical Problems

(take control of our destiny), <u>in order that Ireland may take her place among the Nations of the world as a free and democratic state.</u> (In the exercise of our sovereign right as a free people), <u>and to promote the welfare, and to preserve and to develop the heritage</u> and the spiritual aspirations of our people, (we do hereby create Saorstát Éireann and give it this Constitution.)

KEY

( ) Common meaning – the shared basis of community
==== Shared reference point
—— Irish-Enlightenment reference
---- Gaelic-Romantic reference

A reading of the Preamble reveals elements of both the Gaelic-Romantic and Irish-Enlightenment traditions. But the Preamble also possesses elements that affirm a sense of national unity transcending these competing traditions. Finally, there are parts that, although central to both traditions, if further explicated would reveal different substantive interpretations of national purpose and aspiration.

For example, the first words of the Preamble, "We the people of Ireland in our resolve . . ." constitute an assertion of nationhood standing above any fractious divisions. But to speak of "renew[ing] our state" clearly reflects a Gaelic-Romantic conception of the meaning of independence, implying that the Irish state that existed prior to colonial conquest would be reestablished. The phrase "establish our state" refers to the Irish-Enlightenment conception of an Ireland possessing, for the first time, political independence. Each clause standing alone has substantive meaning, but the expression "to renew and establish our state," taken together, makes sense only with reference to the particular tension in Irish cultural thinking. Unable to offer a transcendent formulation for national purpose after independence, the drafters sought only to embrace and combine the two competing understandings. "Taking control of our destiny," again as an expression of national sentiment, has a common transcendent meaning, whereas the phrase "in order that Ireland may take her place among the nations of the world as a free democratic state" evokes general consensus only because each tradition remains free to apply its own distinctive meanings to that sentiment. "To preserve the heritage and the spiritual aspirations of our people" claims that the integrity of Irish culture has been jeopardized because Ireland has not been a sovereign nation, but rather subject to British rule. Such a view falls solidly within the Gaelic-Romantic rendering of Irish history, whereas the clause "to develop the heritage and spiritual aspirations of our people" expresses Irish-Enlightenment convictions. In this case, independence and self-determination are presented as necessary for a national culture to flourish. Rather than emphasizing the perversion or atrophy of Irish culture prior to independence, as the Gaelic-Romantics do, this conception asserts only the conditions necessary for a national culture to thrive. To speak of "preserving and developing" the Irish heritage is not inherently contradictory, yet the inclusion of both clauses again constitutes an effort to embrace both traditions of Irish nationalism.

The Preamble, in short, was a valiant effort to transcend these cultural and political divisions by incorporating both within a civic, national, and moral document. Like all other efforts to bridge the two polarized worlds in Ireland in the pre–Civil War period, this effort collapsed. What Michael Collins had failed to appreciate when he instructed the committee not to include the Treaty provisions in the Constitution was that the divisions in Ireland ran deeper than merely support for or opposition to the Anglo-Irish Treaty. To remove the symptom from public view would not rid the nation of the disorder that was plaguing it; of this the Constitution became living proof.

Some members, with Figgis at the fore, although accepting Collins's instructions and acting in good faith to produce a document acceptable to the Irish people, understood their task to be a legalistic one, namely, to establish the machinery of state for an independent Irish government that violated neither the spirit nor the letter of the Anglo-Irish Treaty. Like the pro-Treatyites generally, who placed the British constraints on Irish action at center stage, these drafters worked with an eye on the British, arguing that only a Constitution that could pass British approval should be drafted.

Other members, however, of whom Collins was the most prominent, saw in the drafting process an opportunity to circumvent the restrictive features of the Treaty. Drafting the Constitution represented a chance to present the Irish people with a radical document of independence capable of receiving widespread national support and, therefore, of halting political polarization. Similar to the anti-Treatyites, these drafters rejected placing the British at the center of their deliberations and, instead, wished to write a constitution that would heal the divisions within the Irish polity. Bridging the gulf between Irish nationalists, they asserted, should be the preeminent purpose of the Constitution.

This division within the Drafting Committee was but a microcosm of the larger split in Irish society. Despite Michael Collins's hopes, the same political divisions, animated in part by the cultural polarities in

Irish society, were reproduced in the Constitution Drafting Committee. Because there was no functioning public that could successfully mediate between the polarities of thought, there appeared what seems almost a natural "sociocultural" process of breakdown. The fact that it occurred among supporters of the Treaty and not among radical idealists on either side of the political spectrum reveals, once more, the strength of the two cultural strands in Irish thought. On the one side, there was the realistic and pragmatic appraisal of the political and legal constraints facing the Irish nation. A constitution was conceived that would ensure Irish independence by circumventing British objections. Ireland would enter the modern world and assume a modest place in the community of nations. On the other side, members of the Drafting Committee were inspired by a spirit of national unity, common resolve, and a sense of the uniqueness of the Irish experience. More romantic in vision, these drafters sought to forge the kind of national unity that would help usher in the new age for Ireland. Rather than producing a single Draft Constitution, the committee broke up into two factions and presented to Michael Collins not one constitution to be submitted to the British for approval, but two.[13]

An analysis of the two documents reveals important areas of contest in the conception of constitutional government. These alternatives, although not reducible merely to differences in cultural perspective, were filtered through the increasingly strong poles of Gaelic-Romantic and Irish-Enlightenment thought. These draft constitutions, in short, were the material embodiment of the divergent conceptions of state and nationhood coexisting in Irish thought. And yet, if the two drafts expressed political-cultural tensions, they also contained shared elements representing common nationalist agreement, transcending differences, and expressing Irish civic unity. This was the first time that the unique Irish understanding of itself vis-à-vis Britain and the rest of the world had been embodied in a written document.

Those areas of consensus, in effect, established the definition of and agenda for a transcendent civic consciousness based upon principles neither exclusively Irish-Enlightenment nor Gaelic-Romantic. Instead, these sentiments expressed the nationalist struggle against external rule. Yet, to achieve a consensus based on these principles, as the following chapters will show, would prove to be extremely difficult. The cultural tension, as expressed in the constitutional debate, focused on the extent to which political authority was to be centralized in the state government. Irish-Enlightenment thought encouraged a strong state, so that primordial connections and political alliances would be subordinated to an individualized, egalitarian civil order. A strong, centralized state would protect minority rights and strengthen the influence of the individual citizen. But the Gaelic-Romantic tradition was largely at odds with a political elite attempting to establish a more universalistic political system.

Gaelic-Romantic thinking embraces a decentralized political authority in which the community plays a pivotal role in developing policy. Further, it is suspicious of political authority in general, preferring to have the "natural" Catholic majority determine the political course for the nation. Its antihierarchical commitments, its suspicion of secular authority, and its yearning for a reestablishment of a community of brethren posed formidable problems for the new government. In attempting to create a state apparatus separate from the private sphere and possessing authority to regulate it, in asserting its popular mandate, and in seeking to integrate not only Irish nationalists but Protestants – many of them Unionists – into the new state, this political elite was compelled to moderate Gaelic-Romantic commitments sharply, consistent with the establishment of a more universalistic political system.

The constitutional drafting process that will be described in the following pages illustrates the difficulty faced by the political elite in forging any compromise position acceptable to both traditions. In fact, as I will argue, the first Free State Government in time abandoned its efforts to promote a transcendent political form that blended both cultural understandings into a new, uniquely Irish political expression. Instead, the new government sought to promote strong, effective institutions capable of sustaining oppositional politics; in a fashion, it adopted Irish-Enlightenment forms characterized by strong political institutions and suppressed Gaelic-Romantic politics. But this is to get ahead of the story; it is first necessary to appreciate the inability of the Irish politicians to forge a mutually satisfactory and meaningful Constitution. What was produced instead were two draft constitutions that embodied very different understandings of the appropriate character of political authority.

Cultural polarization and the drafting process

As already described, the Drafting Committee, upon convening, almost immediately began to break down into different factions. Despite its good intention to find a consensus, the antinomies of cultural thinking were quickly revealed. Yet, prior to total polarization, most of the committee members cooperated sufficiently to produce "Document No. 39," not a draft constitution but a working paper from which it was hoped that a draft would be drawn. The preamble discussed earlier was the preamble to this document. Like the preamble, the document attempted to blend elements from both traditions of thought; where agreement could not be reached, alternatives were placed in the text.

In attempting to proceed beyond the working paper, members of the Draft Committee sought to use Document No. 39 to produce an actual draft constitution. It was here that the consensus-building process broke down: Two draft constitutions were written. Draft A, which Darrell Figgis helped write, bore the strong imprint of Irish-Enlightenment thinking, with no further compromises to Gaelic-Romanticism than those offered in Document No. 39. Draft B, in contrast, which James Douglas, Collins's original choice for committee chairman, helped write, rejected much of Document No. 39 and offered instead a version that expressed a clearer Gaelic-Romantic perspective.

The preamble to Draft A, for all intents and purposes, was the same as the preamble to Document No. 39. But the preamble to Draft B was fundamentally different, expressing sentiments and convictions distinctly Gaelic-Romantic. That it was offered as a possible constitution and that it resembled the initial preamble so little reveals how quickly the polarization process was occurring, not only in the country but also within the committee itself.

Draft A Preamble

We, the people of Ireland, in our resolve to renew and re-establish our State and to found it upon principles of freedom and justice, take control of our destiny in order that Ireland may take her place among the Nations of the world as a free democratic State. In the exercise of our sovereign right as a free people and to provide the welfare and to preserve and develop the heritage and the spiritual aspirations of our people, we hereby declare Saorstát Éireann established and give it this Constitution.

Draft B Preamble

We, the people of Ireland, acknowledging that all authority comes from God, and in the exercise of our right as a free people, do hereby create Saorstát Éireann and give it this Constitution. Through it we shall endeavor to re-establish our national life and unity that Ireland may take her rightful place among the Nations of the earth.

A comparison of the Draft A preamble with Document No. 39 shows few alterations. Except for minor grammatical and punctuation changes, there is nothing different in the two texts. However, the Draft B preamble bears very little resemblance to the first preamble or to Draft A's, and the ways in which it is different are important. Unlike Document No. 39, which could be read as an effort to incorporate within one body politic certain Gaelic-Romantic and Irish-Enlightenment sentiments, Draft B reveals little of the same catholic spirit. The latter preamble, in the context of Irish politics at the time it was drafted, is nearly an admission that no common consensus would be forthcoming.

First, the secularism of the Irish-Enlightenment tradition is abridged in the declaration that "all authority comes from God." By introducing God into the preamble, where no reference was made in Document No. 39, these drafters were offering a conception of authority radically different from that shared by adherents to the Irish-Enlightenment tradition. The people of Ireland, in acting for God, were establishing a holy nation where decisions were providentially legitimated. This constituted an absolutist conception of a political community whose actions were not determined by an emergent and indeterminate collectivity, but were teleologically justified.

Second, Draft B made no reference to the state, to principles of freedom and justice, or to the aspiration to achieve a free, democratic political system. In other words, Draft B, although intended as a preamble to a national constitution, reflected no commitment to principles of civic life. Unlike Document No. 39, this preamble refused to acknowledge the rightfulness of a state apparatus exercising authority and administering justice to the nation. Had it expressed a commitment to a free, democratic state, it would have been endorsing a political system not based on a predetermined sense of right, but one in which the wishes of the free individual, whatever they might be, would be protected and honored by the state. This unwillingness to endorse a modern form of civility based upon the rights of the individual represented a romantic reassertion that the collective will of the Irish community, primordially defined, would and could harmoniously establish patterns of interaction belying any need for hierarchy and authority relations superior to the community.

Finally, this preamble interpreted the Constitution only as a means to "re-establish our national life and unity," not as an end in itself. Rather than offering a new conception, as Document No. 39 proposed, of civic integration, capable of incorporating the heterogeneous elements of Irish society through the Constitution itself, this preamble saw the Constitution – whose authority came from God – as the stepping stone to that Republican image of a homogeneous and unified Irish people. Where Document No. 39 identified the establishment of a free, democratic state as the precondition for Ireland to "take her place among the Nations of the world," Draft B asserted that only when national life and unity were reestablished could Ireland "take her rightful place among the Nations of the earth." One was a conception of a modern society where political rule was differentiated and where the private interests of the individual citizen were protected. The other was a conviction that moral community could be re-created, composed of all who shared in a mutual collective interest.

The two preambles, then, expressed two sharply divergent understandings of the Irish community. In fairness, Document No. 39 and Draft A had made concessions to incorporate the Gaelic-Romantic strain of thought and Draft B, merely by accepting the need for a constitution, had given some ground to the Irish-Enlightenment way of perceiving the Irish nation. But despite these modest movements toward the center, the two preambles illustrate the fundamentally different value commitments that were dividing the Drafting Committee. This fact is even more striking when one recalls that these men were selected because of their nonpolitical moral commitment to Ireland, their devotion to constitutionalism, and their fundamental humanitarianism.

Value dissension and normative divergence: the two draft constitutions

These value differences, as reflected in the different preambles, were reflected in several key provisions of the Constitution itself. Because the document intended to regulate institutional and interpersonal relations in an independent Ireland, the Draft Constitutions expressed the divergent value commitments revealed in the two preambles. Draft B possessed, in short, specific normative provisions for the structure and processes of independent Irish life that reflected the Gaelic-Romantic values that were motivating certain of the drafters.

One cannot predict easily how those committed to Gaelic-Romantic principles might have translated those convictions into constitutional idiom. The creation of an abstract legal document allowing certain individuals to assume power and to regulate the population already represented an abridgment of those sentiments. Similarly, the idea of a constitutional document is itself a negation of conflict resolution through violence. The drafting of the Constitution, by its very nature, succeeded in compromising a significant dimension of Gaelic-Romantic thought. Yet the Gaelic-Romantic tradition was expressed by offering a Constitution deeply suspicious of secular authority; it was a document that attempted to restrict centralized power and that introduced substantive popular checks on elite actions.

In a word, just as the two draft preambles revealed two distinct conceptions of the appropriate relationship between the people and the government, so did the provisions of the Constitution itself. The authors of Draft A, although certainly not undemocratic, were content to develop political institutions that closely paralleled those of Great Britain. Although the Crown was not involved, these provisions were seen as protection of the political apparatus against a less disciplined popular will. The writers of Draft B, in contrast, not having this distrust of the masses, were intent on weakening the power of the political elite and enhancing the role of the Irish citizen.

There were two significant disagreements in the drafts that illustrate the divergent approaches to a modern constitutional order. First, the drafts differed on the appropriate role of the Senate in a new Irish government. Although it was originally conceived as a counterpart to the British House of Lords without the hereditary privilege of that institution, drafters of Document B sought to restrict the Senate's power. Although both Draft A and Draft B provided for the first Senate to be elected, Draft A asserted that the members of the lower house would elect Senate members, whereas Draft B proposed a popular election. Further, whereas Draft A looked to the Senate to play an important regulatory role in preventing the lower house from acting excessively, Draft B demonstrated a considerable distrust of that body, which was further distant from the popular voice. In this latter draft, the Senate was excluded from both appropriating and raising taxes, and it was denied any function in regard to money bills. In short, Draft A looked to the Senate as an agency of moderation and responsibility, whereas Draft B, although accepting the institution of the upper house, sought to limit the role of elitism and privilege in Irish political life.

An even more significant and revealing difference between the two drafts concerned the organization of the executive branch of the Free State. These differences had already been presented as alternatives in Document No. 39 and were now formalized in two separate drafts. Draft A proposed a cabinet government identical to the British system, except for the role of the Crown. The president was to be elected by the Dáil and was to appoint his cabinet ministers from among its members. They would be the heads of the various executive departments, comprising the executive council, and would be bound by the principle of collective responsibility.

Draft B offered a novel alternative. According to this proposal, four ministers would be chosen from the Dáil: the president, the vice-president, the minister for external affairs, and the minister for finance. The last three officers would be appointed by the president. In addition, there would be ministers nominated by a committee of the Dáil who would be chosen "with due regard to their suitability for office and should as far as possible be generally representative of Saorstát Éireann as a whole rather than of groups or parties."[14] Not members of the Dáil but subject to Dáil approval, these ministers, who came to be known as "extern ministers," would serve for four years, and except for incompetence or malfeasance, could not be removed from office even if the Dáil was dissolved. What was proposed was a two-tiered Executive Council in which the four ministers who were members of the Dáil were collectively responsible, that is, acting as a single authority, for external affairs, whereas collective responsibility for domestic affairs would be shared by all ministers, including the extern ones.

Extern ministers, for those drafters who conceived the idea, represented an ingenious way to circumvent the full proscriptive authority of the Anglo-Irish Treaty. By these provisions, cabinet ministers might serve in that capacity without first sitting in the Dáil and, more importantly, without having to first take the oath of allegiance to the Crown. Moreover, in this dual form of collective responsibility, extern ministers would not have to approve of the Free State's relations with Great Britain. At the same time, they could still serve on behalf of the Free State.

Clearly, as Akenson and Fallin suggest, these provisions of Draft B were motivated by the framers' desire to generate support for the Constitution by the anti-Treatyites.[15] The institution of extern ministers would prevent the Treaty from blocking the political participation of those opposed to it. But these provisions were motivated, more fundamentally, by a Gaelic-Romantic cultural orientation whose understanding of state and society required an executive system different from the British cabinet one.

The political solution offered in Draft B represented as much a cultural alternative as a political agenda. The idea that the political system ought to draw a majority of its ministers from the nonpolitical arena revealed a strong suspicion of political authority. The fact that there were "politicians" and "experts," mutually exclusive categories, and that both should be represented in the Cabinet runs counter to the more common notion that politicians are best equipped to conduct political affairs. In this more unusual rendering, a mechanism was offered to ensure that the community – not politicians – would prevent complete state control by politicians. Further, and in the same vein, these proposals revealed the conviction that national unity ought to be the principal purpose of the state. In contrast to Draft A, which sought to promote those conditions necessary for an effective and efficient state apparatus, Draft B was mainly concerned with reestablishing national integration. This would be accomplished by weakening the autonomy of the political structure by having the community represented directly in the executive council through extern ministers. In this sense, too, the Gaelic-Romantic response to independence was to offer a superdemocratic conception of political order. Depending on the context, this could mean either direct participation of the electorate in political affairs, militating against a feared political elitism, or it could mean weakening of the government through popular representation, militating against a feared isolation of the government from the community.

The Draft Constitutions and the British response

In late March 1922, Michael Collins was presented with the two draft constitutions. It was his unenviable task to create from them one constitutional draft that would be satisfactory to the Irish population as well as to the British Government. To be sure, substantial portions of the two drafts were identical and reflected those beliefs shared by all Irish nationalists. With respect to these elements, Collins's task was not difficult. It is important to identify briefly the parts of the Constitution that both drafts adopted.

In both drafts, the basic structures of government differed little from the British model, with distinct legislative, executive, and judicial branches. To protect minorities, like Southern Unionists, a system of proportional representation, first introduced into Ireland by the British, was maintained in the independent state. Undoubtedly, Ireland's century-long involvement with the British parliamentary system promoted an understanding of and a comfort with the British model, with which no other form of governance could effectively compete.

But the Draft Constitution also possessed some important modifications of the British model, reflecting, in part, the Irish exposure to continental constitutions and the American one. These provisions also expressed the drafters' perception of the political-cultural differences between the English and Irish nations and their interest in making the Free State Constitution uniquely representative of the Irish spirit. In these respects, when compared to the British Constitution, both Draft A and Draft B were thoroughly Republican.[16] First, they rejected the empiricism of British constitutional practice by defining carefully and thoroughly the scope and functions of the branches of government. Even more significantly, both drafts, adopting the wording of Document No. 39, began the Constitution with a declaration of the fundamental rights guaranteed to the citizen. Both drafts began by referring not to the state but to the nation: "The Nation's sovereignty extends not only to all the men and women of the Nation, but to all the material possessions of the Nation, the Nation's soil and all its resources and all the wealth and wealth-producing processes within the Nation; and all right to private property is subordinated to the public right and welfare of the Nation." This provision, Article 1, reminiscent both of Wolfe Tone's demand for national sovereignty over natural resources and, more recently, of the Democratic Program of 1919 espoused in the first Republican Dáil, asserted the preeminence of the nation – the men, women, and material resources – over any political apparatus. Article 3 states that "all powers of government are derived from the people of Ireland," clearly establishing the causal link between nationhood to statehood. Articles 7 to 11 specify the fundamental rights guaranteed to Irish citizens: liberty, dwellings, conscience, free expression of opinion, assembly, and education.

In specifying these rights, the drafters distinguished their Constitution from other Dominion constitutions; for the Dominions, the civil liberties and rights were guaranteed by the British Crown. These drafts claimed that fundamental rights would be guaranteed by the Irish Constitution, not British statute. But probably more to the point, a declaration of fundamental rights reflected the Irish assertion of the limits to parliamentary authority.[17] Placed prior to the legislative provisions, this declaration of individual rights is testimony to the democratic spirit that inspired the nationalist movement and motivated the drafters of the Constitution.

There are two other constitutional provisions that both drafts included and that further reflected the democratic spirit of the drafters. Manifesting again a common distrust of parliamentary authority, the drafters established a system of initiative and referendum that ensured the ability of the electorate to counteract legislative action. Any law passed by the House or Senate could be suspended for 90 days if either two-fifths of the members of Dáil Eireann or a majority of the members of the Seanad (Senate) demanded it. If 30,000 voters (in the Draft Constitution that Collins submitted to the British, this was changed to one-twentieth of the registered voters) signed a petition, the law in question would be submitted by referendum to the population. The only qualification was that the referendum process would not apply to tax or money bills or to any bills declared by the Dáil or Seanad "to be necessary for the immediate preservation of the public peace, health or safety." This latter clause would prove to be very significant in later developments in the Free State, and will be discussed in forthcoming chapters.

Through initiative, further, citizens could make proposals for laws or constitutional amendments. If, within two years, the Dáil or Seanad failed to consider these proposals, they could, if certain qualifications were met, be submitted by referendum to the Irish people. Although the two sets of drafters might have had different minority populations and different issues in mind when they introduced these provisions protecting minorities from abusive governmental power, all of them agreed on these democratic provisions.

The fact that Drafts A and B had substantial elements of agreement, that they reflected a common heritage of nationalist opposition to British rule, and that both, in their own way, wished to protect the individual from a potentially abusive state apparatus surely made Michael Collins's task of creating from the two documents one draft easier.

As I have suggested, these areas of agreement represented both the common exposure to British parliamentarianism and the convergence that resulted from the long-term nationalist movement. Yet the degree of discord between the two cannot be minimized, nor can the fact that the disagreements were not ad hoc but reflected deeply rooted differences in cultural perception. What may appear to be mere differences in nuance or emphasis were, for the Irish, features of extraordinarily powerful meaning. The challenge of finding a compromise satisfactory both to the British and to the various factions represented in the constitutional drafting process could hardly have been more formidable. As Akenson and Fallin show, Collins arranged negotiations with the Southern Unionists, the British government, and the anti-Treatyites.[18] The most important set of talks, and those that would prove to have the most lasting consequence, were the ones with the anti-Treatyites.

The original agreement that Griffith helped arrange with Sinn Féin to give the Drafting Committee time to operate was, by late April, close to expiration. Collins, already under pressure from the right wing (e.g., the Unionists) of his government, who were disturbed by the radical ring of both drafts, needed cooperation from de Valéra to justify such an independent-minded Constitution. Unlike Collins, Griffith was not enthusiastic about the proposed Constitutions. As already stated, he was prepared to offer the British a Constitution explicitly incorporating the provisions of the Treaty.[19] De Valéra, for his part, remained hopeful that the Constitution, if sufficiently a document of independence, would rescue Ireland from the threat of civil war and guarantee him a key role in the government of an independent Ireland. For their own separate reasons, and because of their common interest in avoiding civil war, Collins and de Valéra entered into what came to be known as the "Collins–de Valéra pact." It was an agreement that the upcoming election, which threatened to be a referendum on the Treaty and the Constitution, would circumvent those issues. Sinn Féin, the nationalist party, would maintain the appearance of a national consensus by putting forward a panel of candidates; sixty-six of the candidates would be pro-Treaty and fifty-eight anti-Treaty, representing the exact division in the Treaty vote that had already occurred in the Dáil.

It has been suggested that the pact, in addition, was an arrangement between de Valéra and Collins over the specific content of the Draft Constitution to be submitted to the British. Akenson and Fallin argue that at least those provisions regarding extern ministers in the executive branch were part of the bargain struck by Collins and de Valéra.[20] Although there is some circumstantial evidence to support this view, it is equally plausible that those provisions contained in Draft B were the ones that Collins himself favored; in any event, the pact with de Valéra gave him further justification to submit this to the British, rather than Draft A.

The Free State Constitution: the juxtaposition of symbols of national unity and monarchy

The draft that Collins submitted to the British combined elements of both drafts, with a decided bias toward Draft B. Collins included Draft B's provisions concerning the Seanad and those sections detailing the special place of extern ministers in the executive branch. Perhaps the most noteworthy aspect of the Draft Constitution was that it was submitted to the British Government without a preamble, probably indicating Collins's belief that the preamble to either Draft A or Draft B would be read by the British as an objectionable assertion of Irish national independence.

Collins need not have been so wary of the British reaction to any particular clause of the draft, for they immediately rejected the entire document. They viewed the draft, as a whole, as an Irish attempt to circumvent the constraints of the Treaty. The rigidity of the British response was undoubtedly fueled by the increasingly fragile public order in Ireland. With the anti-Treatyites apparently gaining ground and the onset of civil war more and more imminent, the British believed it was necessary to pressure the Provisional Government to protect both the

Treaty and British interests.[21] In this milieu, they were not about to allow a reassertion of radical Irish nationalism, even in the form of a constitution.

Lloyd George drafted a series of six questions to the Provisional Government concerning the Draft Constitution. Each was concerned with the relationship of the draft to the Anglo-Irish Treaty, querying whether the Irish nation was willing to assume its rightful place in the British Commonwealth and to publicly swear its allegiance to the Crown. It was clear that these were hardly innocent questions; the acceptance of the Draft Constitution by the British Government depended upon the appropriate Irish response.

Arthur Griffith responded to these questions and, for all intents and purposes, conceded nearly every point. The British were assured that the Treaty would figure prominently in the Free State Constitution. It is not clear how pivotal Griffith was in the surrender to British interests, but his cultural convictions, as described earlier and as distinct from those of Collins and other members of the Draft Committee, lend credence to those who suggest that he broke fundamentally with Collins on this score.[22]

Within the next two weeks, during the first weeks of June 1922, the Free State Constitution was redrafted by the Draft Committee and Sir Gordon Hewart, representing the British Government. Griffith's letter of response to the British queries constituted the basis of the revision. Nearly all of the changes were to make crystal clear Ireland's status as a Dominion of the Commonwealth and bound by the Anglo-Irish Treaty. In addition, there was some concern to protect the rights of Southern Unionists. As a result, certain measures strengthening the role of the Senate were included. Aside from those changes, the integrity of the original draft was intact. Britain paid little mind to the specific provisions of the Constitution other than those that had a bearing on their role in Irish affairs. As a result, the Free State Constitution embraced both the symbols of monarchy, to which virtually no one in Ireland subscribed, and the elements of radical independence, emphasizing the power of the nation over even the government; the latter provisions were introduced largely to induce Republican acceptance.

The consequence was a document rife with ambiguity, incorporating symbols that were totally incompatible. In the Free State Constitution, approved first by the British Government and later by the Dáil Éireann, a preamble was written that was essentially taken directly from the Gaelic-Romantic Draft B:

> Dáil Éireann sitting as a Constituent Assembly in this Provisional
> Parliament, acknowledging that all lawful authority comes from

God to the people and in the confidence that the National life and unity of Ireland shall thus be restored, hereby proclaims the establishment of the Irish Free State (otherwise called Saorstát Éireann) and in the exercise of undoubted right, decrees and enacts as follows . . .

Immediately following this assertion of Irish sovereignty and its commitment to the re-creation of a unified national community, the following caveat was introduced:

The said Constitution shall be construed with reference to the Articles of Agreement for a Treaty between Great Britain and Ireland . . . which are hereby given the force of law, and if any provision of the said Constitution or of any amendment thereof or of any law made there under is in any respect repugnant to any of the provisions of the Scheduled Treaty, it shall, to the extent only of such repugnancy, be absolutely void and inoperative and the Parliament and the Executive Council of the Irish Free State (Saorstát Éireann) shall respectively pass such further legislation and do all such other things as may be necessary to implement the Scheduled Treaty.

Further, the first article, referred to earlier, which proclaimed that national sovereignty extended not only to all men and women of Ireland but to all the material possessions of the nation, was removed because it obscured Ireland's Dominion status. Replacing this impressively progressive assertion of national authority was the following statement: "The Irish Free State is a co-equal member of the Community of Nations forming the British Commonwealth of Nations."[23] Other changes in the Constitution included the following: Irish armed forces were restricted, consistent with the Treaty; amendments to the Constitution could not supersede the Treaty; and extern ministers were required to take the oath of allegiance to the Crown, like all other members of the Dáil and the Executive Council.

Thus, in the Constitution that finally emerged, Irish sovereignty was limited by the parameters of the Anglo-Irish Treaty. Upon its approval by the British Government, the *Sunday Times* (London) wrote, "The English victory is plain. Everything which left the question of the Imperial connection in doubt in the Irish draft has been positively and successfully restored."[24] Nevertheless, the Constitution reflected a popular constraint on political authority. Ironically, the provisions that made the Irish Constitution especially democratic, allowing for substantial popular control over political authority as presented in Draft B, were included to secure Republican support. Yet with the Anglo-Irish Treaty now so prominent in the Constitution, this effort was futile. No Republican would consider accepting the legitimacy of the new Free State, no matter how democratic its structures.

The Constitution symbolically incorporated the most extreme elements of Irish life – its connection with British monarchy on the one side, its deep suspicion of political authority, and its assertion of national unity standing above political power on the other. Leo Kohn, in commenting on this document, characterizes it positively:

> Its archaic symbols had to be introduced, but their meaninglessness for Ireland was writ large on every page. The monarchical forms paled into insignificance in the light of the formal enunciation and the consistent application of the principle of the sovereignty of the people as the fundamental and the exclusive source of all political authority. . . . It was instinct with a supreme faith in the inherent ethos of democratic principle, but that faith was permeated by a critical realization of the inadequacy of the traditional forms of parliamentary government to ensure a more than formal democracy, a scepticism intensified by a deeply rooted distrust of governmental authority – the peculiar Irish heritage of centuries of opposition.[25]

Yet, despite Kohn's celebration of the document, the Constitution would make the task of governing especially difficult for two reasons. First, the Free State would be born as a result of a document that sharply restricted its ability to exercise political power. On the one side, its actions were constrained by provisions of the Anglo-Irish Treaty; no action – even in the interest of greater political inclusion of dissident Irish Republicans – could be taken that abridged the Treaty. On the other hand, the Constitution, expressing a strong commitment to the popular will and the rights of individuals, limited the capacity of the government to enact those measures designed to reduce the Republican challenge to political order. In both respects, political power was limited. The consequence of these constraints will become apparent in subsequent chapters.

The Constitution impeded governing in an additional way. In incorporating the symbols of British monarchy and Irish populism, it failed to represent the symbolic commitments of the vast majority of the Irish population. To be sure, it possessed nationalist elements with which most people identified, but neither the references to the British Crown nor those elements intended to mollify Republican opposition to the Free State captured the spirit and concern of the Irish majority. Support for and commitment to the new Free State would have to be won despite the Constitution, not through it. The government would have to demonstrate that it was neither an arm of British authority nor a vehicle of intransigent Republicanism (of course, its role in defeating Republican forces in the Civil War helped in the latter respect). But the fact was that the new government was unable to wrap itself around a symbolic flag to which the majority of the population could respond. Because the government could not celebrate the Constitution, it would be evaluated by its actions and by a population not entirely sure of its moral and political commitments. Rather than acclaiming the Constitution and thereby attempting to create a connection between the Government and the constitutional symbols, the Free State had to apologize for the Constitution. It would have to gain popular support by its ability to act expediently and pragmatically. That was hardly a way to produce strong emotional attachments and support. Kevin O'Higgins, minister for home affairs and Government spokesman in the Constitution of Ireland Bill, stated:

> . . . had circumstances here been other than what they were, I do believe that we could have got a more pleasantly worded Constitution; but I do not believe that we could have got a better Constitution than we have in fact got. It was our duty – it was the duty of the Irish representatives to hug the safety line; to walk as it were the cliff's edge while being very careful not to hurl their country over that cliff's edge and I know that the cliff's edge was walked and I know that the safety line was hugged.[26]

Later in the debate, O'Higgins argued:

> . . . people do not expect to eliminate from the Constitution features of the Treaty which, while undoubtedly unpleasant to the sentiments of a vast majority are yet explicitly and implicitly embodied in the document which the Plenipotentiaries signed. . . . On the face of it, this Constitution is not a Republican Constitution; perhaps I would not be wrong in saying that it is as little a Republican Constitution as a British Constitution. It contains the trappings, the insignia, the fiction and the symbols of a monarchical institution, but the real power is in the hands of the people.[27]

The Constitution, rather than saving the Irish nation from civil war, became a victim of the same forces propelling the country inexorably into battle. It became but another weapon in the arsenal of the Provisional Government to prevent war, one hardly successful in achieving its objective. In failing to slow the march toward civil war, the Constitution – a document intended to unify a nation around common moral sentiments and aspirations – became instead a partisan political tract.

Not only was it widely viewed, even after the Civil War, as a replica of the polarities besetting the Irish nation but at the same time, it restricted the capacity of the new government to heal the rifts.

If cultural antinomies writ large helped characterize the challenges faced by the new Irish Government following the Civil War, the institutionalization of these traditions in the Constitution more precisely describe the cultural impact on political rule. In a certain sense, the Constitution celebrated those symbols – of British monarchy and national life and unity – that the new government was incapable of embracing.

As the following chapters will demonstrate, independence began largely without a supportive symbolic system. The Civil War denied the new government the chance to present itself as the inheritor of the nationalist legacy, and the government certainly was not interested in being perceived as the agent of British monarchy. In short, the political events surrounding independence and the strength of cultural antinomies required the new government to forge political order through the exercise of institutional strength alone. The Constitution would be an obstacle to both symbolic integration – for it celebrated the wrong symbols – and to effective governance. The government could rule, as subsequent developments would prove, only by demonstrating its capacity to preserve stability and to isolate the expression of extremist political sympathy, while attempting, at the same time, to forge symbolic integration anew. As in other new nations of the twentieth century, the Constitution proved to be an ineffective weapon in promoting democratic stability. In its place, the government would have to rely on far less noble sentiments and actions to ensure that democracy would prevail.

Part II. Patterns of Crisis Resolution in the Irish Free State, 1922–1932

4. The Army Mutiny and Normative Political Challenges

Introduction: the political context of crisis politics

The following three chapters will examine a major political crisis in the Free State during its first decade. As I will argue, these crises revealed the kinds of political obstacles – and how they changed over time – that the political leaders had to confront and overcome in their efforts to construct a modern, democratic order. Most broadly, these crises were political expressions of the competing cultural currents in Irish society. Especially in the early part of the decade, challenges to political order were understood and typically expressed through these cultural prisms. As I suggested in Chapter 3, these cultural strains became institutionalized through the constitutional drafting process. As I indicated, the result was paradoxical. Rather than solving the problem of contending cultural currents, the Constitution only amalgamated them into a single document. As the decade progressed, as the next chapters will detail, challenges to the political regime were less frequently expressed in broad cultural terms and increasingly in constitutional, even public policy, terms.

But I will argue that the shift in political language over the decade cannot be interpreted as the result of decreasing cultural opposition. Rather, different understandings of the Irish government continued to animate political life, but as the regime became increasingly adept at demonstrating its political control and authority, and as it appropriated greater political resources on its own behalf, political discourse became less general and confrontational. This new discourse, in short, was a function of the increasing capacity of the government to respond to political challenge, not its success in converting or integrating cultural orientations. Only with the rise of Fianna Fáil, a development I discuss in Chapter 7, did the government move toward greater cultural integration.

Yet if we examine the political and social context in which the Free State Government was forced to operate in 1922 and 1923, its failure to resolve the cultural problem early on can be better appreciated. Consider these features of the Irish nation. By the end of the Civil War, the Free State had condemned more people to death than the British had executed throughout the entire 1916–21 period. More than 10,000 had been interned without trial.[1] About 4,000 people in all were killed between July 1922 and May 1923.[2] When the anti-Treaty forces were finally defeated and a cease-fire was declared in late May 1923, the Republican forces, although conceding military defeat, neither surrendered their arms nor recognized the political authority of the Free State. Instead, the political wing of the anti-Treaty forces, Sinn Féin, proceeded to establish, to the best of its ability, a dual government complete with a parliament, army (IRA), legal institutions, educational institutions, and social services. De Valéra was named president.

This Republican government continued to seek a unified Ireland, one completely independent of the British Commonwealth. Relatively weak, it did not pose a real political alternative. Nevertheless, its presence demonstrated the difficulties faced by the Free State Government. In the first general election following the end of formal hostilities, 44 of the officials elected to the Dáil (almost 30% of the 152-member house) were Sinn Féiners, who, although standing for election, refused to take the oath of allegiance and sit in the Free State Dáil. Thus, despite the Republican defeat on the battlefield, antigovernment sentiment was well entrenched, even institutionalized, in the Free State.

The difficulties faced by the Free State Government were not only military-cum-political. The Irish economy was already weak because of chronic disruptions, a result first of the Anglo-Irish conflicts and later of the Civil War. But it was worsened as the worldwide wartime boom gave way to a severe economic downturn. Credit was almost impossible to obtain, and prices fell sharply.[3] Ireland was simultaneously contending with adverse political and economic circumstances; conditions hardly augured well for the new state.

As if these problems were not sufficient to make stability precarious, the Free State lost, within 10 days of each other, its two most important leaders. On August 12, 1922, Arthur Griffith, not yet fifty years old, collapsed and died. His death was attributed to strain and exhaustion. On August 22, Michael Collins was ambushed and killed by Republican Irregulars, depriving the Free State of its most dynamic and capable leader. The consequence was that the burden of government was now shared by William Cosgrave, formerly a minister for local government in the Republican Dáil of 1919, a stolid, if not charismatic, member of the Provisional Government; Kevin O'Higgins, once Cosgrave's assistant; and General Richard Mulcahy, who assumed Collins's place as commander-in-chief. Cosgrave would become president of the new government, with O'Higgins assuming the post of minister for home affairs and Mulcahy that of minister for defense. The new leadership was young and, when compared to the challenges it faced, of relatively little political experience.

Clearly, the presence of an ambiguous Constitution did not promote the stability of the Free State. Because the Constitution could not offer a way to eliminate the value strains caused by the two cultural and political positions, and because it institutionalized both the British and the Republican presence in Free State politics, political opposition would surely reflect a general critique of the values (or the perceived lack of them) of the Free State Government. In addition, the government's opponents rejected not only the right of the leaders to lead but also the authority of the government itself.

Thus the first crisis to be discussed, the army mutiny of 1924, was not only the first major crisis following the Civil War but also the most serious. Although it was concerned mainly with principles of allocation and distribution, that is, normative questions concerning promotion and demobilization in the Free State army, the crisis would not have occurred had the government possessed, and the Constitution reflected, greater value consensus.

As I will demonstrate, the crisis reflected the suspicion of some people that the new government was not representing the national interest. The Constitution's symbology and the Free State's role in forcibly suppressing part of the national community together required a clear and forthright demonstration, following the Civil War, of the Free State's true aims and convictions. The army mutiny reflected, in part, a belief that the new government, to the extent that it was revealing its commitments when it adopted a particular demobilization scheme for the army, was more interested in demonstrating its continuity with British power and authority than it was in identifying itself with a uniquely Irish conception of political rule.

But this analysis of the army mutiny is not only intended to demonstrate the connection between political and cultural strains and specific forms of political expression. Its purpose is to explain, in addition, how the Free State leaders successfully began to contain and specify political opposition – to move from challenges to basic political values and norms to the development of an opposition contained within a party system, whereby the institutions of rule and the "rules of the game" were widely accepted. The achievement of democratic stability in Ireland cannot be seen merely as a function of a brutal suppression of the government's opposition. That is only a partial reason for its success. Were that the only mechanism, the democratic experiment in Ireland would probably have long since failed. Nevertheless, the efforts to restore a public in which discourse could operate freely was a preeminent task of the new government. Those forces that were attempting to prevent the renewal of civility in the Free State – the extremist Republicans – were to be isolated and squelched. But this was to be accomplished by a response whereby the party in power rather than the government itself increasingly bore the brunt of political opposition.

Kevin O'Higgins, as minister for home affairs, had the principal responsibility for restoring political order. He was a remarkable young man (thirty-one years old in 1923) with extraordinary administrative and leadership skills. If anything, he was overzealous in his political realism. His assessment of what needed to be done led to the passage of two public safety bills in 1923 and 1924 that granted the government exceptional powers to establish Free State authority throughout the nation. The Public Safety Bill of 1923 allowed the government to continue the internment of prisoners that was deemed necessary for public order and to detain anyone suspected of being a danger to public safety. There were further provisions to control possession of firearms. In the face of continued challenges to public authority throughout 1923 – with arson, robbery, and refusal to pay outstanding debts being the most evident examples of disrespect for the government – O'Higgins passed in 1924 a further Public Safety Bill. This bill continued the sanctions of the 1923 Bill and increased the power of the sheriff to recover debts. There was nothing benign about this emergency legislation, and the government was not timid in enforcing it.

These draconian measures could be justified only by the Civil War. Violating the expectations of some nationalists about the nature of independence and stretching the bounds of legitimate authority, the Free State was compelled to assert more positively its role in promoting a modern democratic nation. This was done, in part, by asserting the preeminent authority of the state and even by defining more narrowly the meaning of democratic rights. But as the government was well aware, a secure state apparatus could not be achieved solely by repression. Stability would go hand in hand with increasing public acceptance of the Free State's political apparatus. If democratic order were to be achieved, it would have to be the result of demonstrably "good works" by the government. But that would take time; meanwhile, the new government concentrated on demonstrating its constitutional strength and its capacity to respond to challenge.

The Free State leaders achieved democratic stability partly by an aggressive demonstration of constitutional power and the use of political authority by every means available. Cosgrave, O'Higgins, Mulcahy, and others, upon assuming office, sought to make their presence known throughout the nation in an administrative rather than a repressive mode. And by their very ubiquity, they hoped to wear the opposition down. Their goal was to demonstrate the government's resolve in establishing an efficient and effective government. During their first years they pushed through the Dáil impressive legislation affecting every major social institution. For example, the Civil Service Regulation Act of 1923 established commissioners to recruit candidates according to criteria of efficiency and impartiality, producing an effective, rationalized administrative branch modeled after the British service. Cosgrave had established an unarmed police force, Garda Siorchanna (Civic Guard), that became widely perceived as an apolitical law enforcement body. The court system was revamped. Although roughly paralleling the British system, it was more rationally organized and efficient. The government completely reorganized the administration of local government, ensuring greater administrative uniformity and a larger national role in local affairs.

In short, the Free State Government sought to remake the administration of the nation and, in so doing, to assert its preeminent authority throughout the land. As F. S. L. Lyons comments, "At any time this task of rebuilding virtually the entire administration of the country would have been tremendous. But to begin it in the midst of a Civil War and to carry it on despite the sullen opposition of bitter, inveterate enemies was to take a fearful gamble."[4] In taking these steps, the Free State began to demonstrate its determination and capacity to rule. Each day that it governed, passed legislation, and implemented policy, it enhanced its authority. In the face of several years of political disorder, the establishment of routine political processes – a government constrained by rules and determined to rule by law – benefited from a population yearning for such an order. Yet despite the popular wish, the Free State emerged amid a population by and large not hostile to its rule but deeply suspicious of its capacity to fend off its detractors. And in this milieu, the progress made each day toward greater popular acceptance could be quickly eroded when an unusual crisis beset the new government.

Patterns of Crisis Resolution

The army mutiny crisis, erupting not long after the Civil War, dramatized, in a way that routine politics could not, the fragility of the Free State's political apparatus. In the face of popular skepticism about its capacity to respond to challenge, the mutiny provided the first real opportunity for the government to present itself as competent and authoritative, to enhance confidence and reduce skepticism. At the same time, any failure to respond adequately threatened to undermine all the gains that had been made on a day-to-day basis. The government had to respond to the substantive political issue that the mutiny raised while appearing to be in complete charge of the situation. Otherwise, the fear shared by so many that the Free State could not secure stability would more quickly become a reality.

The fact that the first major political crisis of the new government centered on the army was not surprising. Every other department that the Free State attempted to reform had existed prior to independence. But the Free State army – designed to maintain political authority, not to overthrow it – had to be created anew. And for reasons that will be made clear, the government's treatment of the army came to be viewed, prior to this crisis, as the litmus test of the government's political and moral commitments.

Background: the army and national politics

On March 6, 1924, President Cosgrave was handed an ultimatum on behalf of the IRA organization in the Irish Free State army. It was signed by Major-General Liam Tobin and Colonel Charles Dalton. Their position was stated as follows:

> The IRA only accepted the Treaty as a means of achieving its objectives, namely, to secure and maintain a Republican form of Government in this country.
>
> After many months of discussion with your Government it is our considered opinion that your Government has not those objects in view, and that their policy is not reconcilable with the Irish people's acceptance of the Treaty.
>
> Furthermore, our interpretation of the Treaty was that expressed by the late Commander-in-Chief, General Michael Collins, when he stated: "I have taken an oath of allegiance to the Irish Republic and that oath I will keep, Treaty or no Treaty." We claim Michael Collins as our leader, and again remind you that even after the Treaty was signed, that drastic action was taken against enemies of the unity and complete independence of our country. Both in

oath and honour bound, it is our duty to continue his policy, and therefore present this Ultimatum.

We demand a conference with our representatives of your Government to discuss our interpretation of the Treaty on the following conditions:

a) the removal of the Army Council
b) the immediate suspension of Army demobilisation and reorganisation

In the event of your Government rejecting these proposals we will take such action that will make clear to the Irish people that we are not renegades to the ideals that induced them to accept the Treaty. Our organisation fully realizes the seriousness of the action that we may be compelled to take, but we can no longer be party to the treachery that threatens to destroy the aspirations of the nation.[5]

After reading this document to the Dáil, President Cosgrave appropriately interpreted it as an "attempt . . . not against a particular Government, it is a challenge to the democratic foundations of the State, to the very basis of Parliamentary representation and of responsible Government."[6] The "army mutiny," as it came to be known, was the first major threat, following the Civil War, to the government's political supremacy. And as the ultimatum so clearly indicates, the issues that had fueled the Civil War were replicated in this challenge to the government. The Cosgrave government's failure to resolve this conflict would have serious consequences for the stability of the state; the specter of renewed civil war arose.

A political challenge from the army directed at the parliamentary government was not entirely a surprise. Even prior to independence, relations between the army and government had been strained. Political independence did not erase political or ideological tensions within the army or between the army and the Dáil. As the ultimatum indicates, Major-General Tobin and Colonel Dalton made two substantive demands on the government: (1) the removal of the Army Council and (2) the immediate suspension of army demobilization and reorganization plans. To put these demands in the context of these long-standing tensions is a good way to understand the background of the army mutiny.

The army mutiny coincided, almost to the day, with the final stage of an elaborate and ambitious government program to reorganize the army and demobilize a large proportion of it. As a result of the Civil War, the government had inherited an enormous, top-heavy army, one far larger than a nation in peacetime required and far more costly than a poor nation could afford.[7] In 1922, the army totaled 55,000 men with 3,300 officers. The demobilization program, conceived and executed by Richard Mulcahy, minister for defense, called for a peacetime force of 18,000 men with 1,300 officers.[8] The reduction of the Army by almost two-thirds, accompanied by an almost 60 percent decrease in the number of officers, was an extremely difficult and politically dangerous undertaking for a new government. To increase the difficulty, Ireland in the early 1920s was experiencing high unemployment. Although the government encouraged the preferential hiring of demobilized veterans, no assurance could be given that work would be provided.[9]

For this reason alone, discontent among army men was understandable. But there were other factors as well. The army held itself in high esteem, for it possessed a special relationship with the independent Irish nation. Although the Army was legally created by the new government, as a national institution, it had preceded the Irish Free State. The IRB, seeing itself as principally a military organization, it will be recalled, had asserted that the Republic was "virtually established" in February 1867, with its Supreme Council as "the sole government of the Irish Republic until Ireland secures absolute national independence and a permanent Republican government is established."[10] And the IRA, on behalf of the Irish people, again declared the existence of the Irish Republic in 1916. These nationalist military bodies preceded the establishment of parliamentary institutions. And the fact that the army had paved the way for political independence was not lost on army men. As a consequence, the relationship of the armed forces to the government was problematic even prior to formal political independence.

Did the Dáil possess political authority over the army? Would the army acknowledge the supremacy of civilian rule? The opposition that developed in the army over the Free State Government's demobilization program, and the threats to defy the government's actions, demonstrated that political independence had not resolved that problem.

Army men, by and large, perceived themselves as part of an unbroken link with the nationalist army of preindependence days. Had it not been for the voluntary enlistment of thousands of Irishmen in the Irish Volunteers, the IRB, and the Citizen's Army – coalescing into the IRA – the Irish Free State would not have existed. Because of its special place in Ireland's history, many army men believed that the government's efforts to curtail sharply the strength of the army was both presumptuous and offensive. The government's program of demobilization and reorganization was viewed by some as an illegitimate exercise of political power over the army, suggesting a less than full appreciation of the army's role in securing independence. Moreover, the government's inability to ensure work for the ex-army men appeared as a blatant disregard for those who struggled for Irish independence.

The unemployment issue and the controversy over civil authority were not the only sources of tension between the army and the government. Ideological disputes expressed in the Civil War remained within the army after the war had ended. Some Army men supported the Anglo-Irish Treaty and viewed it as the ultimate victory of the nationalist struggle. Others, however, continued to view it as a limited accomplishment, of value only to the extent that it served as a stepping stone to the Republic.

It is important to note that this latter position was taken by the IRB, led by Michael Collins before his death. The IRB supported the Treaty and the new government in the expectation that the stepping stone theory would prevail. In an effort to ensure the continued support of the IRB, the new government appointed some of its prominent members to key positions. Richard Mulcahy, who had once sat on the Supreme Council of the IRB, was appointed minister for defense and was widely viewed as the sympathetic government spokesman for the IRB.

The three members of the Army Council, directly responsible to Mulcahy, were IRB men as well. When army opposition to the government developed because of the Free State's perceived failure to achieve the Republic, the army men could not organize themselves as part of the IRB because of that organization's co-optation by the new government. Nor could they refer to themselves as the "Irish Republican Army," for that title was held by those forces that refused to recognize the legitimacy of any Free State institution, including the army. Thus, this group came to be known as the "old IRA," referring back to the IRA of pre-Treaty days. As the ultimatum indicates, the old IRA men adopted the position of Michael Collins and the IRB, but because of Mulcahy's link to the IRB, they had to differentiate themselves from that organization as it then existed.

Mulcahy's objective as minister for defense was to change the nature of the army. The army was organized for one purpose – the pursuit of national independence – and was now serving another. He was intent on transforming the army from a highly politicized, semiautonomous institution to a depoliticized, efficient arm of the national government. His task was to make the army clearly subservient to the will of the Dáil. Like other government ministers, his task was to retool various institutions to best serve the peacetime interests of the nation. His objective was to transform an army recruited, organized, and committed to waging war in the national interest into one committed to professionalism and proficiency so as to best serve the parliamentary institutions. But because of the strong politicization in the army and the army's key role in the nationalist struggle, this task was especially difficult. Entrenched political interests within the army were reluctant to allow efficiency and rationalization to guide its reorganization.

Mulcahy attempted to use the reorganization and demobilization plans not only to reduce the size of the army but also to rid it of those elements that impeded its change from one kind of institution to another. He wrote about his plan:

> . . . I am concerned particularly, at present, with making and building an efficient and disciplined Army. If you had not an Army such as this no political organisation of any kind is going to be of any use to you. If you have not such an Army and a disciplined efficient Civil Service to carry into effect smoothly and efficiently and with rapidity the intentions of the Government, the Government cannot possibly carry out its programme either quickly or efficiently, and perhaps not at all.[11]

He concluded another memo by stating, "It is no part of my conception of my policy to keep in the Army men who are unfitted for it."[12]

It was Mulcahy's refusal to use nationalist criteria in his reorganization plans and his insistence on efficiency that resulted in increasing opposition to him and to the government. Long before the actual outbreak of the mutiny, criticism was leveled at him for not giving priority to old IRA men in the army. The charge was that in the reorganization scheme, Mulcahy was not giving preference to those men who had served in the nationalist struggle against Britain. In their place, it was claimed, ex-British soldiers were being given places in the army. To the old IRA men, such action typified Mulcahy's insensitivity to the nationalist cause and, more broadly, reflected the government's unwillingness to secure a truly independent Irish Republic.

Although there is no evidence either to support or refute the claims concerning demobilization policy, the charges against Mulcahy grew in intensity as the program progressed through 1923 and into 1924. In fact, given Mulcahy's objectives, it seems likely that well-trained professional ex-British soldiers were given preference over those whose only attribute might have been their previous service in the cause of independence.

Mulcahy, however, was not naive about the problem or about the growing opposition within the army. His efforts to depoliticize the army were resulting in its *increasing* politicization. Efforts to rid it of political

factionalism and to create a commitment to professionalism and efficiency were creating increased polarities, not fewer ones. For certain
army men, Mulcahy's plan came to represent absolute proof that the
government, not just Mulcahy, had abandoned the aspiration for an
Irish Republic. This process, whereby the Free State army itself was
polarizing, led Mulcahy to undertake an even more daring and dangerous maneuver.

Recognizing the old IRA men as the obstacle to the creation of a new
army, Mulcahy sought to introduce a competing political perspective
that was compatible with his aims. He attempted to reorganize the IRB
within the army. He saw this reorganization as a way of transforming
the political ideals of the IRA into support for the government. Parallel
to the manner in which the IRB supported the Treaty and the new
government while retaining a Republican vision of an Irish nation, he
saw an IRB in the army as a solution to the "blind alley organisation of
the IRA."[13] For Mulcahy, the politics of the IRA were both futile and
obstructionist. The IRB represented an opportunity for the army men
to maintain a political vision incorporating a commitment to the present
government.

Speaking to the Dáil in June 1924, Mulcahy read notes he had written
to himself in June 1923 that provided a rationale for his efforts to revive
the IRB in the army. He wrote:

> ... while, ultimately, persons connected with the present Govern-
> ment might not, and, from the point of view of effective national
> development, should not be associated with it [the revival of the
> IRB], it was essential that they control its moulding and develop-
> ment at the present time from the point of view both of giving its
> policy a constructive and un(armed)-revolutionary turn, and from
> the point of view that they were in a position through the organ-
> isation, to be the instruments of allowing the best persons on the
> Irregular side [IRA] to get out of the difficulties they had got into,
> by overreaching themselves.[14]

In the same vein, Mulcahy remarked to the Dáil:

> I want to suggest to the Dáil that there was in that organisation a
> force in existence [IRA] that required to be controlled and that
> required to be directed, and that my responsibility in the matter
> was to take steps to have that force stabilised in the Army, to have
> the constitution of the organisation brought into line with our con-
> stitutional position here, and to take steps at the earliest possible
> moment, consistent with the safety of the State, to take any ele-
> ments of that secret society out of the Army.[15]

There is no question that Mulcahy's efforts to reorganize the IRB in the army stemmed from his desire to transform the army into an institution that served the state and did not conflict with its objectives. It was a bold effort to transform an obstructionist ideology into a constructive one. In his view, an IRB-dominated army, in contrast to an IRA-dominated one, would more likely produce an apolitical army. It would be easier to bring the IRB into line than it would be to gain the support of the IRA. And his goals for a new army, one clearly subservient to the Dáil, would more likely be realized. In this same speech to the Dáil, Mulcahy noted:

> My duty as Minister for Defense has involved me in many considerations, and if it has dictated to me the necessity for recognising the political roots of the Army, and of making allowances and taking precautions because of their nature, it has also dictated a consideration and an appreciation of the principles that are fundamental from the point of view of a good and stable Government.[16]

Good, stable government was Mulcahy's intention. A depoliticized, efficient, professional army was a requisite for such a government. His efforts to reorganize the IRB and control its development were not designed to politicize the army but to provide an ideology that would diminish the importance of politics. Not surprisingly, however, given the IRA's presence in the army and the political atmosphere in the nation as a whole, Mulcahy's intervention was not so benignly interpreted. To the old IRA men, it was Mulcahy who was inserting politics into the army; it was he who was attempting to revive the IRB. Mulcahy's tactics backfired. Objections to the demobilization and reorganization scheme seemed even more appropriate now that the scheme was understood as an opportunity by the IRB minister for defense and his Army Council to promote their secret organization at the expense of the IRA. More importantly, it enabled the old IRA men to express their outrage at the government's failure to transcend politics; the government was violating public trust by directly intervening in political disputes rather than standing above them. These actions confirmed the IRA men's view of the government as having abandoned the nationalist ideals upon which it was founded, thereby legitimating, even requiring, mutiny.

Because of the highly politicized nature of Irish life at the time, even within the government, Mulcahy's actions in regard to the IRB were not viewed simply as bad tactics. Instead, they were interpreted by many in the Executive Council and the Dáil as politically inspired. With that, the developments within the army took on profound national importance. Long before the actual mutiny occurred, Joseph McGrath, minister for industry and commerce, came to share the perceptions of the old IRA men in the army. He viewed Mulcahy as using his political office to promote particular political aims. Moreover, he courted the opposition army men, telling them that their opposition to the reorganization and demobilization scheme was widely shared by the Dáil. He assured them that their threatened mutiny was likely to achieve the reinstatement of the IRA men in the army.

The persistence of political divisions in the army, and a government minister's effort to respond to these divisions in a partisan manner, resulted in a major threat to the stability of the state. The enduring political divisions in Ireland led to a significant split within the Executive Council, with McGrath publicly attacking his fellow minister, Mulcahy. The constitutional doctrine of collective responsibility for the Executive Council was ignored, and the attempt to forge a ruling party made up of individuals with diverse political ideologies was threatening to fail. In the end, the mutiny resulted in the resignation of both McGrath and Mulcahy from the Executive Council, caused the government to fire the entire Army Council, and led to the creation of a new political party led by McGrath. Despite these important political developments, no resolution was achieved on the fundamental question of the army's relationship to civil authority.

The government's response to the mutiny

For Richard Mulcahy and Joseph McGrath, the mutiny came as no surprise. Mulcahy was advised of the growing opposition to his policies months before it actually occurred and was aware of McGrath's encouragement of the opposition. On January 19, 1924, more than six weeks before the government received the ultimatum, Mulcahy got a letter reporting an upcoming meeting in Dublin "to contemplate plans for a series of assassinations of prominent people and the seizure of barracks."[17] Earlier, he had been informed of McGrath's hand in the planned mutiny.[18] Mulcahy remained determined, however, to pursue his program. He believed that "it would practically amount to mutiny on our part to hold conference" with the army officers threatening to revolt.[19] He drew up plans to ask for the resignation of the officers involved, concluding that "the Army at present must be our first and last consideration and cannot be the tool of any political party."[20] Yet between the time he learned of the mutiny and its actual occurrence, no disciplinary action was taken. The weeks passed without incident when, on March 6, 1924, the ultimatum was presented to President Cosgrave.

At the time that Colonel Dalton and Major-General Tobin's letter was received by the government, several mutinous actions in the army occurred. At various posts throughout the country, army officers left their camps and took with them arms, ammunition, and equipment.[21] The number involved, though, was small. In fact, throughout the mutiny and until its resolution in late March, it was estimated that fewer than 100 officers were involved, approximately 40 of whom resigned.[22] Threats to take direct action against the government never materialized. Yet although the mutiny involved only a small segment of the army, the government was deeply alarmed. It was concerned about the deep schism exposed within the Executive Council itself.

Although McGrath and Mulcahy were not surprised by the mutiny, there is no evidence to suggest that either the president or other members of the Executive Council were prepared for it. Nor were they aware, in the first few days, of the extent of the mutineers' support by the army or the likelihood of their taking military action against the state. As a result, the government responded to the ultimatum and the defections within the Army as if the survival of the state was at stake.

President Cosgrave reacted by creating a new administrative position – general officer commanding the defense forces of Saorstát Éireann. It was a position designed to strengthen the president's control over the Army and Army administration. General Eoin O'Duffy was appointed to that position. He had been the chief commissioner of the Civic Guard, the unarmed police force recently created by the government, and had no previous involvement with army administration. As The Irish Times commented, "Obviously the appointment of General O'Duffy to the chief command of the Army is an uncommon step. Under the Defense Forces Act the offices of Commander-in-Chief and Minister of Defense cannot be combined in the one person."[23] The government felt compelled, in light of the conflict between the minister for defense and the minister for industry and commerce, and despite its possible unconstitutionality, to create a position whereby the commissioner would be responsible technically to the Executive Council as a whole but actually to the president himself. It was necessary to appoint a commissioner whose authority was greater than that of the minister for defense.

This government action presaged the kind of response it would make to the army challenge. The president took steps, as the days passed, not only to prohibit the Dáil from playing a meaningful role in resolving the crisis but also to reduce the power of the Executive Council. The president instead consolidated authority in his own hands and in those of his most closely trusted ministers in the Executive Council. It became, as the leader of the parliamentary opposition, Thomas Johnson, would charge, party rule and not democratic rule.[24]

Cosgrave's appointment of O'Duffy to this newly created post was the first sign of this movement toward the consolidation and centralization of authority. It was the first clear recognition that if democracy were to survive, it would depend on strong political institutions buffered from the political community. Despite constitutional claims to the contrary, the Cosgrave government was coming to recognize that it, and not the Irish people, had to govern. Yet the problem was how to achieve that outcome without, at the same time, losing already weak political support. The ability of the Cosgrave Government to solve this problem was its most profound accomplishment of its ten-year tenure in office.

This political course was not apparent at first to Cosgrave; it was only the logic of events during the army mutiny that set him and his government on that path. In the first days of the mutiny, the president sought to involve the Dáil actively in the crisis. In fact, it even appeared that he was prepared to appeal to the public for support. Yet he soon abandoned this approach in favor of an attempt to resolve the crisis within the inner circles of government. The reasons for this shift in strategy are important to understand, since they point to one of the profound ambiguities in the Constitution. Those provisions encouraging open, participatory democracy presumed an integrated, cohesive nation; they were designed to reflect a functioning democratic public. But Ireland in 1924 was hardly integrated; it remained deeply divided, essentially without a public realm. The army mutiny forced the government to acknowledge quickly that a strategy of response dictated by the Constitution would not have worked as intended. Rather, a response had to be made that recognized the polarized and divisive character of Irish political life. The government's response was, as it turned out, ad hoc, dictated not by constitutional considerations but by a more visceral instinct to preserve weak political institutions.

When the president announced to the Dáil his receipt of the ultimatum, he made the following statement:

> The Government relies fully on the Army as well as on the whole body of citizens to support it in whatever action may be necessary to maintain the democratic authority of the people. The attempt, such as it is, is not against a particular Government, it is a challenge to the democratic foundations of the State, to the very basis of Parliamentary representation and of responsible Government. As

such, it is the concern of every Deputy, of every party, and of every citizen.[25]

Cosgrave appealed to the Representative Assembly, to the various political parties, and to the nation as a whole to close ranks behind him in defending the institutions of the state. By appealing to the nation as a whole, he sought to counter the army threat by public condemnation. Seeing the mutiny as a challenge to the state's authority, Cosgrave summoned the nation to demonstrate its commitment to the democratic foundations of the state.

Virtually within hours, however, Cosgrave's insistence on a policy of open government was suspended. By the next day, secrecy in all government actions surrounding the mutiny prevailed. No longer did Cosgrave seek public condemnation of the Army actions, nor did he feel compelled to inform the Dáil of developments except in the most superficial way. Instead, the handling of the mutiny became a private affair, with major and far-reaching developments left unexplained. Second guessing in the Dáil, in the press, and in the nation as a whole became the substitute for an informed, public response previously demanded by the government.

What accounts for this sudden shift in policy? It was Joseph McGrath's public emergence and his qualified support of the mutineers that led to this dramatic shift in Cosgrave's response. Shortly after the president spoke to the Dáil and announced the mutiny, McGrath resigned from the Executive Council and, although stating that he was not in agreement with the ultimatum, charged that the crisis had been brought about by the "absolute muddling, mishandling, and incompetence on the part of a department of the state."[26] He promised to address the Dáil the following day to explain the reasons for his resignation and to detail his charges directed at the minister for defense.

But before the Dáil convened, there were several dramatic developments. The government agreed to appoint a cabinet committee to inquire into the situation that had led up to the army's dissatisfaction. Moreover, in announcing that inquiry, Cosgrave stated that the government was "prepared to consult with the Minister for Industry and Commerce [McGrath] in view of his statement yesterday with regard to how this enquiry is to be carried out."[27] In return, the government received a document from the mutineers. This second document, signed by Tobin and Dalton and dated March 12, 1924, read as follows:

> The document dated the 6th March was sent you with the sole object of exposing to the Government and the representatives of

the people what we consider to be a serious menace to the proper administration of the Army.

We were forced to present the document to bring to your notice and that of the Dáil the seriousness of the situation. We say and have always maintained that we fully recognise that the Army, just as the Police, must be subject to the absolute control of the Civil Authority, and further, that the Army should not have within its ranks any sections or organisations tending to sap allegiance from the only and proper constitutional authority, viz., the Government of the people, which we fully recognise.

We are satisfied that we have brought the matter sufficiently before the people, and will consider our object achieved if as a result of our action the Army situation is righted.[28]

Obviously, a very quick arrangement had been made with the mutineers to settle the issue. Dalton and Tobin assured the government that civil authority over the army was not in question, but merely specific policy decisions by members of the government. With that document, the challenge was no longer to the democratic foundations of the state; it was now a more delimited, though still potentially explosive, policy dispute. Richard Mulcahy and his actions as minister for defense now became the focus of the conflict. The government inquiry was designed to investigate his policies with the assistance of Joseph McGrath.

The rapidity of this arrangement indicated the importance the Cosgrave Government placed on delimiting the dispute. A quick settlement was necessary in order to prevent McGrath from speaking to the Dáil the following day. McGrath's speech and his willingness to expose the minister for defense's actions threatened the shaky consensus upon which the government depended. Kevin O'Higgins, confidant and close ally of Cosgrave in the Executive Council, in a revealing speech to the Dáil some days later, articulated the government's concern with McGrath's promise to address the Dáil:

I would like to suggest to the Dáil that in a certain delicate complexity of circumstances it is not always advisable, not always in the public interest, to drag everything out for mongers of gossip, every relevant circumstance, every charge and counter-charge, every allegation, true, or half true, or not true at all. It is factors like that which weighed with the Executive Council ever since this Army pot boiled over. The Minister for Industry and Commerce was to make a statement here. From what we knew of what the Minister for Industry and Commerce was prepared to state here, and from our judgment of the situation, it would not be in the public interest that that statement should be made. . . . And time was spent, a long time was spent, in an endeavor to convince Deputy McGrath that such a statement ought not to be made, and an undertaking was given that an enquiry would be set up into Army administration, and that he would get every opportunity of having such charges as he might care to formulate thoroughly sifted.[29]

McGrath's speech to the Dáil intended to expose the deep political divisions in the Executive Council, divisions that, in a sense, mirrored those in the army and in the nation as a whole. Imagine the consequences of one minister for state publicly charging another with promoting in the army a secret political organization, the IRB, and with discriminating against old veterans of the war of national independence. The constitutional doctrine of collective responsibility of the Executive Council would have come undone, as well as the ability of the government to present itself as a strong, unified, and transcendent political force. Coupled with the external challenge to the government, such political disarray at the center of government could have proved disastrous. To prevent this from occurring was precisely O'Higgins's purpose when he spoke of protecting the public interest by dissuading McGrath from addressing the Dáil.

McGrath's role in the controversy in many ways dictated the government's response. Certainly Cosgrave, if he had not previously known of McGrath's link with the mutiny, must have been relieved to find that the mutineers had a responsible spokesman on the Executive Council. As long as McGrath was able to maintain the tie with the mutineers, the danger of military action would be reduced. McGrath, as spokesman, made it possible to handle the crisis by discussion and compromise. But at the same time, McGrath had the upper hand in determining the character of the compromise that was to be achieved. It was not certain that this new and insecure government could have withstood McGrath's accusations. To have revealed the weakness of its coalition might have secured the government's downfall. Whether or not it would have occurred, the government leaders had no assurance. In the context of the mutineers' challenge to the government, such a downfall would have involved not merely the ruling elite, but conceivably the whole structure of parliamentary rule.

As a result of this situation, the government was compelled to reach a compromise with the mutineers and McGrath. This meant abandoning support for Richard Mulcahy and, although it was not viewed this way, essentially capitulating to the demands of the mutineers. Because of the divisions in the Executive Council itself, Cosgrave could not transcend political factionalism, but had to enter the fray. In the interest of putting a quick end to the mutiny, he found himself in the paradoxical position of compromising with the nonconstitutional Republicans in the army while attempting to isolate and silence the constitutional ones.

In the government's view, there was no alternative. It quickly recognized the necessity to abandon a policy that sought to isolate the Mutiny through a unified Dáil and public condemnation of extraparliamentary threats to the government. Had it been able to accomplish this, the government could have presented itself as above politics, representing the public interest and speaking for a single Irish voice. But with McGrath's entry into the picture, the government did not believe itself strong enough to act in that manner. Therefore, it had to do a quick about-face. As *The Manchester Guardian* commented, "The net result of their [the government's] tactics is that, having persisted in one course to the point of dispensing with the Minister of Industry, they have now recognized Mr. McGrath by the process of throwing over General Mulcahy."[30]

In short, Cosgrave wished to delimit the dispute by insisting that the mutiny was merely a criticism of a specific government policy orchestrated by Mulcahy. In so doing, Cosgrave hoped to maintain the appearance of a strong, unified state. He wanted to protect the integrity of government institutions and to demonstrate their ability to secure order. Acting on behalf of the government, Cosgrave intuitively appreciated the fact that a debate over particular government policies – demobilization, for example – implicitly assumed the right of the government to make policy.

This strategy of separating political policy from government commitments would prove to be a hallmark of the Cosgrave administration. And it was precisely this approach, as later discussions will illustrate, that secured widespread political support for the government even when the personalities involved in it were widely identified as unsympathetic to Irish national aspirations. Cosgrave's ability to transform disputes into policy questions resulted in an increasingly strong public conviction that the policies adopted by his ministers did not represent public will, but rather abrogated it. It was, as Cosgrave's first foray into crisis politics would demonstrate, a willingness by the politicians to bear the brunt of public opposition while protecting the regime that ensured, in the end, a politics of democratic stability.

The irony of Cosgrave's response to the army mutiny was that his efforts to turn it into a policy dispute reflected the fragility of the government, not its strength. Cosgrave felt compelled to turn on a member of his own Executive Council, Mulcahy, so as to avoid continued assault on the regime by the mutineers and to prevent the dissolution of the governing coalition. Only by succumbing to the demands of McGrath and the mutineers could the difficult fundamental questions posed be avoided. To secure political order and protect the only political coalition capable of representing a large segment of the Irish population, Cosgrave quickly agreed to a compromise with McGrath, Dalton, and Tobin. He believed that he had no other choice.

The early compromise agreement, however, did not end the matter; it simply moved it out of the public view. Although direct government intervention dispelled the fear of a military challenge to the state and protected internal divisions from public exposure, it also succeeded in intensifying the divisions within the Executive Council. The compromise in no way resolved the fundamental political and philosophical differences between Mulcahy and McGrath. Nor did it resolve the conflict in political and cultural principles that permeated government.

For McGrath and his followers, the government's *raison d'être* was to secure complete and total independence from Britain. The Irish Free State, although bound by the Treaty, was to be a stepping stone toward the Irish Republic. For this faction, all government actions were to be evaluated according to this standard. Thus, McGrath viewed the compromise agreement that recognized the claims of the old IRA men as only a first-step corrective in what, for him, had been a history of misguided policy. The government was still on trial, and only subsequent actions could prove to him that it was serious in its commitment to change in a manner consistent with his principles of nationalist rule. Of course, as I have already suggested, the compromise represented no such principled change but was made solely for political expediency. It was inevitable that McGrath would ultimately be disappointed with the policies of the government.

Mulcahy's actions as minister for defense, on the other hand, indicated a far greater commitment to stable, transcendent political rule. Despite his link with the IRB – the original proponent of the stepping-stone theory – and his encouragement of the IRB in the army, Mulcahy was guided by principles of competence and professionalism in government; he was unmoved by charges against him of being antinationalist. For Mulcahy, the compromise agreement by the government represented the abandonment of a commitment to a politically neutral state. In Cosgrave's statement that he would consult with McGrath on the army inquiry, Mulcahy correctly perceived the government as having capitulated to blatantly political demands. It was a response, Mulcahy believed, that ultimately would prevent the government from establishing the stable political institutions for which it hoped. In the Free State's rush to compromise, Mulcahy saw his influence in the Executive Council dwindle to the point where he believed himself to be the only member of the government concerned with the establishment of a professional, efficient army. As I shall shortly describe, this view led Mulcahy to act directly contrary to the Free State's wishes, challenging the compromise agreement. In the end, these actions led to Mulcahy's resignation from the Executive Council.

Cosgrave and his closest political associates were caught between McGrath and his army allies and Mulcahy and his unbroken determination to accomplish his goals for the army. And although the government had compromised with the mutineers in the interest of politics and stability, it certainly was not prepared to cede all authority to the Army or subject all of its actions with respect to the army to a nationalist criterion. At the same time, it could not ignore the potential danger McGrath and the mutineers posed to the state. Cosgrave was presented with the unpleasant challenge of tiptoeing gently through a minefield of opposition, attempting to avoid mines laid by both McGrath and Mulcahy. The government was unable to emerge from this crisis unscathed. Yet, throughout the crisis, political expedience dictated continued compromise with the mutineers, thus setting the stage for a counterattack by Mulcahy.

What the compromise agreement left unresolved, and thus subject to controversy, was how Tobin, Dalton, and other participants in the army were to be apprehended and dealt with. When Cosgrave announced the mutiny to the Dáil, he stated that an order had been put out for their arrest. In the spirit of compromise, however, in the days following the receipt of the second document, Cosgrave was negotiating with McGrath, Mulcahy, and other members of the Executive Council on the attitude to be adopted toward the officers involved in the mutiny.

Two policy directives emerged from these negotiations. One grew out of a meeting of the Executive Council in which Mulcahy participated. A memo was drawn up in which conditions and deadlines were laid down for the surrender of the mutinous officers and the return of the arms and equipment taken. It was agreed that by March 20, all arms and equipment were to be returned; those involved in their appropriation were to surrender, as well as all those who had absented themselves from Army duty. It was further agreed that after their surrender, they would be released under open arrest.[31] Both McGrath and Mulcahy were presented similar memos stating these agreed-upon terms.

A second government document was also drawn up, but it was not circulated to Mulcahy. The Executive Council, assembled as a meeting of the Cumann na nGaedheal Party – the recently formed party organization representing the governing elite – and not as government representatives, composed a document that McGrath was to present to the leaders of the mutiny. Mulcahy was not included in these deliberations, nor was he aware of these actions. The document was signed by Cosgrave as chairman of the party, but it was understood as binding on the Executive Council. The document read, "The men concerned in the recent trouble in the Army undertake to undo, as far as they can, the mischief created by their action, and on their so doing the incident will be regarded as closed."[32] The memo and the document were not patently contradictory, for the officers' surrender was assumed to be part of the process of undoing the "mischief." But the document was intended to indicate to the mutineers that penalties would be light if they cooperated in quickly ending the dispute. Moreover, the employment of McGrath as government messenger was to imply the Free State's sympathy with the mutineers' complaint about Army policy.

What emerged from these two statements – the memo and the document – was an official, explicit *Executive Council policy* in which Mulcahy was included and an unofficial, implicit *party policy* intended to undermine his position in the government. Unofficially, the government was determined to settle the dispute as quickly and quietly as possible. For the sake of the party, it sought to convince the mutineers that punishment would be light and that their grievances would be addressed sympathetically. Implicitly, as the McGrath document demonstrates, it was assumed that the surrender would be accomplished through the active intervention of McGrath, who was in contact with the Army officers.

However, the reconciliation of official with unofficial policy created considerable difficulty for the government. It was the spirit of compromise that motivated the unofficial party policy. Nevertheless, the mutinous officers had acted illegally and had challenged the authority of the state. For that reason, an arrest order had been issued; to rescind that order, for whatever reason, would have been legally indefensible, contravening the basis of constitutional order. To retract the order for arrest or to back away from a determination to apprehend the mutineers – leaving the administration of justice to the personal intervention of one individual, that is, McGrath – would have jeopardized the government's standing as the public enforcer of law and order. The official memo, setting the ground rules for surrender, was an effort to bridge the gap between the official and explicit government policy and the unofficial and implicit party policy. And it was party policy, not official policy, that the government was attempting to enforce. But still sharp discrepancy between public policy and private actions remained.

This discrepancy enabled Mulcahy to circumvent the government's attempt to minimize the conflict between the Free State and the army. On March 18, 1924, two days prior to the deadline for surrender, Mulcahy learned that several of the mutinous officers, including Tobin and Dalton, were meeting in a public house on Parnell Street in Dublin. In consultation only with his Army Council, he ordered a raid on the house. As a result, ten officers were arrested, although Tobin and Dalton escaped. McGrath appeared on the scene but could not prevent the arrests.[33] Because the government was unable to rescind the order, despite the fact that it had no intention of arresting the officers before the date of surrender, Mulcahy's actions were technically legal.

A second factor enabled Mulcahy to act legally. Shortly after General O'Duffy assumed his new position as general officer commanding the defense forces of Saorstát Éireann, he became aware that, despite the government's intentions to the contrary, his authority over the army was limited. In accordance with the powers granted by the government, O'Duffy found that he had no authority over the Army Council and it had no responsibility to him. When the Executive Council became aware of this situation, they appointed him, in addition to his post as general officer, as inspector-general of the defense forces of Saorstát Éireann, which gave him full authority over the Army Council. But at the time of the raid, a list of his full powers in this position was only being drawn up, and he was not formally instated. The Army Council, then, still maintained freedom of action. The raid, approved by the Army Council, was still legal. A furious McGrath described Mulcahy's decision and the Army Council's approval of that decision as follows:

> Did any of you ever wonder why . . . that raid should have taken place on that particular night? . . . Apparently, there was no need for the raid until a few hours before they felt they were losing the grip of power, and that their authority was being taken from them . . . the raid took place just a few hours before General O'Duffy would have in his hand, in writing, the complete draft of his powers . . . it was because they knew they were losing their grasp of the

hammer, that a few hours or a few days before they were prepared to strike with, that they made this one last effort to cause the conflict.[34]

The raid occurred, as McGrath argued, because the Army Council still possessed the legal authority to act independently of O'Duffy. Moreover, it still represented the official policy of the government. But, more substantively, it was perhaps Mulcahy's and the Army Council's last opportunity to influence the course of the government's actions in response to the mutiny. Despite McGrath's Machiavellian claims, the raid was intended, once again, to demonstrate civil authority over the army. Mulcahy defended the raid by arguing that he was merely enforcing the Defense Forces Act of 1923; his actions were determined by the legal responsibilities with which he was entrusted. Mulcahy claimed that the adjutant-general of the Army Council, who was responsible to him, "had no alternative but to enforce the statutory provisions of the Defense Forces Act against those who had been guilty of indiscipline and mutiny."[35] A failure to arrest mutinous officers, in the face of an order for their arrest, he argued, would have constituted a dereliction of duty.[36]

Mulcahy's defense of the raid as a simple exercise of duty was not entirely honest. He understood as well as anyone that the raid would have far-ranging political consequences in upsetting the government's efforts at compromise. Perhaps in anticipation of the consequences, Mulcahy's raid attempted to expose the presence of a dual policy – one official, one unofficial – of the Executive Council.

The raid only served to highlight the untenable position of the government. Although Mulcahy's actions were legally justified, the raid countered the government's unofficial desire to bring the mutiny to an uneventful end; it ignored what Kevin O'Higgins referred to as "the obvious and necessary implication" of the memo.[37] It threatened to renew the conflict between the government and the mutinous officers. Moreover, it jeopardized McGrath's special relationship with these officers, for the raid appeared to indicate government duplicity in the negotiations.

At this new stage in the crisis, the logic of events continued to dictate a government response similar to the previous one. To support Mulcahy's actions and his raid – that is to enforce the letter of the law, to forcefully condemn mutiny, and to bring to bear the full weight of public opinion against the mutineers – remained far too risky for the fragile political structures. Instead, the government's wrath was turned not on the mutineers but on Mulcahy and the Army Council.

The Free State's reaction to the raid was immediate. First, it asked for the resignation of the entire Army Council and the minister for defense. Second, it began a campaign to discredit Mulcahy, his policies, and the actions of the Army Council extending beyond the raid itself. It was an attack on the implementation of the entire demobilization scheme. Third, President Cosgrave nominated himself to the position of acting minister for defense upon Mulcahy's resignation, further consolidating his political control. Finally, to demonstrate the government's good faith to the mutineers, the surrender deadline was extended for two days; until then, it was stated, "no arrests, searches, or other action of an aggressive nature will be undertaken against these officers."[38]

The Free State's response was determined by its need to legitimate its earlier compromises with McGrath and the mutineers. To respond in any other way would have meant a public refutation of its unofficial policy of accommodation to its political challengers. As I have already described, such a policy reversal could have been disastrous to the party and possibly to the democratic political institution. But, ironically, in responding as it did to the raid, the government came to adopt every demand and every criticism of army policy originally made by the mutineers. The Free State's position unwittingly became almost indistinguishable from theirs.

It was on the day following the raid that the Executive Council asked for the resignation of the Army Council and the minister for defense. Kevin O'Higgins, in announcing their resignation, felt compelled to state publicly that the action did not stem from the mutineers' demand for the removal of the Army Council. He insisted that the action was not caused by the raid alone. Instead, he argued, it was a carefully thought-out policy that had been germinating in the Executive Council since the mutiny began; the raid only served to confirm the Free State's suspicions.[39] The reason that O'Higgins gave for the government's demand of the resignation of the Army Council was that there was increasing evidence of political factionalism in the Army fostered by the Army Council and by Mulcahy:

we were not without evidence that that impersonal discipline does not exist in the Army, that generally, naturally with diffidence, as being Ministers in the political headships of other Departments, naturally with a certain reluctance, a certain hesitation, the view was forming in the minds of members of the Executive Council that there was danger that the Army was not unequivocably, unquestionably, without reserve, simply the instrument of the people's will, expressed constitutionally through the Dáil, and through the Executive appointed by the Dáil. If that view is right, if that half-formed view – shall I call it – is right, that it was a question of rival combinations, there was a lot to be said for the view that you could not strike at one of these combinations through the medium of another.[40]

What had been feared in McGrath's threatened address to the Dáil some weeks before – the exposure of political factionalism in the Army and the fostering of the IRB by a government minister – was now publicly proclaimed by Kevin O'Higgins, the minister closest to the president. O'Higgins's admission to the Dáil of the existence of "rival combinations" in the army represented the abandonment, in part, of the Free State's earlier policy of secrecy in handling the mutiny. However, its openness was to justify its predetermined policies and not to seek guidelines from the representative assembly. With the raid, the hope of preserving a semblance of unity with the Executive Council had collapsed. (Notice, however, how timidly O'Higgins made a charge against a fellow minister.) The only alternative was to make the Army Council and General Mulcahy the scapegoats and precipitators of the disunity.

Because of the continued policy of compromise with McGrath, Mulcahy had felt compelled to force the Free State's hand. The raid presented the government with the choice of supporting its official, explicit policy and, thereby supporting the raid, or of condemning it in favor of continued compromise with McGrath and the mutineers. Mulcahy had made it impossible for the two policies to coexist. The demand for the resignation of the Army Council and Mulcahy signified the government's continued commitment to compromise. But only by charging Mulcahy and the Army Council with irresponsible behavior, with promoting political factionalism, and by expelling them from positions of political power was it possible to justify the continuation of this policy. Only by making Mulcahy and the Army Council the guilty parties could the government persist in a policy of compromise and condemn the legal actions taken by Mulcahy. Not coincidentally, the charge O'Higgins leveled at Mulcahy and the Army Council of political partiality in the administration of the army was the same charge the mutineers and McGrath had made. But the government sought to protect itself by pointing to errors in judgment by certain persons and to their misplaced political interests.

Following the raid and the Free State's swift response to it, events proceeded much as the government had intended. It appointed a committee to inquire into the mutiny, and after being challenged by the Dáil for including only party and non-Dáil members, it consented to have representatives from all of the parties in the Dáil. The Army Inquiry Committee conducted forty-one meetings and examined twenty-seven witnesses.[41] In early June 1924, three months after the start of the mutiny, it presented its report to the Dáil. This unimpressive nine-page document essentially restated the Free State's earlier charge of political factionalism in the army. The report stated:

> We consider that the reorganisation of the I.R.B. carried out as it appears to have been by the actual heads of the Army, was a disastrous error of judgement, and accentuated a mutiny which might not have occurred at all, and which could have been more firmly suppressed, if those in authority had not weakened their position by leaving themselves open to the charge of acting in the interest of a hostile secret society.[42]

At the same time, the report found no evidence that IRB members in the army had received preferential treatment in terms of appointments or promotions.[43] Further, it specifically refuted McGrath's earlier charges of "muddling, mismanagement and incompetence" on the part of General Mulcahy.[44] But by the time the inquiry report was released, the mutiny was essentially history and the inquiry had little public impact. Except for McGrath's and Mulcahy's personal interest in it, it received little attention in the Dáil. In fact, more important than the report itself was the Free State's decision not to release the evidence compiled for it. This suppression of evidence by Cosgrave, reminiscent of his entire policy vis-à-vis the Dáil and the public toward the mutiny, reflected his desire to "protect" the public from the controversies that were so much a part of his administration. Demands from the Dáil for the evidence were ignored in the same way that they had been ignored during the entire crisis.

As a consequence of this policy, however, the government was successful in containing the mutiny and securing a sense of stability in Ireland. This accomplishment should not be minimized. But it is significant that, instead of gaining accolades for Cosgrave and his party, it increased public suspicion of them. Part of the reason that their response to the mutiny failed to win the party greater support was the confusion their policies produced. To the public, no coherent policy seemed to be emerging from the Executive Council; the government appeared to be responding to events haphazardly as they occurred, and the public had little comprehension of either the meaning of those events or the rationale behind the response. The actions of the mutineers, McGrath, and Mulcahy had seemingly caught the government off guard.

The Executive Council appeared not to be in control of the events, but controlled by them. This confusion prompted *The Leader*, a Dublin periodical, to write:

> The new row is disedifying. And the issues are far from clear. It is easy, in a general way, to suggest personalities, jealousies, jobs and temperaments – those things we have always with us disturbing the even tenor of the States. The mutineers letters, the action of the Government, the second letter, the complacence of the Government, the seige of the public house, the resignations, and all these leave our mind in somewhat of a maze. We don't know, as we write, where Mr. McGrath stands in the picture. He appears to be against the O'Higgins crowd as against the Mulcahy crowd. . . . So far as we can understand the confused matter, the mutineers were given until Thursday 6 p.m. to report themselves while on Tuesday night a public house was raided for wanted officers. At the Dáil on Thursday, McGrath referred to what he called "a miserable, dirty attempt to mix up matters". . . . O'Higgins is clearly out against Mulcahy. . . . We are inclined to look upon the matter as a storm in a teacup and we do not attach very much national significance to it.[45]

The secrecy in the government's response and its unwillingness to involve the public in the crisis created both considerable confusion and increasing distrust of the Cumann na nGaedheal Party. Yet, this secrecy both from the public and from the Dáil was believed by government members to be necessary in protecting the party from irreparable division and essential in changing the dispute to one of policy. Although the institutions of government were protected, the party sacrificed considerable popular support. Its secret dealings and its unwillingness to make the matter public meant that although the public had greater respect for the government because of its successful management of the crisis, the party itself did not receive greater public support. If anything, because of its secret dealings, it lost support.

It was not only the public that was concerned with the party's response, but also key figures in the controversy. Neither Mulcahy nor McGrath was satisfied with the course of events as dictated by expedient compromise. Although such a policy may have increased the stability of the state, it did not protect the party from further divisiveness or create greater support for it by the various participants.

Mulcahy, upon learning of the firing of the Army Council, and before he was asked, resigned as minister for defense. Announcing his resignation before the Dáil, he explicitly criticized the Executive Council. He said that he had been tempted in the past several days to appeal to the Dáil to contravene party policy but, in the end, had decided against it. As he stated, his decision not to appeal directly to the Dáil stemmed from his concern with the constitutional difficulties that would have arisen from such an action:

> I had to take into consideration that an Executive Council has its important constitutional position in our Constitution here. I was deterred, as I say, from appealing to the Dáil over the Party by the fact that the Executive Council had very serious responsibilities on it from the point of view of administration, and I was not willing to interfere with the Executive Council's work even to that particular extent.[46]

Thus, Mulcahy observed the process by which the Executive Council had closed off the Dáil from governmental deliberations and the process by which the Executive Council became reconstituted as an agency of the party. But if Mulcahy can be taken at his word, his decision not to appeal directly to the Dáil to challenge these developments stemmed from his belief that the political repercussions were potentially too explosive. The legitimacy of the political structures and the Constitution would have been called into question; Mulcahy's commitment to those structures was too great for him to jeopardize them by a direct appeal to the Dáil.

Mulcahy's decision to order the raid appeared to be a challenge to the government to alter its policy. When this did not happen, Mulcahy resigned. He explained his reasons to the Dáil:

> My reasons for tendering my resignation now are simply that I cannot stand over condoning mutiny to such an extent as to foster it and to prejudice discipline in the Army, and that I cannot stand over ill-considered changes in Army control, from the point of view of the effectiveness of that control. . . .[47]

Although deeply disturbed by the course of events, Mulcahy simply bowed out of the dispute without challenging what he saw to be a substantial movement away from popular democracy that had occurred in response to the mutiny. Some weeks later, he introduced into the Dáil a motion to censure the Executive Council for its dismissal of the Army Council.[48] Although this provided an opportunity to articulate his dissatisfaction with the government's response to the army mutiny and the Army Inquiry Report, he limited his criticism to the government's army policy, justified his own policies, but withheld those criticisms that would have challenged the legality of the Executive Council's actions. The censure was defeated in the Dáil.

Although it is understandable why the government did not make a friend of Mulcahy in dealing with the mutineers, it is less clear why McGrath continued to be an outspoken opponent of the government's policy. In fact, he resigned from the party and established his own National Party. McGrath's actions perhaps can be understood, as it was suggested at the time, because of his own ambitions to become the president of Ireland.[49] With this aspiration, he may have recognized the political power of an alliance with old IRA men challenging Cumann na nGaedheal's insufficient nationalist commitment. Yet, even after it became clear that the government was in control of the situation and had made significant compromises to the mutineers, McGrath persisted in his opposition. His support for the mutiny and his opposition to the government was more than merely tactical; it was a result of fundamental disagreement with the orientation and direction of government policies. For McGrath, Mulcahy's policies towards the army epitomized the government's disinterest in using the Anglo-Irish Treaty to achieve the Irish Republic. The government's policy of compromise with him and with the mutineers represented for McGrath, as later developments would prove, only political expediency and constituted no fundamental alteration of policy. Thus, even after the compromise, McGrath continued to remain suspicious of the government's intentions.

Two conditions demonstrated McGrath's distrust of and increasing dissatisfaction with government policy. Both centered on the raid, which had proved to be a pivotal event in the crisis. First, the raid had placed McGrath in an untenable position with the mutineers. Having promised them immunity from arrest until the date set for surrender, and speaking on behalf of the government, he was publicly compelled to accept sole responsibility for the arrest of the officers in Parnell Street.[50] He saw the raid as evidence of the government's continued violation of its agreements. Although he surely recognized that the raid occurred at Mulcahy's instigation, not the Executive Council's, the fact that the government was unaware of those plans did not, in his mind, lessen its culpability. He observed a deeply divided government incapable of implementing a policy that would engender trust. At that point, and in response to the difficult position in which he found himself, McGrath decided to retire from public life while using his remaining influence with the officers to end the mutiny. He stated:

> I cannot expect a continuance of this confidence [with the officers] but in the interests of the peace of the country I have made an appeal to the officers and men concerned to get out, as it were,

and leave the arena of what appears to me, and I think the public generally, to the elements within the Government fighting for power.[51]

McGrath encouraged other Dáil deputies to resign in protest of the government's policy.[52] Despite the government's efforts to reach a compromise with him, McGrath turned his back on the party for its inability to control the government. And yet, ironically, it was the party's excessive concern with compromise that exacerbated such internal power struggles and ensured the government's loss of control over the developments surrounding the mutiny.

In addition to condemning the raid, McGrath was deeply dissatisfied with the government's reaction once it had occurred. The Executive Council, as already described, demanded the resignation of the Army Council and Mulcahy. The reason given, however, was not that the officers should have been immune to arrest but simply that the action was taken without the approval of the Executive Council and General O'Duffy. McGrath insisted that the raid was improper because the government had violated the "McGrath document" – which asked that the mutineers "undo their mischief" and stated that the "incident will be regarded as closed." For McGrath, the document implied that the mutineers would be reinstated in the army without punishment. He believed that the document marked the adoption of a "no-victimisation" policy by the government.[53] When Cosgrave and others challenged his interpretation of that document, McGrath could only conclude that the government was backing down. It could not be trusted; it was not sympathetic to the claims of the old IRA men in the army or interested in the creation of an Irish Republic. Without knowing precisely what occurred in the party meeting that drafted the document, it is not possible to assess the party's intent. Only the reinstatement of the army officers without penalty would have satisfied McGrath; this policy was impossible for the government, given the officers' illegal conduct.

As it happened, McGrath did not resign from public life; instead, he and eight other Dáil members resigned from the Cumann na nGaedheal and founded the National Party. It was a party of constitutional Republicans pledged to work for the establishment of the Republic by recognized constitutional methods.[54] Although these men proved to be no threat to Cumann na nGaedheal rule, since they were all decisively defeated in the 1925 by-elections, their resignation from Cumann na nGaedheal indicated, in at least one sense, the futility of the government's policy of compromise.

Conclusion

The lessons of the army mutiny were fundamental. On the one hand, the government proved to be strong enough and legitimate enough in the eyes of the Irish people to contain the mutiny. It succeeded in transforming a challenge to the institutions of rule to one merely critical of specific policies. In contrast to the Civil War, which had wound down only months before the mutiny and reflected the inability of the Provisional government to assert its authority through parliamentary rule, the mutiny illustrated the remarkable increase in the strength of the parliamentary structures and in the government's ability to respond to political challenge. The government's successful containment of the mutiny was conclusive proof of the new strength of the Free State as the dominant political agency in the nation.

On the other hand, the mutiny also demonstrated the continuing impact of value conflicts on the functioning of the new political apparatus. Because of the divisions within the nation and the absence of a public sphere capable of mediating between the powerful contending commitments represented by McGrath and Mulcahy, the government was incapable of using the Mutiny to promote democratic consciousness. This failure was expressed in a number of ways.

First, the government was unable to insist upon the supremacy of the civil authority over the military. The former's policy of compromise only sidestepped that issue. Thomas Johnson, spokesman for the opposition Labour Party, perceived immediately that the compromise avoided a final settlement of this thorny problem. When Cosgrave announced the establishment of an Army Inquiry Committee in return for a retraction (the second document) from the mutineers, Johnson commented:

> I am afraid that the two statements we have heard do not give us an assurance that the Government has insisted upon supremacy of civil power. The Dáil has a right to know, and to insist on knowing tonight, whether the Government is maintaining its authority or whether it has submitted to the ultimatum.[55]

Later, when the Executive Council asked for the resignation of the military officers from the Army Council, Johnson astutely observed:

> It seems to me that the Executive Council in deciding to ask for the resignation of military officers from particular posts, not in asking them to resign their commissions, was in itself a kind of admission that these officers were in a position of independence – or semi-independence – of the Executive Council and did actively occupy a place which many of us feared they would and uttered

warnings about, viz. that the Army Council was being placed in a position of autonomy and independence.[56]

It might be argued that the persistence of an Irish military man's consciousness of having a special status in the new government and of being entitled to a special voice in Irish affairs was a consequence of the government's failure to resolve the issue of army subordination decisively. In a certain sense, as Frank Munger has argued, the government's response to the mutiny was "to remove from the Army its most political elements" in the sense that the proponents of further army politicization left the political scene.[57] Further, it is true that on a practical, day-to-day level, the army subsequently accepted its subordination to the parliament. Yet, in the government's failure to address this question head on, and instead to seek compromise at all costs, the fiction of the Irish army warrior – always more vigilant than the politician in protecting Irish nationhood – was a sentiment that was allowed to survive in the army. The emergence in the late 1920s of the National Defense Association and the later growth of the fascist Army Comrades Association reflected, in part, a continuing resentment by army men of their subservience to the parliament.[58]

But the normative consequences of the government's compromise proved to be even more profound than the failure to resolve the ambiguous relationship between the parliament and the army. The army mutiny raised the important question of the criteria for allocation of political resources to members of the community. Because of its need for a quick resolution to the crisis, the government criticized the principles behind Mulcahy's demobilization scheme, suggesting that they were both unfair and ill-conceived. In so doing, the government appeared to be endorsing the use of an ideological criterion, that is, service in the nationalist cause, and to be foregoing an absolute commitment to the freedom of the individual. The government had buckled under to the charge that former British officers were not equally entitled to political rewards. In short, in the interest of maintaining democratic institutions, the government was forced to forego what would seem to be a principal underpinning of a democratic community. Implicitly asserting a particular definition of the national community, that is, commitment to a nationalist Ireland, and endorsing criteria of rewards that excluded certain individuals from equal consideration, the government's actions served to strengthen certain seemingly undemocratic tendencies in the polity.

This strain between individualism and contra-individual forces is a part of all democratic orders. Yet, in the Irish case, the government –

forced to articulate its preference early in its term – was incapable of asserting its preeminent commitment to the individual. As a result, its concern for political expedience produced further disenchantment with the government leaders among those who had expected a thoroughly Irish-Enlightenment democratic state. To those who shared such convictions, government actions revealed the strong presence of Gaelic-Romantic contaminants.

This incapacity to promote democratic consciousness was demonstrated more specifically within the government itself. The intrinsic strain within democracy between popular rule and elitism was strongly expressed during this crisis. Despite constitutional assertions of a strong popular voice in governance, the government felt compelled to separate the decision-making process from the more egalitarian checks and balances.

Because of the government's need to offer a quick compromise, Cosgrave was required to consolidate power around himself and his most trusted ministers. Splits within the party and the Executive Council required the limitation of decision making to only a handful of officials. The government's response to the mutiny established troubling precedents for open, participatory rule in Ireland. The Dáil was informed afterward of the events; the Executive Council existed, for this issue at least, in form only. The Party Council, in this crisis situation, became the decision-making body of the state.

Thomas Johnson, who in the course of the mutiny became the most articulate critic of the government's policy as it affected the democratic political institutions, quickly perceived the tendency toward secrecy in the Executive Council and the movement toward party rule. He suggested that such a policy, rather than enhancing stability, might ultimately undermine it. Speaking in the Dáil following Cosgrave's announcement of the Army Inquiry, Johnson said:

> The President speak(s) of democratic authority and say(s) that the document [the original ultimatum] was a challenge to the democratic foundations of the State and to the very basis of all Parliamentary representation and of responsible Government. Responsible to whom? The Executive Council is not responsible to the Party Meeting. The Executive Council is responsible to the Dáil and to the country for the government of the country. I make the assertion that much of this trouble has resulted from a failure to recognise responsibility to the Dáil as distinct from responsibility to the Party.[59]

In a similar vein, and also in response to Cosgrave's sudden change in policy to achieve compromise, *The Irish Times*, a politically conservative newspaper and a supporter of Cosgrave, nonetheless sharply criticized the government's actions. In an editorial, it stated:

> Not the least disquieting feature of yesterday's arrangement was the manner in which it was taken out of the hands of the Parliament. On Tuesday President Cosgrave said that the military challenge to the Government was "the concern of every deputy, of every party and of every citizen." On Wednesday, after a private conference to which the deputies of only a single party were admitted, the Government confronted Parliament with a *fait accompli*. In fact, the crisis which began with an ultimatum to the Government ended with an ultimatum from the Government to the Dáil. Necessity is an urgent plea, but it cannot be held to condone either a military or a political dictatorship. Dáil Éireann must insist that in the future adjustment of relations between the Army and the State the Government shall allow a livelier regard for the authority of the people.[60]

Yet, as I have already described, the government, although abrogating participation, was hardly involved in the destruction of democratic rule. Its policy was designed to preserve the structures of parliamentary rule through the creation of more rigid political domination. This strategy was determined by the belief in the fragility of those structures; only by consolidating authority in the hands of a few could the government be assured of containing the mutiny and of not further undermining the public's faith in the political structures. To do otherwise would have exposed to the public the political weakness of the new government.

The government's normative and organizational solutions to the crisis produced a problem for the political system. They stripped the government of nearly all of the symbolic claims – either those embodied in the Constitution or those of the nationalist movement – necessary to legitimate its rule. Its inability to enforce norms of individualism and its movement toward a system of closed party rule helped ensure that the party would not be perceived as the one graced with a nationalist vision. In its need to demonstrate institutional capacity, the party leaders abandoned any concern with the symbolic meaning of rule. This strategy, although seemingly a prerequisite for stability, ensured that the party could not strengthen political institutions while enhancing its own place in the government. As we shall see, the relations between party and government would become increasingly weakened throughout the decade. The irony of Irish politics during the 1920s would be that the party that secured political stability for the nation ensured, by that very accomplishment, its own decline as a potent force in Irish politics.

Cosgrave's party accomplished this rather extraordinary feat by focusing almost exclusively on preserving the integrity of the political structures. In ending the mutiny without violence and within the parameters of democracy, the government succeeded in expanding the state's legitimacy. But by solidifying the structures of political rule through the containment of the mutiny, the Party was challenged for its failure to embody the principles upon which those structures were founded.

In place of a national political community integrated around the symbols of the Irish population – those variants of nationalism and constitutionalism – the Cosgrave government sought a commitment to the state because it was effective and efficient. At least implicitly, the government sought legitimacy for a colorless yet competent and efficacious state. This effort to promote a legitimate order in which specific meanings in Irish history would be replaced by a demonstrably effective institution would ultimately prove unsuccessful. Not surprisingly, Cosgrave's attempts to replace the given cultural world for one that would give complete license to the state interest were to no avail. Yet, at the same time, it should not be forgotten that the policies of the Cosgrave government with respect to the army mutiny helped pave the way for an ever sharper distinction between the democratic rule and the party in power. And in sharpening that distinction, the party secured the conditions necessary for a democratic public, ensured the stable functioning of a political order, and guaranteed the party's political decline.

5. The Boundary Commission Crisis and the Development of Strategies of Political Efficacy

The army mutiny revealed the fragile and contentious character of democratic norms in a society with deeply rooted value conflicts. But the government's success in quieting the political challenge meant that contending normative claims were no longer the stuff of political opposition movements, even though these issues had hardly been resolved decisively. Contending beliefs concerning the allocation and distribution of resources remained intense; only the government's efficacy in changing the mutiny to a question of political policy prevented that issue from further undermining a weak public sphere. The normative question receded into the background of Free State politics.

As this chapter will illustrate, successful crisis resolution in the Free State would have important consequences for subsequent politics. The government's success in handling one crisis helped shape the character of political expression following it. We can posit a kind of "value-added" political analysis. The Free State, in suppressing the Civil War, weakened the power of value-oriented political conflicts while paving the way for a norm-oriented political challenge, that is, the army mutiny. Similarly, by demonstrating the strength of the political structures in containing the mutiny – the government's ability to subdue normative challenges, to transform principled opposition into issues of policy, and to preserve social order – meant that the subsequent political contests in the Free State shifted downward to organizational battles between political units. The efficacy of the state reduced the potency of both value conflicts and normative disputes; instead, Free State politics increasingly became more stable contests over power and influence by well-institutionalized political interests.

In this sense, the politics of the Free State after the mutiny increasingly appeared to resemble those of other democratic nations – where political challenges, although ubiquitous, never really challenged the basic structures of the political system. This form of interest politics, which developed rapidly given the depth of the division, made the stability of Ireland in the 1920s appear both relatively simple and largely foreordained. Yet this achievement, which was neither, rested squarely on the shoulders of the political elite, who suppressed their Civil War opponents and co-opted their less extreme army mutiny challengers.

Despite appearances, the Free State in the early and mid-1920s was hardly a model of stability. Political battles were no longer fought out over issues of values and norms, but this hardly meant that a new post–Civil War consensus was forged or that a new, better-integrated public was yet created. Instead, the situation was one in which the political institutions, with increasing effectiveness, were pitting their power against a badly split and deeply divided body politic. To be sure, with every political victory, the state was gaining converts from a suspicious community. Yet, as I have described, the state, although strong, was symbolically bankrupt, unable to embrace as its own either Irish nationalism or even constitutionalism. The Free State was securing order, but without creating a well-integrated polity. Instead, the political elite achieved or enhanced its institutional capacity while failing to establish the state at the center of the Irish symbolic universe.

In this chapter, I examine the complicated process whereby the state strengthened its political hold while becoming increasingly remote from public convictions and concerns. This chapter focuses first on the organization of the Irish party system, which contributed to this split between symbol and power. In the same way that the intense value conflicts in Ireland produced severe normative strains that the government could only sidestep, these same conflicts produced a party organization that prevented the emergence of a state symbolically integrated with the polity. The exercise of effective political power and cultural integration constituted, for now, incompatible agendas.

In the next section of this chapter, I examine the convening of the Boundary Commission and argue that the Free State government sought the establishment of this commission in an attempt to have itself identified with a symbolic concern of the Irish political community: the end of partition between Northern Ireland and the Free State. Its convening, I will argue, represented a recognition by the Free State leaders of the limits of power without moral authority; it was their effort to bridge the worlds of political efficacy and symbolic identity. In the final part of the chapter, I examine the political crisis that ensued when the Boundary Commission failed to produce the outcome the government had hoped for. Not surprisingly, the government's response to this political crisis was roughly equivalent to that of earlier crises. Political expedience became the single most important concern of the government, and its hopes for greater symbolic identity with the body politic were quickly dashed. The result, as we will see, was a state apparatus that secured further community respect for its ability to respond to crisis – even if this was one of its own making – but was incapable of promoting admiration for or identity with its policies.

The organizational basis for political instability in the Free State

Shortly after the founding of the Free State, President Cosgrave and his ministers organized a political party, Cumann na nGaedheal. It was perceived as the pro-Treaty, pro-Constitution party and provided the organization to gain and enhance support for the new state. Because of the deep political schisms in Irish society, Cumann na nGaedheal could not appeal for popular support on the basis of specific policies or programs. Instead, it had to attempt to create a broad coalition of support from all segments of the population who shared its support for the Free State. In the first convention of the Cumann na nGaedheal party held in April 1923, President Cosgrave spoke of the objectives of the new party organization. He argued:

> ... an important work for the new organisation to do was to bridge the great many differences that arise in a community of so many interests. The Cumann na nGaedheal ought to attract to itself the best elements of the nation, and it ought to bring home to everyone the vital need for a sound national organisation, knowing neither creed nor class, but working for the best interest of the whole of the people and the whole of the nation.[1]

To flourish in the context of early Free State politics, a new party would have had to speak to the "national question" because of the strong and persistent opposition to the Treaty. Until that question was resolved, no mass-based political party could be organized or influential. At this same meeting, Ernest Blythe, the minister for local government, spoke more pointedly of the political problem facing the nation:

> They [Ireland] had not yet reached the stage when an organisation with a definite plank was not needed. He hoped and believed that before many years it would not be necessary, when the various sections and economic interests could put up their own organisations, and the national interest would be safe, and when it did not matter what section of the nation or what political party came into power.[2]

Cumann na nGaedheal's organization according to national principles, rather than to more particular economic and social commitments, ensured that political development in Ireland would be very different from that of other European systems. Neither defined principally by a particular constituency nor committed to any policy except support for the Anglo-Irish Treaty and the Free State Constitution, political affiliation in post–Civil War Ireland would be fundamentally affected by the value conflicts that had produced the Civil War.

The institutionalization of value dissension, rather than the provision of a mechanism by which specific political and economic interests could be contested, had profound consequences. Whereas the institutionalization of political and economic contests have typically promoted political integration – in which the "rules of the game" are commonly adopted and serve as the legitimate basis upon which the outcomes are accepted – the institutionalization of value splits in the party system make political integration all the more difficult. First, value discord produced a political system in which one party, Cumann na nGaedheal, sought to protect the political apparatus of the Free State, whereas the major opposition party, Sinn Féin, sought its destruction. As Ronan Fanning has characterized it, the Treaty split was a "division between those who were prepared to contemplate some kind of party politics and those who were not so prepared."[3] Interparty contests, rather than strengthening the Free State, undermined it. I will return to this point shortly.

In addition, the value conflicts produced a political party, Cumann na nGaedheal, which was organized solely around the issue of adherence to the Treaty. Because those who adhered to the Treaty had diverse political commitments and interests, only the belief in the Treaty, the Constitution, and Free State institutions held them together. Although commitment to the treaty was certainly necessary in the early years of the Free State, it came to constrain the party later, when it adhered to that doctrine despite changes in circumstance. To abandon at any point its national plank, to renounce the Treaty, or to alter the terms of the agreement between Ireland and Britain, would have left the party with no common basis for membership. Ultimately, this problem meant that the party leaders were severely limited in their ability either to reduce the value conflicts or to promote political integration. Working for the preservation of the political structures – as Cumann na nGaedheal leaders so admirably did – represented, in the context of Civil War divisions, an assault on the principles of the anti-Treatyites. Cumann na nGaedheal's actions highlighted rather than muted the differences between the various sectors of the political community. This situation led one political commentator of the time to write:

> Parties, of course, must have more than a fundamental idea to justify their existence. The fundamental idea must take allies to itself of policies and reforms akin to it. But when a country is disordered necessity makes strange bedfellows of ideas. . . . Our politics at present are haphazard, the Government taking up anything which occurs to it as important at the moment, and we suspect that external dangers have united in the one Government men who in a more normal country would be found in opposite camps.[4]

But beyond the inevitable result of inhibiting political integration, the organization of the party system according to these national principles promoted a rather unimaginative response to political crisis. As the discussion of the army mutiny has already demonstrated, the differences in opinion among party members resulted in an inability to respond creatively to political challenge or to assert positions on principle. In place of principle was the singleminded objective of preserving the institutions of rule; indeed, government policies could extend no further. Any broader objective would have generated opposition from some segment of the ruling party that could have proved fatal not only to the party but to the political apparatus as well. To take measures to achieve the Republic, for example, would have only alienated those content with Commonwealth status. As a result, the government party became preoccupied with preserving democratic forms of rule, that is, the structure of the Free State institutions and their legal underpinnings. As a consequence, it was continually giving ground to the opposition party, Sinn Féin, enabling it to voice the substantive concerns and aspirations of the Irish people. As the same commentator noted, "Our Free Staters who rely upon democratic sanction are becoming the centralising bureaucrats. Our Republicans, who speak with contempt of democratic majorities in their propaganda, do yet strongly plead for democratic institutions and decentralization."[5]

Stated differently, members of Cumann na nGaedheal shared only a commitment to the preservation of political institutions, and a strong, effective, centralized bureaucracy was the most effective way of preserving the fragile political coalition and protecting the institutions. As the army mutiny revealed, political challenges resulted in a quick retreat from open, participatory rule toward closed, centralized control of the party elite. Political crises intensified these processes, but they were characteristic of routine, day-to-day practice during the early part of the decade. In contrast and as a consequence, oppositional political forces like Sinn Féin could easily promote principled challenges to state rule, evoking the name of the Irish people and employing themes of Irish nationalism or even constitutionalism against government policy.

This unique organizational arrangement in the Free State produced an ironic situation for the Cumann na nGaedheal Party. The government's capacity to strengthen institutions, to repress dissent, and to consolidate power in the hands of a few people proceeded essentially without a hitch. No party was capable of challenging these centralizing efforts. And at the same time, each step toward further consolidation of state power by Cumann na nGaedheal weakened the relationship between the party in power and the symbolic issues that animated the Irish people.

Because Sinn Féin refused either to reorganize the new state or to participate in the parliamentary process (except to stand for election), the third national party, the Labour Party, was thrust into the role of the loyal opposition. But it was only a formal opposition; despite having highly competent leaders, it was hardly up to the task of serving as an effective parliamentary counterforce. In the elections of 1923, the first following the ratification of the Free State Constitution, the Labour Party had gained only 11.4 percent of the vote compared to the Cumann na nGaedheal's 38.6 percent and Sinn Féin's 27 percent.[6] As a minority party, and with Thomas Johnson, a Protestant, elected as its leader, the Labour Party never seriously challenged Cumann na nGaedheal for control of the government.

Despite serving as the opposition party, the Labour Party remained principally concerned with particular social and economic policies. It was not inspired by the same national questions that motivated both Cumann na nGaedheal and Sinn Féin. In the opening session of the Fourth Dáil (the first of the Free State), Thomas Johnson remarked:

> But our interests rather lie in questions of social and economic difficulty, problems that I fear are going to prevent the re-establishment of peace and the stabilisation of the State, unless they are dealt with on lines very different from those hinted at and suggested by the Government, and the Government supporters.[7]

Since the Labour Party served as the loyal opposition without any real interest in so doing, its political effectiveness was greatly reduced. As Arthur Mitchell writes, in his book on the Labour Party:

> Had the Labour Party restricted itself to social and economic matters, an almost impossible situation would have been created for

both the party and the Dáil. The party would have exposed itself to the criticism that it was simply a special interest group, a delegation from the Trade Unions. The Dáil, without an active opposition, would have been reduced practically to a one-party assembly. No other group in the Dáil could have formed a meaningful opposition.[8]

Instead, the Labour Party, informally serving as the opposition, promoted the appearance of an effective two-party system while simultaneously providing Cumann na nGaedheal with a license to take any measure it deemed necessary to preserve the democratic structures. In its desire to promote a strong, centralized state buffered against political challenges, Cumann na nGaedheal had the best of both worlds: While putatively operating within a contest-oriented two-party system, it functioned much like a one-party government.[9] Upholding democratic forms, it was able to secure institutional stability without concern about an opposition party seriously aspiring to assume power.

Irish politics in the early years of the Free State was confronted with this odd situation. The party willing to engage in politics, Cumann na nGaedheal, did so in form; in substance, however, there was little need for it to do so. With no real political parliamentary opposition, many critical questions concerning the course of the new nation went undiscussed. As I have already described, Cumann na nGaedheal was at liberty to respond to political challenges decisively. As *The Statesman* noted:

> ... conflict, whether civil or external, abolishes democracy for the time being and the disorder which follows all conflict enables the autocratic and bureaucratic elements to make almost an unanswerable case for more or less centralized control of local as well as national and departmental administration.[10]

Cumann na nGaedheal, the product of such conflict, made precisely this case. The absence of an effective opposition enabled it to rapidly establish a centralized bureaucratic state, thereby promoting the strength of the political apparatus.

On the other hand, Sinn Féin, the party unwilling to engage in party politics, was the real political opposition. It alone truly competed with the government for popular support. Although refusing to assume its role as the formal opposition, it was the de facto opposition party. Not only was it the largest minority party, with 27 percent of the vote, it also addressed, unlike the Labour Party, the central concern that divided the nation.

As the extraparliamentary opposition party, Sinn Féin organized itself around the national question. The principles of organization, like those of Cumann na nGaedheal, were products of the Treaty dispute and the Civil War. Its organization according to these general national principles has been identified as a primary reason for its failure to remain a potent political force throughout the decade. Although this is undoubtedly true, since the national question waned in importance over the decade, any imputation that Sinn Féin would have been more successful had it been organized according to more specific economic or social commitments, or that it did have a realistic option to organize differently, ignores the political conditions that prevailed early in the decade. Peter Pyne writes about the "third" Sinn Féin party, the Sinn Féin of post-Treaty Ireland:

> ... the leaders of the Republican party in the post–civil war era made the error of regarding their organisation as a national party, in a sense that the previous Sinn Féin had been national, i.e. supported by all classes in all sections of the country outside of the six north-eastern counties. Because the Second Sinn Féin party had been determined not to confuse the struggle for independence by becoming involved in any class of social interests that might divide its heterogeneous supporters, the Republican leaders of the new party, anxious to emulate the success of the earlier organisation, considered the placing of emphasis on social ideals as both unnecessary and a political cause of division. The Third Sinn Féin party wanted all sections of Irish society to present a united front to secure independence.[11]

But it must be recalled that Sinn Féin was seriously challenging Cumann na nGaedheal for the allegiance of the Irish people. The newly organized Cumann na nGaedheal Party and the persistence of the divisive treaty issue left Sinn Féin with little alternative but to be similarly broad-based and to attempt to appeal to a heterogeneous population. This was hardly an error in judgment, as Pyne suggests; rather, it was a political necessity.

Yet, as the Free State institutions became stronger and more secure throughout the decade, Sinn Féin's fate was similar to that of Cumann na nGaedheal. Both parties were products of the Civil War, and both were unable to break out of their original organizational mold. There was, in fact, little that Sinn Féin could do to increase its declining appeal. Bound together only by the party's opposition to the Treaty and by competition with the broad-based Cumann na nGaedheal Party, its leaders could neither abandon their principled opposition and reenter parliamentary politics nor relinquish the party's national plank. Either action would only have ensured the party's becoming a small, interest-articulating party with no legitimacy as the de facto national opposition. As the Treaty issue began to decline in centrality and the existence of the Free State became increasingly taken for granted, as I will detail in this chapter and the next, Sinn Féin appeared more and more anachronistic. It continued to expound even more virulently upon issues of decreasing public concern.

But there was another way in which the course of Sinn Féin was inextricably bound to the fate of Cumann na nGaedheal. I have already suggested that the Free State Government's effectiveness in securing order had the consequence of dividing the party's power increasingly from the potent symbols of the new Irish nation. A commentator in *The Leader* described the political situation as follows:

> The result is that the Government are fairly safe in power for some time, but we do not believe that the country is in favour of the Government. What makes them safe is the lack of alternatives. . . . If there was a working national alternative to the present Government, the present Government would probably be out of office at a general election.[12]

Power was securely in the government's hands, but its leaders were hardly admired. Sinn Féin's history over the decade presented a strong contrast. Both the minority status of Republican forces and their defeat in the Civil War promoted a politics that were largely symbolic. The party's refusal to sit in the Dáil so as not to take the oath of allegiance to the king of England, and its refusal to recognize the legitimacy of the Free State because it accepted the partition of the thirty-two counties into two separate nations, although highly symbolic actions, ensured Sinn Féin a largely peripheral role in post–Civil War politics.

Ironically, the defeat of the anti-Treaty forces enabled the party to remain, for a time, the conscience of the country. Because the Republicans stood outside the formal political arena, untarnished by political exigency, their symbolic politics crystallized into a constant and perennial irritant. Republican politics was consistently directed against those who attempted to establish political normalcy in the country and against those who had little defense–except the most pragmatic one–against these claims. As a consequence, Northern Ireland as a symbolic issue remained significant in post–Civil War politics because the issue of partition was now fused with the principles of Republicanism and political independence from Britain. As a symbol, the persistence of partition, like the oath of allegiance, confirmed for Republicans the Free State's lack of commitment to the ideals of the nationalist revolution. Partition was a living testimony to the incomplete, and therefore suspect, realization of national principles.

Republicanism in Ireland had successfully appropriated for itself the symbols associated with the nationalist struggle against Britain. The principles around which the Irish had originally mobilized against the British – political independence from Britain, autonomy and self-determination, and unification of Ireland – became increasingly possessed by those outside of government and were used as political weapons against those inside. Further, the ambiguities of the Free State Constitution – which prominently featured the Anglo-Irish Treaty – made even the nationalism of the Irish-Enlightenment tradition inaccessible to the Free State leaders. Power, in contrast, was held by those inside the government, who now defended themselves against principled attack by using instrumental politics.

For reasons largely beyond its control, Cumann na nGaedheal opted for a centralized, bureaucratic state sheltered from the populace. As that process intensified, principled criticisms by Sinn Féin became all the more damaging. It was impossible to assert as principle the protection of the state at all costs, as Cumann na nGaedheal attempted, and expect it to counteract effectively the more emotional, and perhaps more fundamental, national symbols of unity and independence. The power politics of Cumann na nGaedheal were counteracted by the "cultural politics" of Sinn Féin, and although those who held power had the upper hand, this division of symbolic and instrumental concerns disturbed the development of stable democracy.

The inability of the two parties to alter their policies produced a new political problem for the party in power; it was a problem they appreciated, but they had few options to reconcile the two political worlds. The remainder of this chapter – a look at the work of the Boundary Commission and its aftermath – will examine the consequences of this fundamental political split between those on the inside of the Free State and those on the outside, and the dangers it posed for post–Civil War politics.

Background of the crisis: Northern Ireland and Irish politics

Northern Ireland, a six-county area in northeast Ireland, was partitioned in 1920 from the remaining twenty-six-county area of Ireland that came to be known as the Irish Free State. This partition was accomplished by the Government of Ireland Act, whereby the British government, in the last of a series of home rule acts, attempted to accommodate Irish Republican demands for independence with the Northern Protestant majority's adamant opposition to it. With this act, two governments were established, one whose center was in Belfast, the other in Dublin.

The Anglo-Irish Treaty in 1921 formally granted political independence to the twenty-six-county area of Ireland. At the same time, the Treaty honored the six-county-area's right to self-determination; its government had the option of maintaining Northern Ireland's political sovereignty if it so desired. If it chose that alternative, the Treaty provided (Article XII) for the establishment of a Boundary Commission to determine, in a more careful and systematic manner, the boundary between Northern Ireland and the rest of the country. Predictably, the Northern Irish government chose to remain independent of the Free State. With that decision, Irish nationalists in both the North and in the Free State looked to Article XII in the hope that it would provide the mechanism for the abolition of partition.

Article XII provided that the Boundary Commission, if convened, would consist of three members. One was to be appointed by the government of the Irish Free State, one by the government of Northern Ireland, and the chairman by the British government. The commission's purpose, according to Article XII, was to "determine in accordance with the wishes of the inhabitants, so far as may be compatible with economic and geographic conditions, the boundaries between Northern Ireland and the rest of Ireland."[13]

The circumstances under which Article XII became part of the Anglo-Irish Treaty, and the article's subsequent history in Irish politics, illustrate an important fact about the role that Northern Ireland played in the politics of the Irish Free State during the 1920s.[14] As a symbol, Irish unity remained extremely important. Partition and the presence of Northern Ireland were expressions of continued British rule in Ireland. As such, they were an affront to the sensibilities of a nationalist-minded, anti-British Irish populace. Yet, although people were capable of mobilizing against the idea of partition, at the same time they were, by and large, resigned to a divided Ireland. In practice, they were not willing to sacrifice gains won from the British in their quest for political independence in order to win back the six counties.

The disparity between the normative importance of the North and its relative unimportance in practical political terms helps to explain why Article XII of the Anglo-Irish Treaty took the form it did and why it was invested with expectations that proved to be unrealistic. In one sense, treaty negotiations with the British could not succeed before some resolution of the problem of partition occurred. Its symbolic importance was too great for it to be ignored. Yet, the primary objective of the negotiations was to provide political independence for the twenty-six counties of Ireland. An intransigent Ulster was not a sufficient cause to give up the struggle for a free Ireland. Irish negotiators, for example, were instructed that should the negotiations with the British fail, it would be best if the break appeared to be over the Ulster question.[15] This strategy reveals both the recognition by political leaders of the symbolic importance of the North and its lesser importance to the Irish negotiators.

As further evidence, when the Dáil considered whether or not to approve the Treaty, the issue of partition was practically ignored. As Maureen Wall has noted, of more than 300 pages of Treaty debate, only nine were devoted to the subject of partition.[16] The question of a united or divided Ireland was largely peripheral to the central issues at home. As already described, those who opposed the Treaty opposed it on terms other than partition. Criticism focused on the oath of allegiance to the king and Ireland's relationship to the British Empire. Even de Valéra's Document No. 2, intended as an alternative to the Anglo-Irish Treaty, provided no counterproposals to Article XII.[17] All, however, hoped at some time for an end to partition, and for this they looked to Article XII. Michael Collins, for example, defended Article XII by arguing that it would "lead very rapidly to good-will, and the entry of the north-east under the Irish Parliament."[18]

Article XII, then, accomplished two important objectives. First, it offered a compromise on Ulster. It provided the opportunity for the negotiators to defer consideration of partition and thereby enabled the negotiators to proceed on the issues of political independence. Second, it allowed the Irish to defer the problem of the North without abandoning its symbolic significance in nationalist self-understanding. The Irish signatories to the Treaty genuinely believed that the convening of the Boundary Commission, as provided by Article XII, would result in significant land gains for the Irish Free State.[19] They laid considerable claim on the "wishes of the inhabitants" clause of the article. The British negotiators, as the evidence well documents, encouraged the Irish delegation to believe that the desires of the inhabitants of the six-county area would be the primary criterion for determining the new boundary; economic and geographic factors, although considered, would be secondary.

Reasoning that Catholics at the district level, with the exception of a few areas in the six counties, were in the majority, the Irish believed that a Boundary Commission would be compelled to cede large portions of the North to the Free State. Moreover, it was believed that with such significant secession from the North, the areas remaining independent of the Free State would not be economically viable. As a result, these areas, too, would seek entry into the Free State.[20] Partially because of Catholic strength at the local level, it was widely felt that when the wishes of the inhabitants were determined, much of the North would join the Irish Free State.

That interpretation of Article XII was presented to, and widely accepted by, the population in the twenty-six-county area as well as northern nationalists. The inclusion of Article XII in the Anglo-Irish Treaty allowed for the continuing negotiations between the British and Irish over issues of political independence for the twenty-six counties. It further provided a substantive doctrine for Irish nationalists that appeared to indicate that the goal of one Ireland was close to being realized.

The readiness with which the Irish were willing to believe in the likely end to partition because of Article XII suggests the strength and importance of the wish. Despite British deception (the British were assuring the North at the same time that their territorial sovereignty was secure), the Irish expectation that a three-member commission, chaired by a British government appointee along with a delegate appointed by the Northern Ireland government, would cede large portions of land to the Free State demonstrates the large gap between wishful thinking and real political possibilities.

The Cosgrave government, despite its politics of practicality, similarly saw Article XII as a means to achieve a unified Ireland. But even more importantly, it perceived the Boundary Commission as a way of being strongly identified with the passionate concerns of nationalist Ireland. To press the British government to convene the Boundary Commission was powerful symbolic politics, and the Cosgrave government took full advantage of the opportunity.

As I have described, following the Civil War, the new government had to demonstrate that a commitment to the Anglo-Irish Treaty did not inherently mean an abandonment of nationalist goals. Further, it had to prove that such goals could be achieved through parliamentary processes. For these reasons, Article XII became the vehicle by which the government sought to prove that the important symbols of Irish nationalism – like ending partition – could be achieved on their political terms, and not on those of the anti-Treatyites. The question of the North, therefore, was intimately linked with the government's efforts to gain legitimacy. From the outset, the issue of partition became the acid test of the government's ability to fuse symbolic politics with the practical political process. In the early months of the Free State, political stability seemed to depend on this fusion.

Before 1922 ended, the government created an agency, the North-Eastern Boundary Bureau, to examine the boundary problem. But the Republican forces, sometimes joined by the Labour Party, continued to criticize the government for its inactivity on the issue.[21] Especially in the Catholic areas adjoining the six northern counties, the Government was criticized for not pressing for the convening of the Boundary Commission. In July 1923, Cosgrave tried to quell criticism by appointing the Free State commissioner to the Boundary Commission. This was Eoin MacNeill – the minister for education, a northerner, and a Catholic.

Not coincidentally, his appointment came only weeks before the first general election following the Civil War. It was a clear response by Cosgrave to the mounting criticism of his government and revealed the importance of the government's ability to manipulate the partition issue for political gains. After the election, the boundary issue receded once again to the background, prompting a popular periodical of the time to comment:

> Now that the election is over the Boundary Question has disappeared again, so the folks who said that it was just an electioneering stunt, seemed to have whacked the nail right on the blinkin' nut. Quite a good scheme for it can be trotted out again when required.[22]

In March 1924, it was indeed trotted out again. At that time, no further progress had been made in convening the commission. In fact, Sir James Craig, the ardent Unionist leader of the North, had made it clear on numerous occasions that the North would not participate in the commission and would not cede to its rulings.[23] Nevertheless, the Free State government sent a strong letter to the British government demanding that the Boundary Commission be set up immediately.[24] March 1924, it will be recalled, was the month in which the government was confronted by the army mutineers and attacked for their insufficient commitment to a nationalist Ireland. Under attack because it failed to embody Irish national symbols, the government used Article XII as the single most important mechanism to undercut parliamentary and extraparliamentary criticism on this score. After meeting with Cosgrave and other members of his cabinet in late March, Thomas Jones, the British Cabinet secretariat, said, "The fear of the growing opposition to the government and of its rallying around the failure to operate Article XII is having more and more weight in their minds."[25]

The decision to press for the convening of the Boundary Commission, in short, was more for the purpose of securing a stable twenty-six counties than it was to achieve a united Ireland. And once the decision was made, once the government had identified itself with the successful outcome of the Boundary Commission, there was no turning back. Cosgrave, despite discouraging political events both in the North and in Britain, was compelled to carry through on convening the commission. The credibility of the party as one committed to principles of Irish nationalism and unification was at stake.

Britain was not anxious for the Boundary Commission to be convened. In the first place, the early 1920s in Britain was the most unstable political period in over fifty years. Between 1921 and 1925 there were four different governments – a liberal coalition government, two Tory governments, and a socialist government. As Geoffrey Hand notes, "Continuity of policy was a good deal to expect in such circumstances."[26] In addition, British politicians were as concerned with their relations with the Northern Irish government as they were with the Irish Free State. The Boundary Commission could not be expected to please both sides. As a result, the British politicians were making it clear that their interpretation of Article XII differed substantially from the official interpretation of the Free State Government. As early as December 1921, just after the signing of the Anglo-Irish Treaty, Lloyd George referred to Article XII as intended to "readjust" the boundaries.[27] Unlike the Irish government, the British felt that the article was not designed to transfer large territories. As the Boundary Commission began to take shape in the summer of 1924, the British signatories to the Treaty declared unanimously that "they never had any intention of interfering with the essential integrity of the Six Counties."[28] These statements led President Cosgrave to comment in the Dáil:

> I have observed references by British politicians and British signatories to the Treaty, opinions which were carefully concealed when the negotiations, that resulted in the Treaty, were being undertaken. Had these pronouncements been made at the time there would not have been Irish signatories to the Treaty.[29]

Nonetheless, for reasons that make sense only in terms of internal political needs, such pronouncements by British political leaders did not lessen the Irish government's determination to have the Boundary Commission convened.

Conditions in the North proved no more promising for a successful resolution of the boundary problem than those in Britain. In fact, in May 1924, the Northern Irish government, which did not recognize the Anglo-Irish Treaty, formally declined a request to appoint a member to the Boundary Commission. The Free State Government insisted that the

North's refusal was Great Britain's problem; Britain was responsible for finding a solution, since it was legally bound by the Anglo-Irish Treaty to convene the Boundary Commission.[30] When a Judicial Committee of the Privy Council, appointed by the British government, determined that Britain was not legally empowered to appoint a Northern Irish minister under the terms of the Treaty, nor would the commission be legal with only two members, the British government agreed to pass legislation enabling it to appoint a Northern Irish delegate to the commission. No doubt that legislation was motivated by Cosgrave's assurance that failure to convene the Boundary Commission would result in the fall of his government because of its inability to implement the Treaty.[31]

By November 1924, the necessary enabling legislation was passed in Britain and approved in the Irish Free State. Justice Richard Feetham of the South African Supreme Court had been appointed some months previously by the British as the chairman of the Boundary Commission. Joseph Fischer, a seventy-year-old Ulster Unionist and a barrister, was now appointed by the British government to be the Northern Irish delegate. With Eoin MacNeill representing the Irish Free State, the Boundary Commission was fully constituted and formally met for the first time on November 6, 1924.

The Boundary Commission became a reality only because of the Cosgrave government's insistence. By the end of the year, even the people of the Irish Free State were no longer optimistic about the prospects of the Boundary Commission. An Irish periodical commented in September 1924:

> ... all the clamour for the Boundary Commission is based on the assumption that we do want the Commission, that it is going to be a good thing for the Free State of Ireland, and the assumption is not based on any reasoned argument or supported by any sober consideration of the probable results of the Commission.[32]

Several Dáil representatives expressed a sentiment similar to that of Representative O'Connel when he remarked, "I think the number of people in this country who believe that any good will come out of this Commission is exceedingly small. The belief that we had when the Treaty was accepted has disappeared."[33]

Even at this early stage, the difficulties that the government confronted in fusing symbolic and practical politics were clear.[34] The pressures on the Government to press for the Boundary Commission – reflecting, on the one hand, the popular suspicion that the government was not committed to unification and, on the other, the government's interest in demonstrating the capacity of the Free State to realize nationalist goals through moderate politics – meant that the government had to pursue the implementation of Article XII even if political realities clearly suggested that this would hardly help to abolish partition. Yet, the writing was already on the wall: The Cosgrave government, despite its best intentions, could not be identified with the central symbolic concern of nationalism while responding to the practical requisites for governance in a weakly integrated polity. That lesson was first learned at the time of the army mutiny; it would be driven home clearly as the Boundary Commission, in subsequent months, failed to produce the desired results.

The political crisis unfolds: the collapse of the Boundary Commission

On November 7, 1925, almost a year to the day after the first meeting of the Boundary Commission, the *Morning Post*, a London newspaper, published a "forecast" of the award that the commission was soon expected to make. The paper's account, with an accompanying map detailing the boundary changes, proved to be largely accurate. It claimed that the commission would make only minor adjustments in the existing boundary, and it included for the North a considerable area of East Donegal, the richest part of the county. The award was to transfer land from both the Irish Free State side and Northern Ireland. Had the award been made, the Irish Free State would have had a net gain of 134,000 acres of land, increasing its population by almost 24,000.[35]

Yet, the mere suggestion that some land was to be ceded to the North, regardless of the net effect of the transfers, led to a storm of protest. The possibility of losing land to the North had never been seriously considered in the Free State. In those areas likely to be transferred, protest was most intense. The Monoghan County Council, for example, adopted a resolution pledging resistance to any attempt "to dismember our county as well as Donegal and to bind in perpetual bondage, in defiance of the wishes of the inhabitants, large areas of Down, Armagh, Tyrone, Fermanagh and Derry."[36] Members of the Dáil, cognizant of the political repercussions of such an award, did not hesitate to object strenuously. Representative McCullough, of Donegal, for example, said:

> I do not want to act as a prophet here as to what would result if any such findings as was forecasted by the *Morning Post* was brought in by the Boundary Commission, but I venture to say there would result a state of affairs that at least would not be desirable. Threats of trouble are made by those who are threatened with removal

from the jurisdiction of this Government, and, while I recognise that this Government can probably deal with any difficulty that may arise, I say that position will not be a happy one, or one that they can look forward to with any pleasure. In the case of any trouble, the Border would be the rallying ground for every discontented element in the 26 counties, and it is quite possible that a fire may be lit that would present grave difficulties in extinguishing.[37]

With opposition to the government mounting in the countryside, Thomas Johnson, chairman of the Labour Party, sought to make political capital of the situation. In an interview, he called for the resignation of the entire government:

> The position with respect to the boundary and the position in which the country has been placed by Mr. Cosgrave, Dr. MacNeill and the whole Executive Council acting with them is one of deep humiliation, and one out of which I cannot see themselves extricating themselves with any regard to honourable conduct.[38]

The president himself was acutely aware of the political dangers his government faced if the Boundary Commission announced such an award. After the Executive Council consulted with its delegate to the commission, Eoin MacNeill, and ascertained that the paper's forecast was largely accurate, Cosgrave traveled to an area in County Monoghan (Emyvale) that was slated to be transferred to the North. He went to reassure and calm a troubled populace, to assert his interpretation of the situation, and to offer his recommendations for appropriate action. He said:

> (T)he Treaty settlement was intended by all parties to mark the end of coercion in Ireland and to substitute the principle of democratic government based on the consent of the governed. No other intrepretation of Article 12 could possibly accord with the general spirit of the Treaty. It was clearly intended, in the event of Northern Ireland deciding to secede from the Irish Free State, to bring relief to the Nationalist inhabitants of the Six Counties, who would otherwise be held under a Government not acceptable to them. . . . It [the grave situation] calls for the exercise of restraint and dignity by all the people of Ireland, and particularly by those most closely and most directly affected. A new and grave situation has undoubtedly arisen, but good citizenship dictates that no heated words or foolish acts should render our task more difficult.[39]

The developing political crisis resulted in the resignation of Eoin MacNeill from the Boundary Commission, presumably under strong encouragement from Cosgrave. It was hoped, for a brief period, that the resignation of one member would invalidate the decision of the other two; a British legal ruling prevented that possibility. With increasing criticism directed at the commissioner, MacNeill, acknowledging errors of judgment in his role as negotiator, resigned from his position as minister for education in the Cumann na nGaedheal government.[40] MacNeill's retirement from the government, like Mulcahy's during the army mutiny crisis, was intended to deflate the growing political opposition. Criticism directed at the government, however, continued unabated.

The Cosgrave government was facing its gravest crisis since the end of the Civil War. The situation was made more serious by the fact that it was not only the viability of the party in power that was being challenged; the resiliency of the political institutions themselves was being tested. As Kevin O'Higgins insisted to the British Cabinet in persuading them to suppress the Boundary Commission award, "The Free State position is too fluid for us to deal without apprehension. It is not a case of six or seven men facing extinction. There is no coherent party ready to take over from us and carry on on the basis of the Treaty."[41] Or, as a "well-known" deputy of the government party responded to the political correspondent of the *Irish Times*:

> The moment that the Boundary Commission presents its award, that moment the life of the Free State Government comes to an end. President Cosgrave could not possibly remain in office, and I am quite certain that he would not want to, just as I am sure that neither myself nor any other member of our party would remain in the Dáil. . . . The Treaty, we all believed, meant an end to all the old prejudices and the old antagonisms, but in the changed circumstances they would be revived and intensified a hundredfold, until it became only a matter of months till a Republican Government displaced the present administration.[42]

The sudden political crisis required a new strategy. With the political survival of the institutions at stake, the government largely abandoned its concern for incorporating nationalist symbols into its rule. Instead, its aim was simply to preserve the political institutions in the most expedient way possible. A compromise with the British was made by the president and his closest political allies, largely in secret. The need for compromise was a reflection, once again, of the government's limited maneuverability. Its options were few. The parallels of the government's response to the army mutiny were striking.

The Irish government was in no position simply to accept and implement the Boundary Commission award, as the British would have preferred. Such an action would have been intolerable to a large segment of the Irish population and would have paved the way, it was believed, for a Republican takeover. Yet, a refusal to implement the award would have constituted a violation of the Anglo-Irish Treaty and would probably have led to the severing of political and economic relations with Britain; this, the Irish political leaders believed, would have been financially disastrous and would have ultimately led to their own downfall. Once again, it was these two external forces – the Irish Republicans and the British politicians – that were largely determining the course and pace of events for those in power; the countervailing and incompatible pressures they were imposing on the government made this policy of compromise necessary.

Yet, even the Irish government's efforts to arrive at a compromise were beset by difficulties. Although seeking to demonstrate the competence of the political institutions, it could not afford to further alienate the parties involved. As the crisis itself indicated, its position was not secure enough for it to ignore its opponents. The British, for their part, although recognizing the necessity for a delay in publishing the Boundary Commission's award, given the Irish Free State's internal political difficulties, were not overeager to compromise on the award.[43] They had to be convinced that its implementation at any time would be fatal to the Free State Government. The Republicans, in contrast, were suspicious of any compromise with the British. For them, the Free State government's negotiations with the British were intolerable. In the words of their spokesman, Éamon de Valéra, it was simply a case of Irishmen "playing her [Britain's] game for her."[44] A compromise agreement, therefore, would have to offer, at a minimum, a British concession to gain Republican support.

The government was also faced with increasing opposition from the political center. In the Dáil, the actions of the Cosgrave government were not unanimously endorsed. Elements within Cumann na nGaedheal, for example, especially among those with a direct interest in the affected border counties, were privately threatening to defect from the party unless Cosgrave produced a satisfactory settlement.[45] The opposition political parties also attempted to make political hay out of the crisis. Unlike the Republican criticism, of course, blame was placed squarely on the shoulders of Cumann na nGaedheal rather than Free State political structures. Significantly, opposition members in the Dáil did not question the right of the Cosgrave government to attempt a compromise with the British, but they were critical of the government's refusal to include the Dáil in the deliberative process.

As Deputy Cooper argued, "The Government may not now find themselves to be in a position to announce a full and complete policy . . . but merely to make the statement that the matter is engaging, or would engage, the attention of the Executive Council is, to renew a metaphor again, asking us for a blank cheque."[46] Or, as Thomas Johnson commented presciently:

> I think that before any tentative agreement is made in London, there should be consultation and discussion of a public character on this side of the water. . . . I fear we are going to be faced next week with some provisional agreement which the Dáil will be told is practically an accomplished fact and that if they do not accept it then something terrible will happen.[47]

In another speech, Johnson argued that if, as it had been rumored, the boundary was to stand as it was, that constituted a violation of the Treaty. A failure to fix the boundaries in accordance with the wishes of the inhabitants, Johnson argued, would not be "in harmony with our Constitution," and the Dáil would not be entitled to confirm such an agreement.[48]

The loyal opposition singled out for criticism the method by which the Cosgrave government sought compromise. Attacking its policy of secrecy, its failure to consult with the Dáil, and its willingness to contravene the spirit of the Treaty, that is, Article XII, in the interest of compromise, the Labour Party renewed the attack first mounted during the army mutiny crisis. Cosgrave was challenged for abridging the democratic process by refusing to involve the Dáil in the decision-making process. Instead, decisions were made by a handful of men – Cosgrave and his most trusted advisors.

In the closing days of November 1925, President Cosgrave and two members of his Executive Council, Kevin O'Higgins and Patrick McGilligan, shuttled off to London to begin a round of negotiations with the British. With the negotiations underway and their outcome uncertain, tensions within Ireland were somewhat relaxed.[49] On December 3, 1925, a tripartite agreement was signed by representatives of the Irish Free State Government, the Northern Irish government, and the British government. The agreement was an amendment of and supplement to the Anglo-Irish Treaty of 1921. The three governments were "resolved mutually to aid one another in a spirit of neighbourly comradeship." The main provisions of the agreement were that (1) the powers conferred on the Boundary Commission were revoked; (2) the boundary would remain as it was; (3) the Irish Free State would be discharged from the liability it had assumed under Article V of the Treaty for a contribution to service the public debt of the United Kingdom and for the payment of war pensions as they existed in December 1921; (4) the Free State would take over the British government's share of payments for malicious damage to property in the Free State and would refund the amounts already paid by the British government; (5) the Free State would increase by 10 percent the amount awarded for posttruce damage to property; and (6) the powers of the Council of Ireland in relation to Northern Ireland and the governments of the Irish Free State and Northern Ireland would meet together as and when necessary to consider matters of common interest arising out of or connected with the exercise and administration of those powers.[50]

The compromise achieved for the Cosgrave government what it had hoped. It had annulled the award and, in addition, had granted some financial relief for the Free State Government. It was believed that the annulment of Article V of the Treaty would enhance the Free State's financial prospects and would make it easier for the government to negotiate loans from British banks. The government negotiators, therefore, were able to return to Ireland having averted publication of the Boundary Commission award while gaining, as evidence of their successful bargaining, an additional concession from the British. In return, and probably necessary for their respective internal political situations, both Northern Ireland and Britain were able to demonstrate similar compromises on their behalf. The most significant compromise was the agreement to abolish the Council of Ireland and place its functions in the hands of the Northern Irish government. The Council of Ireland had been intended to promote greater cooperation between the two Irelands, but it was completely ineffective. Nevertheless, the appropriation of its functions by the Northern Irish Government represented a concession the Free State Government was not happy to make, had it any alternative. This agreement strengthened the Northern Irish Government and increased its sense of legitimacy and permanency.

In fact, the Free State Government made little effort to conceal the fact that the agreement, as a whole, was one of necessity. In its defense, government spokesmen argued that they had achieved as much as could be expected, given the difficult circumstances. As Deputy Thrift of Cumann na nGaedheal summarized the situation, "Our Government was found with a really difficult position. They did not ask how it came about but they set themselves to find out what was the next best move."[51]

Those in opposition, of course, saw the issue differently. Deputy Morrissey succinctly stated the alternative view: "We are asked to agree to a measure which, in effect, surrenders every principle of nationality and democracy in order, I submit, to allow an inefficient – because it has proved to be inefficient – administration to save its face."[52]

The compromise agreement had to be confirmed in the Dáil; what followed was several days of heated and acrimonious debate. In the words of the political correspondent of the *Irish Times*, the debate was "equalled in intensity of feeling only by the historic Treaty debate of 1921."[53] President Cosgrave modestly defended the settlement not by asserting its merits but by contrasting it to the situation that might have prevailed without it:

> This was not a party question; it was a question of the nation. . . .
> One thing and one thing only was perfectly clear, and that was
> the publication of an award by the remaining members of the
> Commission would be a national calamity . . . it spelt immediate
> discontent and disorder. What was the way out? Peace – a lasting
> and secure peace – if it could be found under such favorable
> circumstances.[54]

Kevin O'Higgins, as befitting his personality, was more flamboyant in his defense of the agreement. He boldly suggested that it served the reunification of the two Irelands. Had the Boundary Commission gained new land for the Free State, O'Higgins argued, the nationalist minority in the North would have been smaller and more helpless. With the boundary intact, they represented a more potent force in bringing about ultimate unification.[55] O'Higgins paid no mind to the fact that his argument directly contradicted the original justification for convening the Boundary Commission.

Those opposed to the agreement objected largely on two grounds. First, a few members of Cosgrave's own party and members of the opposition parties attacked the government for making a compromise without consulting the Dáil and, in addition, for attempting to push the agreement without allowing the representative assembly to consider it. Professor Magennis, a member of the ruling party who defected as a consequence of this agreement, stated the case eloquently:

> I protest . . . against the effort, which is part and parcel of the Gov-
> ernment policy of late, to set aside all the principles of represent-
> ative government and to introduce autocracy in its place. . . . The
> President and his colleagues seek to terrify the people with the
> bogey of anarchy. We have always been told that there is no al-
> ternative Government, and that if there was an alternative Gov-

ernment, it was that dreadful thing Republicanism. There is another kind of anarchy, not so palpable but quite as terrible – social confusion and the destruction of public order. There is anarchy – I describe it accurately and, I submit, technically – the anarchy of those who ought to be the champions of the institutions of which they are the personal embodiment: of those who use their position not to discharge the natural functions of that office but to undermine it.[56]

The accord was also widely criticized for it was the first time the Free State Government had made an agreement that acknowledged the boundary and therefore gave it additional permanence. The compromise agreement was viewed as the cooperation of the Free State Government with the Northern Irish and British political leaders in partitioning the country permanently. In speaking of the demise of the Council of Ireland and the absorption of its functions by the government of Northern Ireland, Thomas Johnson argued:

I believe that political institutions are of the greatest importance either to assist or retard the development of that spirit of concord and growing together of a people or peoples. Therefore, it is that I feel very sorely about that particular proposal, because I see in it without any question – and it is not denied – the cutting of whatever has been left of the organic unity between the two parts of the country.[57]

Despite the intensity of the debate, its outcome was never in doubt. The ruling party suffered a few defections as a result of the agreement, but Cumann na nGaedheal had no serious difficulty in garnering the votes necessary to gain passage of the Treaty (Confirmation of Amending Agreement) bill of 1925. Nevertheless, there were serious consequences.

Cumann na nGaedheal's complicity with the British and Northern Irish governments, and its endorsement of partition, although necessary given the political situation, enabled a new coalition of political forces to challenge the party's rule. Its formation was only nascent, but it represented a new kind of politics in the Irish Free State. When the compromise agreement was presented to the Dáil, leaders of the Labour Party encouraged elected Republican deputies, who refused to participate in the Dáil, to enter the Dáil and vote against it. Only by their participation, Labour leaders argued, could the bill be defeated. The Republicans would not cooperate, refusing to take the oath of allegiance to the Crown, and, for their part, encouraged Labour deputies to leave the Dáil in protest against the agreement. The Labour Party would not agree.[58] Nevertheless, about forty Republican deputies did meet with other Dáil representatives in a meeting convened and presided over by Thomas Johnson. At the close of the meeting, Johnson announced that those in attendance were "unanimous in opposition to the Boundary Agreement proposals."[59]

Although nothing further materialized from this Labour–Sinn Féin meeting, its occurrence pointed to three important political developments in the Irish Free State. First, Cumann na nGaedheal was being forced further and further away from the potent national symbols. The need for stability demanded that the ruling party become more detached from the central moral-political concerns of the Irish community. Now clearly identified as among the forces upholding a divided Ireland, the government leaders had to argue only that they had achieved a better partition agreement than what might have been. Instead of being identified as the embodiment of national symbols, Cumann na nGaedheal leaders asserted the virtues of realistic, effective, and competent political institutions. Such claims hardly promoted patriotic fervor. The party's success in demonstrating the competence of its rule – for example, the compromise agreement, which preserved stability – was ensuring its greater symbolic isolation from the body politic. The result was an increasing alienation of the party from mainstream Irish and nationalistic politics.

A second important political development illustrated by the meeting was that the Labour Party was beginning to grow into its role as the opposition party. It was attempting to forge a new political coalition reflecting the changing political conditions in Ireland. Sensing the increasing capacity of the political institutions and the increasing vulnerability of the party to attack because of its inability to incorporate nationalist symbols into its rule, the Labour Party leaders reached out to the Republicans. The opportunity was now available to form a political coalition in which the issue of government legitimacy could take second place to a concern for the nature of the ruling political party. This development would mark a decline in Civil War politics dominating post–Civil War Ireland. It suggested the movement toward a more delimited politics in which the institutions would be largely taken for granted; political divisions would center on the issue of who was to control them. The coalition, as I mentioned, proved premature; the Republicans remained stubborn in their opposition to the Dáil as a legitimate political institution. Nevertheless, the Labour Party's attempt revealed a changing political reality in Ireland.

Finally, the Labour Party's opposition to the settlement agreement was critical in ensuring that opposition to the government was not accompanied by a general disillusionment with the institutions of rule. A principled opposition in the political center, such as that of the Labour Party and Professor Magennis and other defectors from Cumann na nGaedheal, ensured that the Dáil would not lose its place as the dominant political institution in the nation. Their assertion of democratic principles in criticizing the government's policy of compromise was significant in furthering the differentiation of the ruling party from the government. Without such opposition within the government, the Republicans would probably have gained in strength and the government itself would have come under increasing attack.

Instead, Republican opponents of the compromise had to contend with the fact that the sizable vocal group within the Dáil opposed Cumann na nGaedheal's policies as well. It was an effective demonstration that a challenge to the policies of the ruling party did not have to entail the rejection of the government as a whole. In this respect, Cumann na nGaedheal's policy of compromise and the outspoken opposition to it in the Dáil came to serve the same purpose. Both demonstrated the viability of the political institutions; both deflated the Republican opposition and strengthened the institution of moderate politics.

With the imminent passage of the boundary bill, pressure was building both in the Republican camps and among those opposed to it in the Dáil to call a popular referendum on the issue, as provided in the Irish Free State Constitution. It was widely believed that such a referendum would reject the establishment of a permanent boundary. Éamon de Valéra, insisting that the new agreement with Britain was a violation of the Anglo-Irish Treaty, said in a speech in Donegal, "We challenge them to put this agreement to the people. There is a referendum by which they can put it to the people of the 26 counties and I am certain that the people would turn down the new Treaty."[60] Despite the fact that President Cosgrave had agreed in the Dáil debates to call a referendum,[61] he reversed that decision after the bill was passed. Speaking to the Dáil, Cosgrave declared that "the Bill entitled the Treaty (Confirmation of Amending Agreement) Bill, 1925, which has this day been passed by the House, is necessary for the immediate preservation of the public peace and safety and that, accordingly, provisions of Article XLVII [Referendum] of the Constitution of Saorstát Éireann shall not apply to the Bill."[62]

The suspension of the referendum was not surprising because of the government's desire to reestablish stability and order as quickly as possible. A referendum campaign would have led to a wide-open, prolonged debate over the boundary and, quite possibly, over the policies of the government in general. That would not have been in keeping with the policy of suppressing debate through concerted action designed to resolve crisis situations expediently. Through its policy of compromise, and because of its desire to establish effective, competent institutions of rule, the Cosgrave government intended to impose a definition of political reality by presenting its actions as the only available alternative.

The government's refusal to allow political debate on this question was a further elaboration of its rejection of key sentiments in the Constitution that, it will be recalled, stressed participatory democracy. It was further evidence that the government believed the state to be so fragile that the preservation of the political institutions was seen to be at odds with open, participatory rule. When forced to choose, Cosgrave shielded the institutions from a too critical public and sought to secure the state through efficacy rather than popularity.

The government's strategy did result in the preservation of political stability in Ireland. On December 15, 1925, by a vote of 54 to 14, Dáil Éireann passed the Treaty Bill and, by a vote of 52 to 15, adopted a resolution declaring that the measure was necessary for the "immediate preservation of the public peace and safety," thereby preventing a referendum on the issue.[63] President Cosgrave and his close political allies achieved what they had set out to do. Within six weeks of the outbreak of the crisis dating from the *Morning Post*'s forecast, the government had succeeded in demonstrating its control of the situation. It had effectively negotiated with the British to suppress the report of the Boundary Commission; it had gained some financial relief from the British; and, most importantly, it had prevented an assault on the political structure by Irishmen who refused to identify with it.

Conclusion

The Boundary Commission crisis and the government's response to it revealed several important features of politics in the Free State in 1925. First, the government's insistence on convening the Boundary Commission revealed the political leaders' recognition that strong institutions alone could not secure democratic stability. Their hope – however unrealistic it was in the context of British and Northern Irish intransigence on the partition question – of uniting Ireland demonstrated the political imperative to fuse a symbolic politics with an effective political agency in order for democracy to flourish. There was an understanding, however inchoate it might have been, that strong political institutions were insufficient. Political integration was also required so that the government could identify itself with important symbolic goals and so that the community would see in the government the pursuit of those goals. Strong institutions, in themselves, could not produce strong allegiance, and the government leaders appreciated that stable democracy depended upon strong allegiance.

The crisis, however, revealed a second feature of the politics of the Free State in 1925, one more promising for stability. The efficacy of the state during both the Civil War and its aftermath had altered the nature of political expression. Previous successes of the government in securing order promoted a more narrowly focused kind of politics. It was a politics that accepted the essential forms of the state, even if the government's political opponents refused to defer to its moral authority. Although integration remained the most pressing political problem facing the new government, and although the failure of the Boundary Commission only intensified the difficulty, that problem was now expressed institutionally rather than through value or normative challenges. The demonstrable strength of the political institutions, although it did not solve the nation's problems, certainly helped contain political expression in parliamentary channels. The ability of the government to salvage something positive, in the form of concessions from the British, from the failure of the Boundary Commission further assured the permanence of the Free State. It was now clearer than ever that political challenges could be made only in terms of political contests. Specific government policies would have to become the focus of political battles. Although democracy was not yet secure in the Free State of 1925, political stability was now much more possible because political expression assumed this more narrow, policy-oriented form.

Finally, the failure of the Boundary Commission served to end any illusion of members of the government party that they could succeed in singlehandedly performing the two tasks of stable democratic rule: establishing strong, effective institutions while integrating the population within a common symbolic political universe. The Boundary Commission's collapse signaled the government's last major effort to develop a symbolically significant political program paralleling its preeminent objective of establishing a strong state apparatus. The result was that the Cumann na nGaedheal government abandoned its attempt to promote its popularity and became concerned solely with the efficacy of state structures. As I have described, the organization of the party system coupled with the persistent value divisions in the body politic prevented the party from achieving both outcomes. Nevertheless, the decision by Cumann na nGaedheal leaders to sacrifice their own popularity for democratic order probably knows few parallels in other nations. That the party did not bring down the institutions with it or, conversely, seek to enhance its own popularity without respect for the consequences to the state is a rare achievement in modern politics.

This recognition of the party's limits in Free State politics and its comprehension of its own mortality is largely the subject of the next chapter. In recognizing that Cumann na nGaedheal was incapable, given the context of Free State politics, of generating widespread popular identification and allegiance, the problem faced by the leaders was how, through the use of the increasingly strong political apparatus, they could promote some form of symbolic integration. It was the assassination of a powerful and effective political leader that gave the government the opportunity to "legislate" and require such political integration of the body politic.

6. The Limits of Effective Rule: The Assassination of Kevin O'Higgins and its Aftermath

Introduction: the changing political context

In July 1927, Kevin O'Higgins, vice president of the Executive Council and minister for justice, was fatally shot in a street outside of Dublin on his way to Sunday mass. He was one of the most outspoken, prominent, and competent members of Cosgrave's government and one of the chief architects of Cosgrave's program to secure social order in the Free State. He was hardly loved by the Republican forces; in his ferocious commitment to the Free State, he was strongly identified with the repressive side of Cosgrave's rule. His assassination rocked the government and the nation; because of his identification with the forces of order, his death demonstrated the ever-present specter of violence lurking just beneath the political surface. Although it was an isolated event for which no political or military group claimed credit or accepted responsibility, the assassination was widely interpreted, by government leaders and the population in general, as evidence of the persistence of physical force, however weak, and the dangers it posed for political stability.

This chapter examines the government's response; it was the response to the assassination, and not the act itself, I will argue, that constituted this third political crisis. For reasons that will be made clear, this was a crisis of the government's own making. In an important sense, the government took advantage of the assassination to complete the project it had created for itself in responding to the previous two crises.

The features of this political crisis differ markedly from those of the previous two. Nevertheless, the nature of the government's response reveals a common and consistent pattern. In each instance, the concern for the preservation and effective functioning of the political institutions took precedence over strategies to enhance either the party's popularity or the political integration of the nation. At the same time, the greater confidence of the government in responding to the assassination re-

160

vealed the impressive change in the political environment that had oc-curred in the Free State by 1927. Before discussing the government's actions, it is important to understand the political environment in which they occurred.

Irish politics was moving in two directions. The political center – those committed to or accepting of Irish parliamentarianism – was growing ever stronger, while the Republican forces, although commensurately weaker, were growing more extreme. These two developments were not unconnected: Each victory by the Free State forces made the Re-publican abstentionist position more untenable. The result was that the Republican movement kept the allegiance only of those most ideologi-cally committed to the Irish Republic. The success of the Free State institutions, in short, was creating a crisis in Republican ranks.

No event proved more fatal to the Republican movement than the Free State's successful containment of the Boundary Commission crisis. Had the Sinn Féin representatives to the Dáil opted to enter the Dáil and vote against the bill establishing the boundaries, as I described in the last chapter and as the Labour Party encouraged them to do, the compromise arrangement with Great Britain and Northern Ireland would not have become law. The irony was not lost that in its role as principled opposition, Sinn Féin had helped secure a victory for Cumann na nGaedheal as well as more permanent boundaries between the North and the South. Sinn Féin's efforts to establish a political alternative to the Free State government had only facilitated Cumann na nGaedheal's policy of strong political institutions.

The Republican movement's inability to produce changes was affect-ing the movement itself. There was growing disenchantment. On the one side were those who were coming to believe that abstentionism was now a misguided policy; on the other side were those who believed that Sinn Féin was abiding too strictly by the parliamentary rules of action. The first sign of political division came when the IRA, the army irregulars of the Civil War, who had formerly sworn allegiance to the political institutions of the Irish Republic and had been committed to work within Sinn Féin clubs, decided in November of 1925 to reexamine that com-mitment. This was done at the General Army Convention, the first such convention held since the cease-fire of the Civil War.

Many of the Army members who attended were dissatisfied with the performance of Sinn Féin, believing that instead of acting as the leader of the Republican government, it was behaving more and more as a political party, like other parliamentary parties. Peadar O'Donnell, active in Republican politics and in the IRA, introduced a resolution to the convention to sever the army's ties with Sinn Féin. The resolution introduced by the Tirconnail (Donegal) Battalion read as follows:

That in view of the fact that the Government [Sinn Féin] had developed into a mere political party and has apparently lost sight of the fact that all our energies should be devoted to the all-important work of making the Army efficient so that the renegades who, through a coup d'état assumed governmental powers in this country, be dealt with at the earliest possible opportunity, the Army of the Republic sever its connection with the [Republican] Dáil, and act under an independent Executive, such Executive be given the power to declare war when, in its opinion, a suitable opportunity arises to rid the Republic of its enemies and maintain it in accordance with the proclamation of 1916.[1]

By his own account, O'Donnell's reason for introducing that resolution to the convention was to enable the IRA to become actively involved in the land annuity agitation that was resurfacing in the Irish countryside.[2] Land annuities were payments owed by Irish farmers to the British government for the land titles granted to them as a result of the various land acts passed by the British prior to Irish political independence. The Anglo-Irish Treaty provided for the continuation of those payments after independence; the Free State Government naturally insisted on enforcing that provision. Irish farmers, however, for both economic and political reasons, resented these continuing payments to the British. When the Free State government, through the courts and local bailiffs, began demanding payment and, in lieu of it, began seizing cattle as compensation, these farmers looked to the IRA for support.

Although not responsible for the agitation, local units of the IRA became involved in the annuity struggle on behalf of the farmers. In contrast, Sinn Féin political leaders were more reluctant to lend support to these peasant unrests.[3] Because of the more urban and professional background of the political leaders, as well as their less than complete adoption of Gaelic-Romantic commitments, peasant struggles had never been widely supported by the Sinn Féin leaders.[4] Even during Sinn Féin's rule of the Republican Dáil (1919–21) prior to independence, as described briefly in an earlier chapter, land seizures by peasants were strongly discouraged. The then minister for agriculture, Art O'Connor, attacked land seizures as a "grave menace to the Republic." He argued then that "the mind of the people was being diverted from the struggle for freedom by a class war, and there was likelihood that this class war might be carried into the ranks of the Republican Army itself."[5]

Like the land seizures prior to independence, land annuity agitation in 1925 posed political difficulties for the Sinn Féin leaders. But now Sinn Féin's reluctance to support the movement stemmed from its incapacity, as a political organization created to oppose the Treaty, to identify itself with a specific social issue that was seen to have little direct bearing on the national question. The party organization would have been threatened by its support of an issue that had no specific connection with the achievement of an Irish Republic. O'Donnell's concern was that, in its failure to agitate for social issues for fear that it would detract from its political objective of achieving the Irish Republic, Sinn Féin was unwillingly re-creating the conditions of the ineffective, though well-intentioned, Irish parliamentarianism of 1918.[6]

O'Donnell did have some support among the Republicans. He and his supporters later founded Saor Eire, a political organization whose objectives were to overthrow Irish capitalism and to establish an Irish Worker's Republic. Nevertheless, O'Donnell's resolution to the convention would have been soundly defeated had there not been rumors suggesting that certain leaders of Sinn Féin were considering entering the Free State Dáil. Tentative and unsubstantiated as the rumors were, the mere possibility of this action infuriated many members of the army organization. And the cleavage that was developing – this time among Republicans – was familiar. When they were led to believe that members of the Sinn Féin were selling out to parliamentarianism and compromise, the response was to reassert the politics of intransigence and extremism. As a result of these rumors, O'Donnell's resolution gained substantial support at the convention. In backing the proposal, party members condemned the policy of moderation and expressed their dissatisfaction with the Sinn Féin leaders. The resolution was passed: The convention adjourned with the IRA asserting its independence of Sinn Féin's political control and expressing its determination to promote the Republic by whatever means it deemed necessary.

The IRA was moving left as the decade progressed, a frustrated response to its increasingly irrelevant place in Irish politics. At the end of 1926, for example, the IRA attacked twelve police barracks in different regions of the country, killing two unarmed members of the Civic Guard. With this provocation, the government introduced a new Public Safety Bill reinstating detention without trial and suspending habeas corpus. Because of these same political circumstances some members of Sinn Féin felt it necessary to move closer to the political center. Éamon de Valéra most notably, in the closing months of 1925 and into 1926, concluded that the time was right to attempt to promote the Irish Republic by entering the Dáil. Although rumors were rife in the Army Convention, it was not until December 1925 that de Valéra publicly raised the possibility of Sinn Féin delegates entering the Dáil.

In the Sinn Féin Ard Feis (Convention), held in March 1926, de Valéra asked the delegates to accept the proposition that "once the admission oaths of the twenty-six and six-county assemblies are removed, it becomes a question not of principle but of policy whether or not Republican representatives should attend these assemblies."[7] With the Boundary Commission fiasco on the minds of many delegates, de Valéra's proposal seemed to be reasonable, but in the end, a narrow majority in the convention, as F. S. L. Lyons reported it, "preferred the pure milk of revolutionary gospel" and defeated the proposition.[8] At the same time, a resolution that intended to place Sinn Féin in the extreme Republican camp was also defeated. It read: "It is incompatible with the fundamental principle of Sinn Féin to send representatives into any usurping legislature set up by the English law in Ireland."[9] The Sinn Féin delegates knew what they were against, but they were far from clear on what they were for.

Sinn Féin, intransigent in its commitment to remain an extraparliamentary party, condemned itself to irrelevance. Already having lost support from its left wing (the IRA) and braced to lose more popular support for its failure to act effectively on the boundary question, the party, in its rejection of de Valéra's proposal, held to a principled opposition that had not changed since the Civil War. It was a position that failed to respond to the changing political realities of the Free State. Recognizing the futility of Sinn Féin's position, de Valéra resigned as president and withdrew from the party. He said that he resigned because he "was compelled to regard the vote [to consider entry into the Dáil] as one against his policy, the adoption of which he considered necessary at this juncture to unite the people of Ireland against foreign domination."[10]

Through a series of political gyrations and verbal gymnastics, de Valéra methodically moved to enter the mainstream of Irish politics. He organized a new political party, Fianna Fáil (Soldiers of Destiny); through it, he hoped to connect Republican principle and sentiment with the Free State's political effectiveness. At the party's inaugural convention in May 1926, de Valéra explained his motives for creating the new political party:

> [I] would not be doing [my] duty to the rank and file Republicans or to the Irish nation if [I] were to contemplate allowing Republicanism to be put into the position in which it would appear to be nearly nominalistic formalism. The freeing of a nation was not an

easy task, and could not be performed except with the enthusiasm and vigour coming from the passionate feeling of the nation. That passionate feeling could never be aroused if they were to move away from realities.[11]

From its inception, Fianna Fáil attempted to take its inspiration from Republican sentiment while accommodating to the realities of parliamentary politics. Insisting on its continuity with the Republican tradition and, at the same time, expressing its commitment to parliamentary processes, Fianna Fáil attempted to bridge, for the first time since independence, the chasm in Irish politics.

Other constitutional republican parties had emerged since the Civil War. Following the army mutiny, Joseph McGrath and eight other defectors from Cumann na nGaedheal had formed the National Party, whose program was to amend the Treaty and to make it a more Republican document. In the first by-elections for which the party stood, it failed to win a single seat, which resulted in its demise. In 1926, at approximately the time that Fianna Fáil was forming, Professor William Magennis, a deputy of Cumann na nGaedheal, left the party in protest over its handling of the Boundary Commission crisis. With two other members of the Dáil and one member of the Senate, he created Clann Éireann. The party stood for the abolition of the oath of allegiance, a revision of the boundary settlement, and the imposition of trade tariffs.[12] None of its candidates won in the election of June 1927, and the party was not heard from again. Both of these parties had failed to significantly enlarge the pool of voters; instead, they had only drawn upon those who were already active.

The failure of both the National Party and Clann Éireann to moderate between the worlds of Republicanism and parliamentarianism revealed the depth of the cultural and political division between them. Republican sympathizers were hardly moved to switch allegiance from a "politics of opposition" to a handful of Parliamentary "liberalizers." Thus, Fianna Fáil was the most significant political development in post–Civil War Irish politics because, unlike the other constitutional republican parties, it developed from within the Republican movement. De Valéra's prominence, as a nationalist leader until the Civil War and then as a Republican leader, assured the party of at least some degree of success. In fact, perhaps only de Valéra, with his impressive political credentials and his charismatic presence, could ensure that Fianna Fáil, unlike the other breakaway parties, would be a potent force in Irish politics. As I will show later, only Fianna Fáil was successful in getting its delegates elected to the Dáil and in substantially increasing the number of voters.

With de Valéra's move toward the political center, it was again hoped that national political passions could be channeled into constructive nation building through the parliamentary process. For the first time, it was possible that Cumann na nGaedheal might be confronted by a party that could effectively challenge its political control. Organized on a similar broad basis, appealing to a mass constituency, and concerned with common national questions, Fianna Fáil offered the possibility of an effective and popular multiparty system.

The Republican movement was breaking apart as the decade progressed. On the one side, the military wing refused any political control by Sinn Féin, desiring to be free to articulate its extreme opposition to the Free State and the parliamentary process. On the other side, the most important and powerful Republican leader, de Valéra, was attempting to find a way to move toward the parliamentary center without abandoning his claim as the spokesman for Republican principles. As *The Round Table*, the conservative British publication, observed in June 1926, "The outstanding event in the Free State during the last quarter has been the increasing disintegration of its political groups. The Republican party has finally and irrevocably dissolved into its constituent elements."[13] Although the danger of a rise in politically unmediated forms of extremism clearly increased when the IRA broke with Sinn Féin, the more significant development was that of Fianna Fáil. Its rise demonstrated the victory of Cumann na nGaedheal's political strategy. The latter's ability to prove time and again that the political structures were resilient meant that the burden was increasingly placed on the Republicans to respond to changing political realities.

This, then, was the political environment in which the assassination of Kevin O'Higgins occurred. We do not know for certain the broader meaning that the government attached to his murder. Yet it would have been reasonable to interpret it as an act of desperation by some extremists sensing the Republicans' increasing isolation from the political center. Because Republicanism was unable to wage an effective political battle against the Free State forces, terrorism became the only weapon capable of reminding the nation of the Republican presence. Had Cosgrave's government analyzed the killing this way, no strong response would have been necessary. But the government hardly responded calmly and reasonably. Instead, it reacted as if the structures of rule were as fragile as they had been in 1922 – as if only extraordinary measures could prevent the felling of the Free State itself. In attempting to convince the Dáil to act decisively, President Cosgrave presented a lengthy account of the history of Republican insurgency since the Civil War, suggesting that republicanism represented as serious a threat to the Free State institutions in 1927 as it had during the Civil War.[14]

It may be that because of the anguish felt at the loss of O'Higgins, their response was a reflexive one, relying on old coping patterns despite the changed political environment. It may also be true that Cumann na nGaedheal was suffering from internal pressures jeopardizing even the pretense of a coherent party line. Economic policy questions – the debate over free trade versus tariff, in particular – were dividing the party. The opportunity to heal internal wounds by focusing on the external Republican danger was an attractive alternative to party dissolution.

Yet I argue that these are only partial explanations, at best, for the government's extreme response to the assassination. I suggest instead that Cosgrave saw in this murder an opportunity to solidify the gains made for the state in the past and, moreover, to ensure the strength of the Free State's democratic structures. Whether intentional or not, the government's response to the assassination was the denouement of the Cumann na nGaedheal program. It demonstrated that by 1927 the party had given up entirely any hope of achieving political integration by enhancing its popularity. Instead, using the death of O'Higgins as the rationale, the party acted to ensure the effectiveness of its political institutions and to demand that Fianna Fáil assume the integrative role in the Free State. Even in its nascent form, Fianna Fáil was clearly a party more capable of promoting integration. In short, Cumann na nGaedheal implemented policies that would result in its own eclipse by a more popular, symbolically central political party. It was a sacrifice of the highest order – though, in all likelihood, it hardly appeared that way to the actors – for it ensured the survival of a democratically stable political order. It is to that program that we now turn.

The government's response to the assassination of Kevin O'Higgins

Kevin O'Higgins was not a beloved figure in Irish politics, but he was immensely respected for his dedication, his brilliance, and his all-consuming concern for the survival of the nation. He argued, on behalf of the government, for unpopular causes. As minister for justice, he proposed and got passed public safety acts and other laws that attempted to put the government on a firmer footing vis-à-vis Republican insurgency. Thus, his assassination – the killing of the symbol of law and order in the Cosgrave government – was immediately, and probably rightly, attributed to Republican sympathizers. Moreover, the government's response to the assassination was what O'Higgins himself would have wanted. Only days after O'Higgins's death, the government presented a package to the Dáil designed to destroy Republican strength once and for all. The bill itself was a living memory to the man and his goals, for it represented the most far-reaching, repressive proposals yet suggested in a nation where such legislation was not uncommon. O'Higgins's assassination motivated and was used as a pretext to achieve effective political institutions – a process, I have argued, that had been developing haltingly but steadily.

The assassination had disarmed organized Republican groups, for as groups attempting to create their own political institutions and not an anarchic politics, assassination (at least as an isolated act) was not an acceptable tactic. Neither Sinn Féin nor the IRA would accept responsibility for it; both condemned it. De Valéra commented that "it is the duty of every citizen to set his face sternly against anything of the kind. It is a crime that cuts at the root of all representative government, and no one who realises what crime means can do otherwise than deplore and condemn it."[15] In this unique situation, in which Republicans and Free Staters agreed, the government showed less restraint than it might otherwise have exhibited. Acting without compromise and negotiation, as it had done in previous political crises, the government introduced three important and far-reaching bills in an attempt to seize the moment.

The first bill was a Public Safety Bill that empowered the government to use extreme coercion against any organization involved in treason or sedition. It laid down severe penalties for membership in any such association. The bill allowed for drastic powers of search and provided for the establishment of a special court empowered to inflict death or penal servitude for life on those convicted of unlawful possession of firearms. As one authority wrote, "Some of the provisions clearly infringed on the constitutional guarantees of the liberty of the subject and trial by jury."[16] This problem was circumvented by a provision that any section that contradicted the Constitution should operate as an amendment to it.

The second bill was an electoral amendment bill designed to end the abstentionist policy of those parties standing for election and then, upon election, refusing to enter the Dáil. Every candidate for election, when nominated, was required to swear that, if elected, he would take his seat according to the provisions of the Constitution. Otherwise, he would be disqualified as a candidate.

The third bill was a constitutional bill proposing that the right of members of the Dáil to demand a referendum be restricted to those who had taken the oath of allegiance and, furthermore, that the initiation of laws or constitutional amendments by Irish citizens be abolished. It was intended to do away with the initiative and to ensure that the referendum could not be used by abstentionist representatives to rid the Dáil of the oath.

The introduction of these three bills into the Dáil demonstrated, in abbreviated form, the dominant political strategy of the Cosgrave government since the Civil War in response to divided national politics and sentiments. Through suppression of Republican opposition and development of effective institutions, political order continued to be the objective. Political domination continued to be used to integrate the population. Even here, where condemnation of the assassination transcended traditional political divisions in Irish society, Cosgrave quickly reinstated those divisions and asserted his dominance by introducing this legislation. Inevitably, the actions served only to revive the deep splits within the Assembly and among the population as a whole. Cumann na nGaedheal's strategy was as predictable as it was politically divisive.

The public debate over the new legislation in the Dáil and the press vividly revealed the tension underlying the problem of institutionalizing democracy in a culturally and politically divided Ireland. Whereas the opponents of this legislation insisted that it would only further isolate the state from the Irish polity, the government argued that the security of the political institutions had to take precedence over the Constitution itself. No compact between the state and the citizens should be so inviolate, it was argued, that political guarantees as provided by the Constitution could be placed ahead of the security of the state.

The Public Safety Bill provided for an inordinate increase in the power of the Executive Council. It was the Executive Council that could declare unlawful any political association it deemed dangerous to the security of the Free State. Possession of incriminating documents would be taken as prima facie evidence of membership in an unlawful organization. The Executive Council could condemn individuals to penal servitude or expel them from the country for joining such organizations. It had the power to declare at any time a state of emergency, which would enable them to establish special tribunals that could inflict the death penalty. *The Irish Times*, although endorsing the legislation, recognized the enormous implications it would have for Irish society and government. In an editorial, it stated:

> The terms of the Public Safety Bill are drastic and far-reaching to a degree which, perhaps, the country had not anticipated. No

"Coercion Act" under the British *régime* ever flung so thorough a challenge at lawlessness in Ireland. The Bill endows the Government with the most formidable powers over life and liberty. Especially in the matter of the proposed deportations, it puts a tremendous responsibility on the shoulders of a single Minister. It authorises the Government to invade the constitutional rights of the civil courts. . . . If, as we must assume, the Government is able to convince Parliament that a malignant and audacious conspiracy threatens the very life of the State, Parliament will do its duty and the country will endorse its action.[17]

Similarly, in the Dáil's debates over this bill, Deputy Johnson appreciated the inherent dangers in such a bill. He argued:

Executives have to be guarded against. There is nothing more certain in life than that accession of power leads to the desire for more power. The whole of the Constitution provisions are intended to place a check upon an Executive going beyond its powers. . . . When you abrogate the constitutional provision which ensures that a judge shall come between the Executive and the citizen, then you are giving power to the policemen, soldier or any person that is in the service of the Executive. . . . When we set up courts, when we set up Constitutions, we do so in order that some institution may stand between the Executive and the citizen to protect the citizen against the arbitrary action of the Executive. That is what the Constitution is for.[18]

In fact, the government argued just as *The Irish Times* had suggested. These drastic powers were required, government leaders insisted, because of the imminent danger presented by Republicans. The government rejected Labour's argument as being hopelessly naive in the face of these threats to political stability. General Mulcahy responded to Deputy Johnson as follows:

Deputy Johnson seems to me to be appealing to our sense of beauty in matters of the written Constitution, as if the Constitution is a piece of lyric poetry that was to ensure definitely perfect peace and liberty, and fill everyone with full appreciation of the liberties and rights of others, whereas, as I have said before, it can be of no use to us if the institutions that it is supposed to set up and guard are destroyed.[19]

Other members of the government argued similarly. Professor O'Sullivan remarked that "if the safety of the State, which is prior to the Constitution itself, demands it, then these rights in our Constitution must, for the time being, and as long as necessary, be abrogated. That is nothing revolutionary; it is simply plain common sense."[20] President Cosgrave stressed the same theme in a somewhat different fashion:

The Constitution which we have here is not the only instrument which guarantees citizens their liberties, privileges and rights. The institutions of the State, the arms of the State, the Garda Síorchanna, the Army, and the various other institutions ensure the liberties, the rights and the privileges; and those are the institutions which we have had to man from our party here.[21]

The government's position was that only by taking these necessary measures to protect the political institutions from the Republican threat could the nation's founding documents and principles be preserved.

This latest Public Safety bill passed with some minor amendments. President Cosgrave then declared that it was "necessary for the immediate preservation of the public peace and safety," and therefore the provisions of the Constitution that allowed citizens to challenge the law through the initiative did not apply.[22] This action was consistent with a provision of the Constitution, it will be recalled, that allowed for the bypassing of the referendum and initiative in extreme situations, but its application to this legislation only highlighted the extent to which the government had circumvented the participatory principles and sentiments of the Constitution.

Consistent with its effort to establish the Executive Council's dominance over the Constitution and to limit constitutional protection of the citizen, the government sought to amend the Constitution Bill, introduced in the Dáil at the same time as the Public Safety Bill. The bill was designed to remove from the Constitution those articles providing for the use of the initiative and referendum to introduce legislation in the Dáil. It was presented as a specific response to continued threats by abstentionist members of the Dáil to use these provisions in order to eliminate the oath of allegiance from the Constitution. Thus, although the crisis was not directly related to the assassination of Kevin O'Higgins, the government used it to restructure the relationship between the Executive Council, the Dáil, extraparliamentary political parties and the larger polity.

The original intention of the initiative and referendum, it will be recalled, was to encourage the public's political participation and, through Dáil members, to initiate legislation to protect against excessive power of the Executive Council. In the eyes of the Executive Council, the potential for misuse by its Republican adversaries justified efforts to abolish these mechanisms. Opponents to the bill were concerned about the government's abandonment of efforts to encourage the public's participation. As Captain Redmond commented about the effect of the bill if it was passed:

> The only thing it will do as far as I can judge will be to exasperate further a certain section of our people who have been showing some indication at any rate, latterly, of advancing in the direction of constitutionalism. This will not encourage them, but it will discourage any advance towards constitutional action.[23]

The government responded by arguing that effective political rule could only be achieved – in light of the Republican opposition – with a Constitution that more accurately reflected the needs and interests of the state. According to the Government, this meant the need for greater power for the Executive Council and reduced power and influence of both the Dáil and the Irish polity. As Deputy Hogan candidly, though not convincingly, remarked:

> There are a lot of frills in that Constitution. We were all younger four or five years ago. We have learned since. There was a lot of needless things put into the Constitution. There were a lot of things put into the Constitution which leads to confusion and the instability that confusion always brings about.[24]

In a somewhat more lofty defense of the government's bill, Deputy J. J. Byrne argued:

> We suggest that we must have Government; we must have leaders of that Government. We must either do one thing or the other – we must govern or get out. . . . We say to the enemies of the people: "You have refused to recognize the de facto and de jure Government of the country that has been carefully created, and we on our part refuse to allow you to exercise certain provisions of the Constitution with the sole, simple and deliberate object of wrecking that Government." We say: "You have no right or title to come in and take an Article of the Constitution for the purpose of wrecking the State. . . . " The Constitutionalists arguing in the house say to us: "You must not alter the Constitution." I say that if the needs of the State demand the alteration of the Constitution, that alteration should be made. . . . For any man who studies the pages of history there is always one lesson to be learned and that is *salus populi suprema lex*, the safety of the people is the supreme law.[25]

This bill was not passed only because the Dáil was dissolved for new elections before a vote could be taken. A similar bill was introduced the following year, which will be discussed later in the chapter.

The Electoral Amendment Bill provided the most compelling evidence presented thus far that the government seized upon O'Higgins's assassination to conclude its program of ensuring strong, democratic political institutions for Ireland. This third piece of legislation in the assassination package insisted that organized political parties could not operate freely without first subordinating themselves to the Free State's political institutions. The government was demanding that the genuine opposition party participate in parliamentary politics. Because of the strength of the parliamentary institutions, the government was now capable of requiring its political opposition to agree to the terms of participation as dictated by the parliamentary process. Only a confident government could demand that the opposition enter the parliament and serve as the legitimate opposition.

There is little doubt that the government leaders were aware of the consequences Fianna Fáil's entry into the Dáil would hold for Cumann na nGaedheal. They were, in effect, legislating their own political defeat. The Public Safety Bill and the Constitution Bill were hardly measures designed to win popular acclamation for Cumann na nGaedheal. Taken in concert with the demand for Fianna Fáil to enter the Dáil, these measures could only be understood as a package of legislation designed to unequivocally secure a strong state while beginning the "socialization" process needed for a genuine opposition party to assume power. It is not surprising, then, that the government's defense of the Electoral Amendment Bill was somewhat different from its defense of the previous two bills. Instead of defending it by referring to the need for a strong state irrespective of constitutional safeguards, government spokesmen argued on behalf of the needs of the political institutions and the principles which underlay the Constitution.

Cosgrave argued in the Dáil that democratic stability required both strong institutions and full public participation. In other words, he broadened his concern for strong state institutions to include the need for political integration. Both, he insisted, were necessary for democracy to flourish. He argued:

> The purpose of this measure is to tell the people of this country that there must be respect for the Parliament of the people – that those who contest elections must take their places in the Parliament of the people. What is the necessity for it? The necessity for it is the stability of the state. . . . The present position of the Abstentionist Party in this country is unconstitutional, it is anti-constitutional; it is a danger to the Constitution and it invites contempt of the Constitution.[26]

How uncharacteristic of Cosgrave to express such concern for both the viability of the parliament and the sanctity of the Constitution! How different a defense of governmental policy – a policy that had been designed to weaken the influence of the Dáil and circumvent participatory provisions of the Constitution. Even the opposition in the Dáil had a difficult time offering a counterargument; with that bill, Cosgrave had pulled the rug from under those usually capable of challenging the government for its contravention of democratic principles in the interest of preserving democratic political forms. Deputy Baxter of the Labour Party expressed his hesitation, as well as he could, to a policy of "forced political participation." He argued:

> I confess that I feel that the attitude and the policy of Fianna Fáil is injuring, to some extent at least, the credit of the country, but, on the other hand, there is no shortcut to stability, and while we must do all we can to encourage it, after all, stability is rather a thing of natural growth. I feel that we cannot create the right conditions through a method of pressure that will undoubtedly have reactions that will not be favourable to the natural growth which in the end is the only thing that stands or lasts.[27]

The opposition claimed that political integration could not be legislated. Nevertheless, in expressing concern for the problem of an integrated polity and in exercising its political will to help achieve it, Cumann na nGaedheal disarmed its opponents. By employing those same strong institutions that it had carefully constructed throughout the decade, the government sought to complete its development of a stable, democratically integrated political system.

In sum, the political crisis was of Cumann na nGaedheal's own making, coming at a time when the limits of its effectiveness were becoming clear to the government. No state, no matter how strong, could be secure when a sizable, organized sector of the society abstained from political participation. This legislation, then, had two purposes: first, to further isolate and squash the extreme Republican opposition, for which the free functioning of a democratic public held no value; and second, to demand that the more centrist Republicans participate as equal members in public discourse and accept the responsibility that such participation entailed. Cumann na nGaedheal was confident in 1927 that these objectives could be accomplished. They were just as certain, however, that the ultimate political beneficiaries of these policies would be de Valéra and Fianna Fáil, not their own party. In treating the O'Higgins assassination as if it represented a sustained, dangerous conspiracy against the state, the Cosgrave government set the stage for the peaceful transfer of power to a political party more capable of symbolically integrating the Irish nation.

The response: Fianna Fáil enters the Dáil

Because this political crisis was created by the government, the burden of response fell upon those directly affected by the resulting legislation. Republican organizations like Sinn Féin could only condemn the three bills, reiterating their position that the Free State was illegitimate. But the fledgling Fianna Fáil Party found itself in a far more difficult situation, no longer able to move toward centrist politics at its own pace. In June 1927 (prior to O'Higgins's assassination), the party stood for election and, considering its young age, fared extemely well. Cumann na nGaedheal commanded forty-seven seats; Fianna Fáil gained forty-four. The Labour Party was third, with twenty-two seats. But when de Valéra led his deputies to the Dáil and the clerk insisted that they take the oath, the deputies returned to their headquarters, refusing to take their seats. With so many deputies refusing to sit in the Dáil, the long-standing political problem that Cumann na nGaedheal had faced since the Free State's formation was more acute than ever.

The Electoral Amendment Bill demanded that Fianna Fáil immediately take a stand concerning whether or not it would sit in the Dáil. As a party it was being forced to decide, sooner than it had desired, the extent to which it was willing to acknowledge publicly the legitimacy of Free State institutions. In early August 1927, less than a month after the assassination of O'Higgins, Fianna Fáil members met to determine their response.

Not surprisingly, the response was ambiguous: While acceding to the demands of the bill, they reasserted their Republican anti–Free State commitment. Nonetheless, they agreed to sit in the Dáil and, in so doing, ensured the government's political victory. At the close of this meeting, Fianna Fáil delegates issued a statement to the press. It is cited here in full, for it vividly reveals the party's political dilemma and the double talk necessary to save political face. The statement is as follows:

> The Fianna Fáil deputies have met and given careful consideration to the position of national emergency which has been created by the legislation now being pressed through the Free State Parliament. They recognise that this legislation may imperil the general peace and cause widespread suffering; that it disenfranchises, and precludes from engaging in any effective peaceful political movement towards independence, all Irish Republicans who will not acknowledge that any allegiance is due to the English Crown. Nevertheless, they have come unanimously to the decision that even, under these circumstances, it is not competent for them, as

pledged Republicans, and as elected representatives of the Republican section of the community, to transfer their allegiance.

It has, however, been repeatedly stated, and it is not uncommonly believed, that the required declaration is not an oath; that the signing of it implies no contractual obligation, and that it has no binding significance in conscience or in law; that, in short, it is merely an empty political formula which deputies could conscientiously sign without becoming involved, or without involving the nation, in obligations of loyalty to the English Crown.

The Fianna Fáil deputies would certainly not wish to have the feeling that they are allowing themselves to be debarred by nothing more than an empty formula from exercising their functions as public representatives, particularly at a moment like this. They intend, therefore, to present themselves at the Clerk's office of the Free State Dáil "for the purpose of complying with the provisions of Article 17 of the Constitution," by inscribing their names in the book kept for the purpose, among other signatures appended to the required formula. But, so that there may be no doubt as to their attitude, and no misunderstanding of their action, the Fianna Fáil deputies here give public notice in advance to the Irish people, and to all whom it may concern, they purpose [sic] to regard the declaration as an empty formality, and repeat that their only allegiance is to the Irish nation, and that it will be given to no other power or authority.[28]

This statement revealed the dilemma of the Fianna Fáil deputies in being forced to respond to the Government's legislative initiative. To enter the Dáil would be to acknowledge the legitimacy of the Free State; to take the oath would be to recognize the tie between the Free State and the English Crown. A decision to accede to the government's demand, in short, required that Fianna Fáil significantly recast its political positions to conform to the presence of the Free State's political institutions and Constitution. On the other hand, a decision to refuse Cosgrave's demands would probably have proven fatal to the fledgling party. First, had it decided not to enter the Dáil or to take the oath, it could have been treated as a seditious party under the terms of the new Public Safety Bill. Members of the party would have been subject to arrest or deportation. Second, since it had already split with Sinn Féin, a decision to refuse parliamentary participation would have made little political sense. The party would have been required to make such a fine distinction between the abstention of Sinn Féin and the coercive efforts of the Free State that its political terrain would have been very narrow indeed.

Fianna Fáil had little choice but to enter the Dáil. Given the political situation, it could only succumb to the Free State's pressure to publicly acknowledge its intention to enter the Dáil before standing for election. Fianna Fáil's "compromise" was an agreement to enter on the condition that such actions not be interpreted as an endorsement of those institutions or as an abdication of the party's commitment to an independent Ireland. Trying to minimize the symbolic import of its entry into the Free State, Fianna Fáil attempted to transform what had been, as Donal O'Sullivan put it, "a matter of high principle" – the oath of allegiance– into merely "an empty political formula."[29] Cosgrave's party was perfectly content with de Valéra's attempt to cling symbolically to his Republican roots as long as he brought the party into the Free State. Irrespective of the meaning given by de Valéra and other Fianna Fáil deputies of the act of entry, the fact of Fianna Fáil's acquiescence to Free State demands was unmistakable.

On August 12, 1927, de Valéra and forty-three other members of Fianna Fáil took their seats. They did so after signing the book, which indicated their having taken the oath. As de Valéra described the process:

> When we came to take this so-called oath I presented this document to the officer in charge and told him that that was our attitude – there were witnesses present for every word – that this was our attitude; that we are not prepared to take an oath. I am prepared to put my name down in this book in order to get permission to go into the Dáil, but it has no other significance.[30]

At first glance, de Valéra's redefinition appeared to be only a face-saving technique enabling his party to enter the Dáil without renouncing its abstentionist past. But this position toward the Free State – being in it but not of it – proved to be more than a response to the moment: Institutionalized ambivalence became the defining feature of Fianna Fáil's relationship to the Dáil for the next six years. Fianna Fáil deputies did not hesitate to speak of the Dáil as illegitimate. In March 1928, for example, Seán Lemass, a prominent Fianna Fáil deputy, spoke in the Dáil:

> Five years ago the methods we adopted were not the methods we have adopted now. Five years ago we were on the defensive, and perhaps in time we may recoup our strength sufficiently to go on the offensive. Our object is to establish a Republican Government in Ireland. If that can be done by the present methods we will be very pleased, but if not we would not confine ourselves to them.[31]

Even more dramatically, de Valéra addressed the Dáil in March 1929:

I still hold that our right to be regarded as the legitimate government is faulty. There must be somebody in charge to keep order in the community and by virtue of your de facto position you are the only people who are in a position to do that. But as to whether you have come by that position legitimately or not, I say that you have not come by that position legitimately. You brought off a coup d'état in the summer of 1922. . . . My proposition [to Sinn Féin] that the representatives of the people should come in here and unify control so that we would have one Government and one Army was defeated, and for that reason I resigned. Those who continued on in that organization which we have left can claim exactly the same continuity that we claimed up to 1925. They can do it. . . . There is no use in your blinding yourself to the fact that you are regarded here as simply continuing in another form of British authority, that you are the agents of British authority in this country, and any other Executive that gets into your position will have the same moral handicap, except they are able to get the acceptance of some common assembly.[32]

Some two years after Fianna Fáil entered the Dáil and only three years before they themselves assumed control of the government, the party continued to deny its complicity in the actions of the Free State government. In this way they, too, helped to sharpen a popular perception of the parliamentary institutions standing apart from their constituency, whereas political parties were seen to represent more closely various sectors of the community. For Republicans, still suspicious of the Free State but admiring de Valéra's clever use of its institutions, Fianna Fáil's continued ambivalence enabled a similar ambivalent participation by certain citizens. Without it, the political structures would have remained more fragile, and the domination of parliamentary politics would have proven more unlikely.

In the same way, Fianna Fáil's entry, however reluctant, enabled Cumann na nGaedheal to more effectively serve its natural constituency: those more well-to-do and conservative individuals who were quite content with Ireland's commonwealth status, fearful of de Valéra's move toward parliamentary politics, and culturally sympathetic to the staid and colorless handling of the ship of state by Cosgrave and his men. The creation of a more genuine two-party system meant that these more conservative groups rested easier with their own party. At the same time, Cumann na nGaedheal, while acting more decisively in their interests, was also ensuring that their days of political control were numbered. The process of political decline began, as I have described in some detail, prior to O'Higgins's assassination; the entry of Fianna Fáil in the Dáil greatly speeded this process up.

Electoral statistics illustrate this dual process whereby Cumann na nGaedheal continued to appeal to a limited number of electors while Fianna Fáil was bringing first-time voters into the political system. Whereas Fianna Fáil successfully mobilized new voters, Cumann na nGaedheal was unable to increase its share of the vote. In the June 1927 election, for example, Cumann na nGaedheal received 100,000 fewer voters than it had in the 1923 election.[33] Between the two elections, Cumann na nGaedheal's share of the vote declined by 4 percent.[34] The loss would have been even greater had it not been for the decline between 1927 and 1932 of the small interest-group parties, which redirected their support to Cumann na nGaedheal.

A worsening world depression and many years of continued rule would make any party less attractive with each passing year. But specific actions taken by the government surely hastened its decline. For example, just prior to the June 1927 election and just prior to his assassination, O'Higgins, on behalf of the government, worked extremely hard to push through the Dáil an Intoxicating Liquor Act aimed at limiting the number of public houses and the hours of their opening. Probably no single bill could have alienated so many Irishmen from O'Higgins's party. As F. S. L. Lyons comments, "To drive through Parliament on the eve of an election a measure that was certain to infuriate the drink trade seemed, even to some of O'Higgins' faithful supporters, not so much a vindication of principle as an exercise in masochism."[35]

In a similar vein, close to the election of 1932, when the party was finally defeated, Cosgrave persisted in attempting to reduce pay for school teachers and policemen. Further, seemingly to ensure its defeat, the government chose to prosecute de Valéra's paper, *The Irish Press*, for seditious libel. The government insisted, moreover, on prosecuting the paper in a military tribunal rather than an ordinary court. None of these measures sat well with those groups anxious to view the Free State as a progressive, a nationalist, and a politically integrative force.

After Fianna Fáil's entry into the Dáil, Cumann na nGaedheal, seemingly with more relish than before, continued to introduce measures designed to counter the persistent terrorist activity in Ireland. In each case, the power of the Executive Committee was strengthened, its further isolation from the body politic that much more certain. For example, in 1931, over the fierce objections of Fianna Fáil, the government got passed a Constitution (Amendment No. 17) Bill empowering a five-member military tribunal to deal with political crime, including punishment by death. The Executive Council could singlehandedly declare political groups unlawful by a simple order, and the police were granted still further powers of enforcement.

But no bill better represented Cumann na nGaedheal's headlong gallop into political decline than its insistence on introducing the Constitutional Bill to abolish the referendum and initiative. Since the bill had not been passed when it was first introduced because of the dissolution of the Dáil for elections, the government offered it again in June 1928, amid threats from Fianna Fáil to use those mechanisms to abolish the oath of allegiance. Cumann na nGaedheal insisted instead on ending the referendum and the initiative.

The debate over the bill in the Dáil had a familiar ring. De Valéra, arguing against the repeal effort, said:

> At the time [the drafting of the Constitution] it was a very different cry. That was the time when every citizen was told that if he were to be a good citizen at all he ought to consider these matters of community interest, and that it would be utter selfishness on his part if he were to confine himself to his own private business and not think of questions that affected his neighbor and the general good of the community. . . . They [the people] were taken in on every possible measure. It was intended to link them up so closely that the individual in the country would be getting the debates, I suppose, of the assembly in order to follow with intelligent interest the various debates and topics that were being discussed in connection with the general interest. But now, having got the people into the trap, different tactics are necessary in order to prevent the people from ever opening the trap and getting out of it.[36]

Fianna Fáil deputies charged the political rule was already too separate from the body politic. The government's effort to repeal the referendum, it was argued, was yet another attempt to keep decision making in the hands of the few. Deputy Flinn argued:

> If you pass this provision, you are passing into the hands of a Party majority in this house all power over the liberty of the people. Are you prepared to do that? If you destroy this, you destroy the means of large evolutionary change by which the liberty of this country can be attained. That is the issue for you now. That is the issue for every man in the country. Either you are going to hold control and keep it in the hands of the people, continuous control over the Dáil, or you are going to take it away from them.[37]

The government's response was no less predictable. Once again stating that the interests of the state had primacy over the Constitution, Deputy Fitzgerald defended the repeal effort:

> I am satisfied above all things that an alien government is better than no government. I suggest that any form of democracy that is imposed or is accepted in any country is imposed as a test. And the test is: Does it unfailingly provide that there shall be a government to order the affairs of the country? If it meets the test then it is bound to stand for a time.... [The referendum] is pre-eminently a machine that could be used for the negation and for the destruction of government and as such has tremendous potentialities for bad in it.[38]

When the bill to repeal the referendum was passed, Cosgrave, hardly concerned about its public reception, stated in the Dáil that it was necessary for the immediate preservation of public peace and safety as provided by the Constitution; therefore, there would be no referendum on the bill to repeal the referendum.[39] With Fianna Fáil in the Dáil, however, the consequences of Cumann na nGaedheal's move toward still more centralized and isolated rule was clearly different from before. The party, rather than the Free State, became the object of opprobrium; it was identified as the party opposed to popular expression and participatory democracy.

This was just one more example of the ruling party's disregard for popular perception. Unmistakably, once it had engineered Fianna Fáil's entry to the Dáil, it had abandoned any pretense to popular rule and sought to secure, at all political costs, political structures capable of resisting the most strident attack. The problem of political integration– whereby those opposed to the Free State and those ambivalent and tepid in their commitment would come to identify with the purposes of the Free State – fell upon Fianna Fáil. The party's role as the agency for political integration of the Irish community, whereby the various traditions of Irish culture and politics would emerge as a basis of moral support for democratic structures, will be the focus of the next chapter.

Part III. The Character of Irish Democracy

7. The Democratic Achievement in Ireland: The Reconciliation of Culture and Politics

Introduction: the Irish public and its problem

In the past four chapters, attention was directed to the political institutions, with little emphasis on the fractious and fragile character of the Irish public. The Civil War and the persisting debate over the meaning of the Anglo-Irish Treaty, it has been argued, ensured at best a weak public sphere incapable of generating a moral consensus on the role and aims of the state and its relations with other nations. The result was the one-sided achievement of the Cosgrave government; institutional efficacy was secured through the successful manipulation and enhancement of its resources, but political integration did not result.

Given its commitment to strengthen the democratic institutions, Cumann na nGaedheal was unable, at the same time, to strengthen popular identification with the policies and purposes of the state. At its most efficacious, the government was capable only of demanding political participation by the opposition; it could not create the integration necessary for stability to be secured. Although Cumann na nGaedheal could demand – because of the now enhanced resources of the state – a functioning party system, it could not create a party able to end the political and cultural rifts in the nation. As I have suggested, Cumann na nGaedheal's was no modest accomplishment. Nevertheless, if more substantive political integration was to be achieved and a more integrated public produced, Fianna Fáil would have to accomplish it.

The public realm was surely stronger in 1927 than it had been in 1922. That area of debate and discourse, in which members of the community participated and agreed to be influenced by other members, was functioning more effectively as a result of the demonstrated strength of the Free State institutions. The formation of Fianna Fáil and its ambivalence – rather than its out-and-out refusal – about entering the Dáil even before the government made it a condition of election is evidence of the public's newfound capacity to constrain and moderate political action and discourse. Fianna Fáil, predictably, opted to conform to the institutional realities.

Nevertheless, as I shall indicate in the following discussion, the public as an institution in Irish life was hardly a healthy one. Thus far, I have treated the public only as the setting in which the new political institutions had to operate to secure stability. In this chapter, the analysis will shift to the ways in which the political structures had to accommodate to the unique features of the national community in order to achieve a democratically integrated public sphere. The public had to become much more successful in constraining extremist politics and much more vigorous in enhancing broad-based participation in and popular identification with Irish democracy. Because of the government's failure to produce a strong public sphere where discourse was active and the parameters of debate were accepted – where the reality of the political apparatus was presumed – Ireland's democratic achievement was not yet secure.

In this section, I will indicate some of the features of the Irish public during the last years of the 1920s and into the 1930s that made this stability still precarious. The fundamental problem facing the Free State was that of inclusion; a substantial sector of the political community continued to feel apart from the democratic political process. Inclusion, it should be clear, does not mean that all members of the political community support the actions of the state. But it does mean that citizens agree to abide by the terms of the debate over issues, to orient their activity – in attempting to influence policy – toward the state structures, and to acquiesce, however reluctantly, in the decisions of the political leaders.[1] Although Irish citizens were equal in a formal-legal sense, there was no universal identification with the political institutions.

Political parties typically serve as the central vehicles by which formal membership is translated into substantive identification. But in the Irish case, for reasons I have indicated, the political parties had largely failed to promote this connection within the polity and the institutions of political rule. Parties represent, of course, more than an expression of specific interest groups; when institutionalized, they indicate a pattern of social solidarity whereby their members identify their own interests within a scheme of competing and contesting interests. In fact, the identification of interest, or specific interests, cannot occur independently of this process of cultural mapping that occurs through contending political parties. As Parsons has argued, membership in a political party is a cultural as well as a utilitarian statement: a statement of irrational, transfamilial attachments to symbolic commitments and goals in addition to a belief in a party as a national means to given political ends.[2] This is an important reason why party identification often remains constant across generations; in spite of changing locations in the social structure, individuals continue to identify culturally with a given party.

Political parties represent a central conduit between the political institutions and the public; a weak party system and low voter participation, for example, may each indicate the fragility of a democratic public. In Ireland, the sense of membership in the political community was hardly concomitant with the legal status of each citizen. Moreover, the weakness of the party system, as an agent of democratic integration, was evidence of the Cosgrave government's inability to promote stronger patterns of political integration. Because this identification problem cut across regional, class, and political lines, the legitimacy of the state in 1927 was still insecure. This problem of malintegration in the political community had to be solved by Fianna Fáil if democratic stability was to become secure in the Free State.

The persistence of political extremism

There is no more striking evidence of the weakness of the Irish public than the continued vitality of both the IRA and Sinn Féin. In the last chapter, I indicated that the efficacy of the state structures reduced the strength of the IRA and the capacity of Sinn Féin to offer a compelling political alternative to the Free State. There is no question that their super-Republican voices, although still strident, were on the defensive in the latter part of the 1920s. The "Third" Sinn Féin Party certainly lost political support with the formation of Fianna Fáil. The election of 1927 was clearly a watershed; although Fianna Fáil secured forty-four seats – even before deciding to enter the Dáil – Sinn Féin won only five seats. De Valéra's decision to leave Sinn Féin and the creation of Fianna Fáil were but the final nails in the former party's political coffin.

Nevertheless, despite their political weakness, antigovernment forces continued to make their presence known. Their continued voice in Ireland revealed the endurance of an ideology still at odds with and inimical to democratic structures. Standing as staunch opponents of the Free State, the endurance of the IRA and Sinn Féin revealed the failure of moderate discourse to fully constrain and transform the terms of debate to conform to the dictates of a democratic community. Their absolutist commitment to means that, by definition, were inimical to the Free State and the Anglo-Irish Treaty precluded their participation, with citizens of equal standing, in the political community. Further their opposition to any kind of politics of reform demonstrated that the cultural-cum-political divisions that first surfaced clearly in the Civil War continued to persist well into the decade. "Politics," as Tom Garvin succinctly put it, remained largely "divorced from government."[3]

Standing outside of the democratic public, Republicans seized upon diverse issues – persistent ones concerning the Treaty and partition, as well as economic and social problems besetting the nation – and presented them each as functions of the illegitimate political apparatus. By articulating the problems in this way, they sought, often successfully, to elevate those issues to their most general and divisive level. Solutions were to be found not in politics of reform but, rather, in the creation of a whole new order.

For example, the Irish economy in the latter 1920s was suffering badly. Whereas the economic debate within the government centered on a policy of protectionism versus free trade – a debate rather narrowly circumscribed – Republicans insisted on viewing the weak economy as a sign of the failure to create the Republic and of the Free State's embrace of capitalism – a further indication of the government's moral bankruptcy. Peadar O'Donnell offered a compelling argument to encourage Western farmers to withhold land annuity payments as a protest against both economic hard times and, more importantly, political oppression.[4] In continually rejecting the given political and economic arrangements and refusing to recognize the power and authority of the state, these challenges prevented the public from flourishing as a democratic forum. Extremism continued as a feature of debate and discourse, reinforcing a long-standing pattern of Irish political life. Discussion continued to focus, at least to a degree, upon either support for the system or opposition to it.

It is unclear to what extent this ideological debate dissuaded the less politicized Irishmen from participating in political life. Yet it is surely true that that kind of discourse made public participation far more dangerous. The risk of immediately being thrust into one of two polarized camps – supporters or opponents of the government – meant that the ambivalent participant commonly chose not to get involved. The result was a generally low rate of political participation in those areas where Sinn Féin and the IRA were strong, a point to which I will return shortly.

But it was not only ideological argument that dissuaded the average Irishman from participating in civic life. It was also the continued, although sporadic, actions of personal intimidation and random violence by Republicans. A new, radical antigovernment group, Comhairle na

Poblachta (Central Council of the Republic), formed in late 1928 and 1929, was committed to the overthrow of the Free State. Together with the continued military drilling by Republican forces and the persistent outbreaks of shootings, this development reveals the sustained vitality of these antidemocratic orientations.

But no single pattern of opposition undermined the integrity of the public more than the IRA's threats to juries sitting in judgment on IRA members. There is perhaps no greater threat to democratic public participation than the perception that the law is incapable of administering justice fairly. The IRA's action against the legal system, together with its other actions of violence and terror, meant that the public was incapable of protecting itself against its detractors. And although the government passed the Juries Protections Act in 1929, in an effort to solve this problem, people hardly felt secure in exercising these basic democratic rights.

Moreover, with its now institutionalized ambivalence and its desire to maintain its links to its Republican legacy, Fianna Fáil vigorously opposed such legislation. In fact, despite continued Republican maneuvers, shootings, and other acts of terror, Fianna Fáil, as the opposition party, nonetheless attempted to block each subsequent government effort to impose greater measures of public safety. In June 1931, the Republicans and members of Fianna Fáil marched together in the annual memorial pilgrimage to the grave of Wolfe Tone.[5]

This political tension between Cumann na nGaedheal and Fianna Fáil is further evidence of the unhappy situation in which the government party found itself. Each passage of yet another draconian public safety act, although considered necessary – within the logic of effective rule – to secure a democratic public, was typically viewed as further confirmation of the government's alienation from the Irish nation. In declaring illegal all of these extremist organizations and thereby enabling them to be treated as traitors to Ireland, the government became increasingly isolated from the body politic. Again, the task was to fall upon Fianna Fáil to span the divide – to preserve the political institutions and enhance the functioning of the public while simultaneously maintaining its own identification with the Irish people rather than opposing them.

Political parties and their political isolation

The continued vitality of the oppositional Republican groups, despite their small size, was not the only indicator of the weakness of the democratic public. Prior to the entry of Fianna Fáil into Dáil politics, many

Irish citizens – particularly in the West and in rural areas – did not vote. In the 1922 "electoral pact" election, fewer than 50 percent of the eligible voters cast their ballot.[6] The voter turnout in the 1923 election was no more than 60 percent in any part of the country; in the Western peripheral region, less than 56 percent of the electorate voted.[7]

This low voter turnout is especially significant because of the highly politicized nature of Irish life prior to these elections and the nearly universal politicization of Irish men and women during the Civil War. Therefore, it cannot be attributed to an apolitical population; rather, it represented a combination of disinterest and distrust of the new institutions. Further, it revealed the failure, thus far, of a party system to integrate the diverse population within the Free State.

As I have suggested, low voter turnout might be explained by the highly charged political atmosphere in the countryside, where the Republican opposition remained a strong vocal presence. Aggregate electoral data cannot sufficiently capture the inhibiting role that Sinn Féin and the IRA may have played in discouraging popular participation in Free State politics. There is, however, a gross correlation between voter turnout and the success of Republican candidates. The Western periphery, as Garvin indicates, was distinguished not only by the lowest voter turnout in the 1923 election but also by the strongest support for Sinn Féin candidates.[8]

But the Republican presence is but one – and perhaps not the most important – factor that helps account for the low level of political participation early in the Free State's history. Low voter turnout was also a function of the social characteristics of the political elite and the orientation and commitments of the national parties.

First, as Tom Garvin suggests, although the Treaty issue animated the Irish population prior to and during the Civil War, national questions became less important once political order was restored.[9] Yet it was that question that continued to inspire and preoccupy the national elites – both in Sinn Féin and in Cumann na nGaedheal – whose main concern continued to be the Irish nation vis-à-vis the Treaty and the British government. The political elite's interests were hardly congruent with the more mundane ones of the Irish population, who, after the Civil War, increasingly turned to the bread-and-butter issues of economic survival.

This split between the leaders and the led can be seen in two different ways. First, the national political elite were disproportionately represented by men who were cosmopolitan in outlook and professional in occupation – lawyers, civil servants, journalists. They were cosmopolitan in the sense that they recognized a larger economic, political, and social order in which the issues that were affecting any given locality were first viewed in connection to a broader national, even international, order. Thus, the larger farmers and graziers, shopkeepers and urban people, as well as skilled artisans, tended to hold this broader perspective, whereas unskilled laborers and small farmers, particularly those in the more insulated West, tended to have a more local orientation.[10] Nevertheless, the political elite – even those in charge of Sinn Féin – tended to be disproportionately professional and cosmopolitan, whereas their support largely emanated, in the case of Sinn Féin, from the more parochial members of the nation.[11] This distinction between leaders and followers had already produced, as described in a previous chapter, a conflict within Sinn Féin itself. When, prior to independence, landless Irishmen attempted to seize land and when small landholders attempted to withhold land annuities in the name of the Republic, Sinn Féin leaders counseled restraint in the interest of the greater good served by a unified nationalist movement.

A second way in which this tension can be seen is by noting how, in the early years of the Free State, individuals were elected to the Dáil by virtue of their relationship to the nationalist movement, not because of their commitment to a given local constituency.[12] The Civil War and the Treaty debate created for only a short time a heightened nationalist consciousness and the reflection of that concern in the government leaders. When political stability returned, the Free State parties did not seem to be either particularly relevant to or especially concerned with the everyday concerns of the Irish population. Especially for those Irish men and women who identified their world largely in terms of their specific land, town, or village, these nonlocal politicians enhanced the estrangement between nation and government.

The inclusion problem was heightened in the first years of the Free State's existence because the party system that emerged reinforced a feeling, especially in the more provincial sectors, that no political party shared their political commitments and cultural orientations. Because of its own alienation from Dublin politics, Sinn Féin, in certain respects and when compared to other Free State parties, paralleled the countrysiders' own perception of their tenuous relationship to national politics. But if there was some cultural compatibility between Sinn Féin and Western and rural life, the former's insurgency politics hardly appealed to the average staid, hard-working, law-abiding Catholic family man and woman of the countryside.

This is one of the more perplexing features of Irish politics. The Kepublican parties could not command a sizable following; the vast majority of the Irish population rejected their tactics. Nevertheless, many of these same people refused to support the Free State parties' efforts to rid Ireland of its Republicans. If one interprets politics solely as a process of interest maximization, one cannot understand the tepid popular support for the public safety bills passed by the Cosgrave government, the insistence by Fianna Fáil that the government's anti-Republican measures were unconstitutional, and the voters' refusal to endorse Cumann na nGaedheal despite its success in restoring social order. The reason for this popular response to the Free State does not lie in the realm of interest politics; rather, it demonstrates the centrality of cultural politics in the Free State. Neither Cumann na nGaedheal nor the Labour Party shared the same cultural universe as most Irish men and women; the government party's anti-Republican policies produced a cultural unease that Fianna Fáil was able to exploit.

Cumann na nGaedheal was supported predominantly by business leaders, prosperous farmers, and the Catholic Church.[13] The party leaders' early hope for a broad-based constituency quickly dimmed. Michael Collins's death reduced the party's influence on members of the IRB. Moreover, the party had the liability of being the ruling party, thereby alienating some supporters in the normal business of rule. For many reasons, the party was incapable of broadening its base of support; although the decade was marked, as I will describe, by substantial success in mobilizing new voters, Cumann na nGaedheal hardly benefited. In 1932, as Garvin reports, the party's share of the total poll declined by 4 percent.[14] As its constituency declined, the party's role in representing this smaller, more elite sector became more apparent and more marked. Each political crisis had resulted in some disaffection within the party's ranks; by the end of the decade, it had been forced to embrace openly those constituents whom the party's detractors had long accused Cumann na nGaedheal of exclusively serving – namely, ex-Unionists, conservative large farmers, and urban sectors.

More importantly, Cumann na nGaedheal openly presented itself as the embodiment of bourgeois decorum and respectability, self-consciously distancing itself from the "riffraff" of Republicans and, for that matter, Labourites.[15] Both its politics and its image ensured that although it was widely viewed as the ruling party, successful in securing order, it was not perceived as being at the center of the Irish cultural experience. Although the party, in the many ways I have described, moved well beyond a purely Irish-Enlightenment political-cultural orientation in its efforts to incorporate all of the population, it could not shake the popular perception that it was not truly Gaelic-Romantic; indeed, it was perceived as being opposed to those sentiments.

It is this staid Anglo-Irish image of Cumann na nGaedheal that explains why many Irish men and women decried Irish Republican violence while objecting to the repressive government public safety acts. Opposition to the government emanated from a feeling that Cumann na nGaedheal was incapable of or unwilling to comprehend the spirit of Republican terror; because of its insensitivity to nationalist impulses – however despicable their manifestation – no repressive measure by the government could be condoned.

The Republicans were culturally applauded (or, at least, understood) and politically condemned by the public. The political community was capable of holding both views simultaneously. The government was treated less kindly. Cumann na nGaedheal's cultural commitments were distrusted, thereby making all its political actions suspect. However irrational the sentiment, the continued presence of Cumann na nGaedheal as the sole political party willing and able to command power in the Free State (prior to Fianna Fáil) ensured that many people would not participate in the democratic process.

The Labour Party, as the major opposition party in the Dáil, also failed to command support or identification from disaffected voters. The party received its support not from the urban regions, as might be expected, but from the Eastern/Midland regions where commercial farming was strong, that is, where there was a sizable population of landless agricultural laborers and where agriculturally dependent towns were predominant.[16] Those who failed to identify with Cumann na nGaedheal because of a sense of cultural estrangement did not, as a result, support the Labour Party. This was in spite of the fact that the Labour Party always sought to treat national issues as secondary to pressing economic and social problems that directly affected the population.[17]

The party's failure to benefit from the weaknesses of Cumann na nGaedheal derived from the fact that it was perceived as occupying the same cultural terrain. Its failure to make the Treaty an object of controversy was interpreted as a sign of its weak nationalist commitments; it confirmed the sense that the Labour Party was a "modern," secular, rationalist party that identified more strongly with the British working class than with the Irish countryman. Although its policies were clearly different from Cumann na nGaedheal's, its ultimate political convictions, it was believed, were substantially the same. The party's selection of a Protestant spokesman further confirmed its cosmopolitan predilection and separated it more sharply from the average Irish man and woman.[18]

The major political parties, then, failed to serve as the vehicles of public cultural identification with the political institutions. Cumann na nGaedheal and the Labour Party were both viewed as operating in a cultural world incompatible with or incomprehensible to certain disaffected groups. While they had integrated like-minded cosmopolitan factions, substantial segments of provincial Irishmen – those located principally in the Western and rural areas – were unable to see in the Free State anything more than continued foreign rule. In terms of its organization, its central objectives, and those elected to serve, the Free State appeared to be essentially Irish-Enlightenment in vision and in composition. For the same reasons, the view from the countryside was that the Free State was not sufficiently nationalist, Catholic, or agricultural.

The leaders of neither Cumann na nGaedheal nor the Labour Party tried to define the state as anything more than an autonomous institution promoting the interests of individual citizens. The government had no purpose of its own; it held no transcendent mission. Instead, its task was merely to secure the structures of rule necessary to protect the interests of the individual. And despite its efforts to encourage universal political participation and its genuine concern for various groups, it was unable to shake off its Irish-Enlightenment "odor." Because it did not espouse the language of Irish nationalism and because it could not wrap itself around the symbols associated with the Irish nationalist movement – for reasons the last several chapters have made clear – it was unable to integrate within the state, in any but a formal way, the groups who continued to hold Gaelic-Romantic sentiments.

Among these groups, there was still the perceived need to resist the inexorable process of modernity; to protect or seek the reestablishment of the small, agricultural, rural character of Irish life; to distance the nation culturally from British Anglican influence; and to place the family and Catholicism at the heart of the national ethos. Although perhaps rejecting the political and military tactics of Sinn Féin and the IRA, they could not identify with a state from which they felt culturally estranged. It was precisely the modernity of the two major parties that prevented the Gaelic-Romantic impulses from being expressed politically. And it was exactly this fact that ensured the continued insecurity of the democratic order.

Fianna Fáil and the public: the reconciliation of culture and politics

The formation of Fianna Fáil in late 1926, and its standing for election twice in 1927 and in 1932, is a crucial political feature of postindependent

Ireland. In terms of its consequences for the public, no other political event proved more important in securing democratic stability in Ireland. The election of 1932, which produced the first transfer of power between parties in the Free State, has frequently been identified as the most important political demonstration of the success of Irish democracy.[19] Yet, although that event revealed the strength of the institutional structures, the transition probably would not have occurred peacefully had the public sphere not become revitalized prior to 1932; that development was, in part, a result of the birth of Fianna Fáil. Had the party not successfully bridged the two political-cultural worlds – the world of cosmopolitan, secular, democratic institutions and the world of romantic, traditional, and religious commitments – the political situation in 1932 probably would have been very different, and certainly less sanguine.

In terms of the long-term course of Irish democracy, nothing compares in importance to the birth of Fianna Fáil. Since 1932, Fianna Fáil has dominated Irish political life. As Tom Garvin wrote in 1981, characterizing the strength of the party:

> In the forty-nine years since 1932, the party has held office, usually on its own, for a total of nearly forty years, including two periods of continued effective monopoly or near monopoly of governmental power totalling sixteen years each. Non–Fianna Fáil governments have never acquired the air of permanence and "right-to-rule" that Fianna Fáil has managed to assume; no other party has succeeded in assimilating its party symbols so closely to the symbols of the state itself; no other party has managed to acquire a clientele at once so heterogeneous and so apparently undivided as has de Valéra's party; no other party has managed to acquire control over so many bureaucratic, commercial and cultural centres of influence and patronage, the influence networks of Fine Gael [Cumann na nGaedheal] being narrower and apparently concentrated in other institutions. Above all, Fianna Fáil overshadows both the old pro-Treaty party and the Labour party electorally.[20]

It is clear that Fianna Fáil's achievement cannot be conceived in narrowly political terms. As Garvin argues as well, Fianna Fáil resonated with an Irish cultural self-conception with which no other political party could compete.[21] The following sections will identify the political-cultural meaning of Fianna Fáil in its early years, which helped establish it as the preeminent political force in the Irish nation.

The elections of 1927 and 1932 reveal the political impact of Fianna Fáil's entry into parliamentary politics. Fianna Fáil substantially mobi-

Table 1. *Percentage of voters, by region, 1923–32 (in %)*

Year	Total	Center	East of Midlands	Western periphery	Border periphery
1923	58.7	60.0	60.3	55.4	60.0
1927 (1)	66.5	65.5	67.7	64.2	65.0
1927 (2)	67.9	67.3	69.1	66.8	65.7
1932	75.4	70.3	76.8	74.8	76.9

Note: The regions represent the following areas of Ireland: center: Dublin City and County, Laoire County Borough; east of Midlands: rest of Leinster except Louth, and Munster except Clare and Kerry; Western periphery: Connacht, plus Clare and Kerry; border periphery: the Ulster counties, plus Louth. Both the Western and Border peripheries were defined by the size of the farm; peripheral regions consisted of farms averaging 50 acres or less in 1936. The border periphery, in addition, was contiguous with the border of Northern Ireland, making partition a more volatile and central issue. In addition, a significantly larger number of Protestants lived in this area.
Source: Adapted from Garvin (1977): 173.

lized the Irish electorate. Garvin reports that voter turnout increased approximately 10 percent throughout the country between 1923 and 1927; by 1932, voter turnout had increased from approximately 60 percent (in 1923) to 76 percent.[22] A genuinely greater competitive party system, in short, promoted greater interest and participation in the electoral process. Between 1923 and 1932, the number of voters increased by 220,000, with 1,750,000 eligible to vote.[23]

Significantly, Fianna Fáil's entry into politics promoted participation by precisely those groups who, up to then, had refused to identify with Free State politics. The party gained in political strength because of its disproportionate attraction, at the outset, to the poorer, less Anglicized, and peripheral sectors of the nation.[24] Fianna Fáil not only brought into the political process a sizable segment of the population, but was also heavily beholden to those that had refused to participate during the first several years of the Free State.

As Garvin argues, the ascendance of Fianna Fáil represented, in addition, the increasing centrality of the rural, Western, non-Anglican Irish men and women in Irish political life; the political center was being overtaken by the peripheral sectors of the country.[25] With that development, the Free State institutions, which had previously possessed a powerful Irish-Enlightenment cast, adopting forms straight out of the Westminster mold, now took on a distinctly Irish, that is, Gaelic-Romantic, flavor. For the first time, the Free State emerged as a protector

Table 2. *Republican/Fianna Fáil support by region, 1923–32 (in %)*

Year	Total	Center vote for Fianna Fáil	Periphery vote for Fianna Fáil	Difference between center and periphery: Fianna Fáil votes
1923	27	17	39	+22
1927 (1)	26	24	33	+ 9
1927 (2)	35	27	45	+18
1932	44	34	55	+21

Note: The regions represent the following areas of Ireland: center: Dublin and Dun Laoire constituencies; periphery: counties a majority of whose farms were under 30 acres in 1936, excluding border counties (except Leitrim, and Connacht County).
Source: Adapted from Garvin (unpublished): 8.

of a strong Irish public distinguished by its reconciliation of Irish-Enlightenment forms and Gaelic-Romantic sentiments.

In short, by the time Fianna Fáil had gained control of the government in 1932, it was well on its way to solving the cultural problem that had plagued Cumann na nGaedheal. In so doing, it not only produced a stronger public more capable of protecting the democratic institutions, but it also laid the groundwork for the restructuring of the political institutions to conform more closely to a democratic public – now more broadly inclusive – and its particular cultural understandings. Just as Cumann na nGaedheal laid the institutional foundations for a cultural reconciliation, Fianna Fáil offered the substantive terms for that reconciliation. De Valéra's party, in walking the line between Republicanism and parliamentarianism and in attempting to establish its own relation to those traditions, succeeded in charting a political course with which these disaffected sectors could identify.

The party's political success cannot be divorced from its cultural one: Through unique political forms, Fianna Fáil accomplished a cultural integration whereby Gaelic-Romantic and Irish-Enlightenment beliefs both appeared compatible with Free State politics. Fianna Fáil's ultimate accomplishment was its ability to convince previously disaffected groups that the party's role in the Free State was neither a hypocritical pandering for power at the expense of integrity nor an abandonment of its commitment to an Irish Republic. Rather, by walking gingerly between Republican conceptions and Free State institutions, the party proved to this population that the democratic structures could represent, via Fianna Fáil, their interests as well. In that achievement, Fianna Fáil assured a public broader in social composition, no significant sector of which felt disaffected. Moreover, as the party gained increasing dominance over the nation's political life, it helped to define, through the public, the predominant cultural character of Irish political life.

The hybrid cultural amalgam that Fianna Fáil forged and that was supported by a majority of the population came to define the special character of Irish democracy and political life. Thus, while preserving the democratic institutions, Fianna Fáil helped change the character of political life to reflect its uniquely Irish features – in general, a hybrid of Irish-Enlightenment forms and Gaelic-Romantic principles.

This process of cultural integration and Fianna Fáil's role in it cannot be examined simply from one angle. In Chapter 2, where I discussed the cultural schisms in the nation, emphasis was placed upon the ideological debates around which those divisions turned. Before the creation of the state or contending party systems, cultural divisions were expressed only through ideological discourse; and, in that sense, I characterized the Civil War as precisely such a battle over contending ideologies. Yet in the years following the Civil War – those years considered in the subsequent chapters – political life was certainly more than ideological debate. Politics, and with it various patterns of cultural expression, became institutionalized, or embedded, in the everyday practices and structures of social life.

To explore and detail Fianna Fáil's cultural accomplishment, it is necessary first to appreciate that cultural integration via the public, when it occurs, occurs in ways more diffuse and subtle than through debates over the meaning and purposes of the nation, although these remain an important dimension as well.[26] But Fianna Fáil's accomplishment was not only a change of the terms of discourse to bring in a wider segment of the Irish population. It was also a change in the character of relationships, via the party, between members of the public to correspond more closely to Gaelic-Romantic conceptions. Further, the party transformed the character of political exchange to resemble more closely traditional patterns of political life. In the following discussion, I will examine the integrative achievement in terms of political doctrine and the new forms of political organization that Fianna Fáil introduced to Irish parliamentary politics. It should be said that the available evidence is only suggestive; definitive demonstration of the relationship between these features of the party and cultural integration requires a more local, contextual investigation of the party and its supporters. But the evidence presented lends support to the argument that Fianna Fáil played a significant cultural role in Irish Free State politics.

Political doctrine and cultural integration

As I have suggested, doctrinal differences between political parties reflect more than rational alternatives to public policy. More is implied in these presentations of party platforms than the simple articulation of reasonable differences, held by rational men and women, on various issues affecting public welfare. To be sure, political debates – both narrowly and more broadly defined – possess an instrumental core; adherents to any given policy believe in its inherent rationality and rightness. The conviction is that one policy, rather than another, is the best means to achieve given ends and that personal interests will be best served by this policy. But this instrumental dimension of political debate is not the only one. Doctrinal differences, reflected in policy positions, also typically stand as cultural codes whereby one's attitude toward a given policy or political orientation is compatible with the more subtle understanding of the commitments, purposes, and goals of social life. These codes convey a certain common understanding of the character of the nation and its people; political differences often denote important cultural differences.

Fianna Fáil's success can be attributed, in part, to its ability to embody in its leadership and articulate in its program a cultural-political orientation with which previously disaffected groups could now identify. It is instructive to note that the policies adopted by the new party were not entirely novel: As previously described, the decade had already witnessed a number of small parties, breakaways from the parliamentary parties and critical of Cumann na nGaedheal, which were unable to gain a popular following. This occurred despite the fact that the issues raised – the boundary question, the Irish dependence on the British economy, land annuities, and so on – were those that caused the people to rally behind Fianna Fáil. Thus, Fianna Fáil's success in mobilizing a population resistant to Free State politics is hardly a case of being at the right place at the right time or capitalizing on issues waiting to be seized upon.

Rather, Fianna Fáil, with de Valéra as its leader, emerged almost at its inception as the necessary counterbalance to the preponderant Irish-Enlightenment orientation of Cumann na nGaedheal. Emerging from Republican rather than Free State ranks, and expressing the ambivalence toward the parliamentary structures felt by many who still supported Gaelic-Romantic principles, Fianna Fáil allowed the new political institutions to serve as a vehicle for a new pattern of cultural integration based upon Free State structures. Fianna Fáil's political successes, appealing disproportionately at first to those disaffected sectors, also signified the strengthening of that civic realm where cultural differences were now expressed and understood as political alternatives and where debate and discourse were constrained by the common acceptance of parliamentary rule.

This attainment of cultural integration through a stronger public sphere, of course, was not entirely a self-conscious one. It grew out of specific decisions made by the party leaders in their desire to create a party capable of wresting political power away from Cumann na nGaedheal. The formation of the party began in Sinn Féin, led by those who were increasingly frustrated by the party's abstentionist politics. In pressing for an abandonment of that program, the soon-to-be Fianna Fáilers offered an assessment of why Sinn Féin was becoming increasingly impotent as a political force. Seán Lemass, in particular, one of the founders of Fianna Fáil, became sharply critical of Sinn Féin. Once the split occurred, Lemass sought to base Fianna Fáil on different principles. He claimed, first, that Sinn Féin's idealism – in adhering to the principles of the Republic, of unification, and of an end to the Treaty – prevented the party from acting as an effective political force. He wrote:

> We must free ourselves of all the tags and tatters, the remnants of a brighter past that now serve only to bind our arms and deny us freedom of action. We must forget all the petty conceits and formulae which bedeck us, like rouge on the face of a corpse, and face the facts, the hard facts which we must overcome. . . . There are some who would have us sit by the roadside and debate abstruse points about a *de jure* this and a *de facto* that, but the reality we want is away in the distance . . . and we cannot get there unless we move.[27]

In addition to the party's abstract concerns – which commanded less and less popular interest as the decade progressed – Lemass was critical of Sinn Féin for failing to make specific overtures to those who remained politically apathetic. Recognizing that participation in the Free State was low, Lemass believed that an effective political party could mobilize those groups that had refused to become involved. "Teach them that National Independence means real concrete advantages for the common people and not merely an idealists' paradise, and they will be with us," Lemass wrote.[28] Lemass asked that Sinn Féin become a down-to-earth political party. Rather than standing as a moral witness critical of worldly politics, Sinn Féin should identify itself with the concerns of the common people and, in representing the interests of these disaffected elements, enter the political fray.

Sinn Féin's refusal to abandon its abstentionist policies and its adherence to idealistic politics resulted in the formation of Fianna Fáil. Lemass's critique of Sinn Féin became the basis of the new party: Fianna Fáil was to be practical and was to speak to those people who had thus far been silent in Free State politics.

The new party had many advantages, not the least of which was the charismatic de Valéra at its helm. It also enjoyed a ready-made organizational infrastructure, since many of the local branches of Sinn Féin simply shifted their allegiance to Fianna Fáil. As Peter Pyne notes, between March and April 1926 – the time of Fianna Fáil's founding – the local branches of Sinn Féin declined from 275 to 173, with most becoming Fianna Fáil branches. Seventeen of the thirty-seven Standing Committee members of Sinn Féin resigned, and twenty-one of the forty-seven Sinn Féin TDs (Dáil representatives) left the party and joined Fianna Fáil.[29]

Important as these personal and organizational features were in paving the way for electoral success, the party still had to appeal to the population in a way that would transform their political lethargy and/ or parliamentary ambivalence into active political support for the party. Despite the party's resources, this was no easy accomplishment. Their task was, first, to distance themselves politically from the Republican terrorists while demonstrating their sympathy for the nationalist cause and, second, to assert their respect for the parliamentary institutions without capitulating entirely to an establishment position. If spokesmen for Fianna Fáil appeared to be talking out of both sides of their mouth, this was as much a consequence of the tensions within the Irish political community as it was an expression of a more calculating political opportunism.

Largely through its political rhetoric, Fianna Fáil succeeded in convincing the Irish population – first, the disaffected and, later, the converts from other political parties – that they were the genuine voice of a nationalist Ireland. Distinguishing themselves from the Irish-Enlightenment orientation of Cumann na nGaedheal by invoking the romantic images of Gaelic Ireland as the goals of political life, Fianna Fáil succeeded in portraying itself as the inheritor of the revolutionary legacy of Irish nationalism. For those who felt alienated from the Free State institutions because they seemed to operate according to different principles and for different ends, Fianna Fáil came to be viewed as an expression of their convictions, thereby making political participation possible.

A comparison of Fianna Fáil's and Cumann na nGaedheal's political doctrine – both in tone and in substance – reveals two very different appeals. Cumann na nGaedheal defended itself and its political record in a rather uninspired way. In the 1923 election following the Civil War, it presented itself as the party of peace and order, promising "the restoration of National Unity, National Life in security, National prosperity in ordered law and society, and National credit well founded in honor and social and economic stability." It claimed to "have saved the country from anarchy."[30]

Themes struck in the party's first political campaign became the motif in each subsequent campaign. Theirs was the party of order and security, of temperateness and frugality, of reason and rationality. Prior to the June 1927 election, for example, President Cosgrave, speaking to a gathering in his home district of Kilkenny, characterized his regime as follows:

> We have done our part in giving you institutions capable of building up the country in a sound economic way. There are great possibilities for material prosperity in the work that we have done. There is security with the peace and order that we have established, and we look to you to maintain that ordered government without which material prosperity would be impossible.[31]

Resting upon its past accomplishments and, even more importantly, limiting the role of the Irish state in national affairs, Cumann na nGaedheal expressed through its political campaigns and doctrinal pronouncements an Irish-Enlightenment concern for the nation. Cumann na nGaedheal was motivated by a desire for an orderly government, one that responded to the needs of the polity, protected the freedom of the individual, and promoted intercourse between Ireland and other nations. That vision was significant as much for what it failed to see as for what it did see. The party leaders refused to view the state as promoting any given, substantive, uniquely Irish agenda for the nation, a purpose that would distinguish it from other nations. In May 1927, Cosgrave summarized the commitments of his party by stating:

> The urgent need of the country is that its present stability should be maintained. Upon this organisation at the present moment rests the tremendous responsibility of maintaining it. The aim and purposes of the Cumann na nGaedheal Organisation are an ordered society, hard work, constant endeavour, a definite settled policy of reconstruction and rehabilitation, recruitment to the public service on the basis of merit; efficient, upright public service, greater national economy day by day, year by year; balanced budgets, a national revival of Irish culture; the maintenance of peace. The present Government have laid the foundations. They are the proper architects to whom to entrust the completion of the edifice.[32]

This statement, like the policy of Cumann na nGaedheal more generally, reads like a Protestant assault on an Irish Catholic sensibility. It is dispassionate, temperate, reasoned, and cool; it invokes none of the sentiment or emotion that had accompanied so much of modern Irish political history. Cumann na nGaedheal's policies may have been appropriate in the historical context, and they certainly appealed to those who had tired of Irish political passions. But in celebrating its accomplishments in this way, it just as surely alienated sizable sectors of the population in spite of its real achievements. The party refused to call upon the sentiments that had fueled the nationalist movement; its sole aim, in fact, was to create a political environment where such sentiments had no place. It is little wonder, then, that the party – for its excessive concern of propriety and decorum, for its Anglican "taste" – was often accused of doing Britain's bidding. The charge, of course, was foolish, but it reflected a realization by many that had Ireland still been under British rule, the etiquette of politics would not have been much different.

Because Cumann na nGaedheal struck the same themes throughout the decade – the themes of order, responsibility, frugality – despite a dramatically changed political environment, their policies were intended as much to promote this particular cultural agenda as to respond to given political crises. The party sought to make the nation and its political life in its own image. The increasing ferocity of the public safety bills enacted by Cumann na nGaedheal over the course of the decade probably reveals as much a form of cultural indignation at the Republican refusal to conform to Irish-Enlightenment political styles as a rational political response to Republican terror. Even the party's demand that Fianna Fáil enter the Dáil revealed, in part, the party's exquisite attention to the appearance of political propriety. When it lost control of the government in 1932, Cumann na nGaedheal still described itself as the "sole bulwark against terror and Communism," portraying its Fianna Fáil opposition as the party of the gunmen and atheistic Communists.[33]

The cultural issues at stake in governance cannot be neatly differentiated from political ones. Fianna Fáil was more than a party of political opposition; it was simultaneously a cultural alternative to Cumann na nGaedheal. Fianna Fáil was not, as Cumann na nGaedheal leaders suggested, the party of disorder and insecurity, of intemperateness and spendthriftiness, of unreason and irrationality. It was the party that offered, for the first time, a challenge to the dominance of Irish-Enlightenment political commitments while accepting (in a fashion) the given institutions of rule.

Fianna Fáil's program had the sentiments and sentimentality of much of the Irish nationalist rhetoric. In place of the British government, Cumann na nGaedheal became the object of opprobrium. To Fianna Fáil, the ruling party was no less illegal in its control of the government and no less immoral in its policies than were the British prior to the signing of the Anglo-Irish Treaty. Because Irish nationalism had been a struggle against political servitude to the British, Fianna Fáil saw itself as obligated to take power from the enslaving Cumann na nGaedheal party. In the June 1927 campaign, de Valéra argued that the main purpose of Fianna Fáil was to reclaim Ireland from foreign powers and their agents. "We are prepared to take over the machinery of Government, to work it in the interests of the whole nation," de Valéra asserted. "We are prepared to do it as quietly as possible; but we are determined that the people of this land shall work for themselves, and not be shivering slaves before John Bull's [British] threats."[34]

As the past several chapters have described, the ruling party's exclusive focus on the problems of political order rather than integration made them especially vulnerable to Fianna Fáil's charges. That Cumann na nGaedheal questioned Fianna Fáil's commitment to political order while Fianna Fáil challenged the former's tepid nationalist convictions reveals how each came to represent two component and complementary parts of a stable democratic order. "I want to reply to the suggestion now being put forward that our purpose in entering the Free State Dáil is to destroy it. That is a falsehood," de Valéra was pressed to state prior to the September 1927 election. Rather, he answered, Fianna Fáil's purpose was "to broaden and widen the Free State Assembly – to free from it all foreign control or interference, and make it so truly representative of the whole people as to secure for it the necessary authority and influence to have its decisions readily accepted and its laws willingly obeyed."[35]

Although de Valéra's language might seem excessive, Fianna Fáil's imagery of a nation still dominated, in fact, fueled the intense political struggle that ensued after the party's formation. And although party spokesmen often resorted to the use of nationalist platitudes, they did not make Sinn Féin's mistake of expressing only abstract sentiments. The lesson learned was that abstract commitments require concrete referents and that Sinn Féin's belief that the entire nation would rally behind an abstract program was naive. Instead, Fianna Fáil geared its pronouncements to those sectors of the population that might respond to a political challenge to the ruling party. Further, they identified those issues that might improve the position of disaffected sectors so as to encourage their participation.

It was the "peasant farmer and the wage earner" to whom the party could appeal.[36] These common people or have-nots, Fianna Fáil members reasoned, would more likely benefit from and thus support a program designed to break the link between Ireland and Britain. The party, in focusing on specific economic and social issues that affected those groups who had remained politically uninvolved in Free State politics, "sectionalized" its appeal and promised that its political program would improve the conditions of its supporters. "We seek the growing up of a movement," the party paper declared, "by active resistance to hardship and wrong."[37]

The appeal of Fianna Fáil's program lay in its ability to evoke powerful nationalist sentiments while responding to specific economic and social problems. The resonance between its nationalist critique of the Free State government and its concrete program of reform produced increasing support. When party spokesmen used platitudes about the Irish nation, the meanings reverberated more specifically on particular policy issues. When a Fianna Fáil candidate asserted that "poverty and decay have been the fruits of British rule whether it operated direct from London or through a Cumann na nGaedheal Government here," this was both an expression of national chauvinism and a more practical insistence that material prosperity for the average Irishman would result from a policy of Irish isolationism.[38] And when the party came out in support of protectionist tariffs for the nation and the withholding of land annuity payments to the British government, it was also a statement of Fianna Fáil's assertion that only with an autochthonous Irish Republic would genuine freedom be attained.

Fianna Fáil offered both a vision of Ireland that resonated with Gaelic-Romantic sentiments and a practical political program seemingly consistent with that vision. The connection between public policy and cultural vision produced a potent political combination for the party. Linking the rhetoric of national independence to specific policy debates, the party promoted a view of itself as deeply committed to the welfare of all Irish people. Fianna Fáil became the party of the people and the nation, whereas Cumann na nGaedheal in contrast, was seen as the party of particular and privileged interests. Even among its staunchest adherents, the latter party was not seen as one serving the nationalist aspirations of the Irish people.

Fianna Fáil's vision was unequivocally Romantic. It celebrated that uniquely puritanical variant of Irish Catholicism by emphasizing that Ireland could not live beyond its means. The aim, Fianna Fáil insisted, was to develop a self-sufficient Ireland neither dependent on any other nation nor expectant of a rich, luxurious life. The vision was of the rural, frugal, family-oriented Catholic society, cognizant of its limits and not envious of the wealth or economic security of other modern nations. It was an image decisively antibourgeois. De Valéra captured this vision well when he delivered the following comments to the Dáil in July 1928:

> We recognise that we are a comparatively small country, and that we cannot afford to carry on our administrative services here on the same scale as if, for instance, we were part of the British administrative system – the centre of an Empire. We, as I tried by example long ago to point out, had to make the sort of choice that might be open, for instance, to a servant in the big mansion. If the servant was displeased with the kicks of a young master and wanted to have his freedom he had to make up his mind whether or not he was going to have that freedom, and give up the luxuries of a certain kind which were available to him by being in that mansion. He had to give up the idea of having around him the cushions and all the rest that a servant in the mansion might have, and the various things that might come from the lord. He had to forgo these in order to get the liberty of living his life in his own way in simpler surroundings. If a man makes up his mind to go out into a cottage, he must remember that he cannot have in the cottage the luxuries around him which he had when he was bearing the kicks of his master. That is simple common sense. If he goes into the cottage, he has to make up his mind to put up with the frugal fare of that cottage. As far as I am concerned, if I had that choice to make, I would make it quite willingly. I would say: "We are prepared to get out of that mansion, to live our lives in our own way and to live in that frugal manner."[39]

De Valéra, speaking for his party and on behalf of the Irish cottagers, condemned the mansioneers: those who believed that Ireland should be organized and should function like other resource-rich, wealthy nations. Such was, of course, Cumann na nGaedheal's notion; the ruling leadership aspired to bring Ireland into the world of nations. For de Valéra and the Fianna Fáil Party, those aspirations for an Irish modernity that paralleled Britain's violated the essence of the nation and, further, the meaning of the nationalist struggle against the British. In its place, de Valéra and other members of the party offered the picture of Ireland as a self-contained, economically self-sufficient country. He argued that only as many families as practicable should be on the land and that new industries, rather than being concentrated in the cities, should coexist in the countryside so as not to violate the essentially rural character of the nation.[40]

Further, de Valéra objected to having the nation saddled with a strong government. Social services, according to Fianna Fáil doctrine, should be commensurate with the limited resources available. In that sense, Fianna Fáil's program was sharply divergent from Labour's. Unlike Labour, which proposed the expansion of government services, Fianna Fáil argued for individual self-sufficiency and nonreliance on government for support.[41] In fact, however, when Fianna Fáil gained political control in the early 1930s it substantially expanded the welfare state to assist especially the hard-pressed farmers who supported the party. And in many different respects, its political program differed substantially from its political platform. This divergence between doctrine and policy is hardly uncommon in politics and did not weaken the conviction with which the party held to its moral-political doctrines. Throughout, the party maintained the position that the family and the church – not the government – were primarily responsible for offering aid in hard times; to do otherwise would be to violate the spirit of limited government.

Fianna Fáil had other themes and policies besides self-sufficiency. The emphasis on a unified Republic and rejection of the Treaty were uppermost in its political rhetoric. The continued existence of partition, the party argued, revealed the anti-Irish bias of the ruling party, which because of the Treaty, tolerated a divided Ireland.[42] In addition, the party appropriated from the persistent Western agitation the issue of land annuities and argued that the continued payment of those annuities to Britain was only one more example of continued Irish servitude. In their place, Fianna Fáil proposed – and eventually implemented – the continued payment of annuities, but to the Irish government rather than the British. Further, the party continued to charge the ruling party with being more interested in pleasing the ex-Unionists than in serving the average Irish man and woman; it insisted that Cumann na nGaedheal had no vision of a new Ireland.[43] In each case, the issues identified by the party contained both the kernel of an egalitarian political program whereby the proposed policies would clearly assist the common man and woman and a broad-based nationalist critique of the ruling party designed to evoke commitment from those who had been part of the nationalist struggle during the last decade.

These same themes spanned several general elections and the by-elections in between. The cultural motifs of returning Ireland to the Irish, of celebrating its rural and Catholic character, and of extolling Ireland's small-scale, frugal, and modest society were reiterated constantly throughout the elections. The contrast to Cumann na nGaedheal could not be more striking. First, befitting its Irish-Enlightenment understanding of government, the ruling party was not in the business of defining, in any specific or substantive way, a vision of the Irish nation. Serving the state, the party saw itself as, in some senses, standing above politics and refusing to dirty its hands by appealing emotionally to a political image of the Irish nation. But that decision, of course, was as much an adoption of a particular understanding of politics and of the Irish nation as was Fianna Fáil's. Cumann na nGaedheal sought a modern, stable, and strong state that acted impersonally and realized through the political process the collective wishes of the population.

It was a vision of "cool" politics. Attachment to the state would proceed, it was presumed, rationally through its demonstrated effectiveness and capacity to rule. The ruling party could play no more active a role in inspiring commitment than that of appealing for support and compliance to the political institutions. It was the ideological accompaniment to the Irish-Enlightenment commitment to parliamentary institutions and representative government. And although Cumann na nGaedheal had made some practical compromises with the Gaelic-Romantic tradition – its IRB roots ensured that – the party was obdurate in its conviction that politics must proceed in this impersonal, procedural, and abstract fashion.

Fianna Fáil, in contrast, bridged the two cultural traditions. Its political doctrine and program reveal the terms of the compromise. Although agreeing to the rules of parliamentary politics, Fianna Fáil sought to infuse them with passion and conviction, tapping the nationalist sentiments of those who still had a Gaelic-Romantic conception of the world and of politics.

Once Fianna Fáil entered the Dáil, Free State politics was changed forever. Irish-Enlightenment propriety was replaced by Gaelic-Romantic intensity. More importantly, the party ensured that politics was not divorced from convictions and passions. What was at stake in policy debates, Fianna Fáil was quick to remind its opponents, was the meaning of the Irish nation and the fate of the nationalist dream. "Hot" politics was the new order; technical or formal rationality in decision making, divorced from transcendent meaning, could no longer disguise the cultural interests involved in policymaking.

The entry of Fianna Fáil marked the introduction of volatile politics into the democratic structures. Public debate and discourse – whether occurring among representatives in the Dáil or within the broader public – was different from before. The public was greatly enlarged; the party had brought into Free State politics people who had heretofore refused to participate. The party spoke to the common man and woman, but it did more; it was culturally inclusionary. It legitimated the political expression of Gaelic-Romantic sentiments, albeit within the confines of a parliamentary system. Thus the traditionalist, localist and parochial views of rural Ireland – not to mention their Catholicity – were now more powerfully felt in the political system.[44]

With the inclusion of this more rural and peripheral sector of the population, democracy in Ireland was faced with a new problem. Fianna Fáil was to feel this problem acutely when, in 1932, it took over the government and was required to defend the institutions from a broad-scale ideological attack of the party's own making. Nevertheless, by turning nationalist sentiment against the ruling party while accepting the Free State structures, Fianna Fáil created a far more culturally in-tegrated society than had previously existed. It had considerably en-larged the public sector by incorporating within it groups that had previously abstained.

The party by no means created a consensus in the Free State. It could not undo the cultural divisions that had a long and consequential history. But for the first time since the Civil War, Fianna Fáil brought the various groups to the point of speaking to each other by accepting certain com-mon parameters of discourse. In bringing disaffected sectors into the public, the party made democratic stability more secure and promoted a political order more closely connected to the concerns and passions of its people.

Political organization and cultural integration

Thus far, I have treated the two contending cultural systems only as they were expressed through political doctrine. But cultural cohesion was promoted by other means as well. Cultural beliefs informed all of social and political life; they became embedded in the institutional in-frastructure and, in this way, refined and reproduced the structures of belief.[45] The opportunities enabling cultural expression to become embedded in national institutional structures, of course, were greatly expanded with political independence. But, not surprisingly, the per-sistence of cultural malintegration in Irish society meant that the political institutional apparatus, for example, the Dáil, reflected more strongly the Irish-Enlightenment forms than the Gaelic-Romantic ones. The po-litical organization of the Cumann na nGaedheal Party, too, reflected its Irish-Enlightenment commitments; Fianna Fáil's success in strengthen-ing the Irish public was a result, in part, of its ability to forge a political organization more compatible with Gaelic-Romantic convictions.

Cumann na nGaedheal, interested in ushering in an era of modern politics like those of other Western parliamentary democracies, attempted to rationalize the political process as much as possible. Consequently, the party's organizational structure was shaped by an image of politics more instrumental, impersonal, rational, calculating, and national than Irish politics had traditionally been. Order, effectiveness, and efficiency were the inspirations for the party organization. This is not to say that local party organizations – aspiring to modern forms – were not frustrated by the more traditional demands and expectations of their constituents; nevertheless, the Irish-Enlightenment sentiments served as the general organizing principles of the party.

The result was a highly centralized control of the party, especially on matters of policy, and a deemphasis on mass organization. In its early years, there were relatively few local party organizations. Only when Fianna Fáil emerged as a political force did Cumann na nGaedheal more than triple its local branches: from 276 in 1924 to 797 in May, 1926.[46] But in emphasizing its formal organization, Cumann na nGaedheal came to rely heavily on paid organizers to generate and mobilize party support at the local level.[47] But naturally, organizers paid by the national organization, not necessarily from the local community being organized, attempted to rally support around national issues and through formal political channels. The result was that the provincial areas less interested in the country's problems and more interested in their own were hardly persuaded to enter the political arena. Neither national issues nor parliamentary structures fired their imagination. The Cumann na nGaedheal's organization was principally interested in shoring up shaky popular support for often unpopular national policies, not in creating an activist local population deeply committed to the ruling party.

To a certain extent, of course, these problems of Cumann na nGaedheal's political organization were partly a function of unwise political tactics and circumstances that might confront any party in power. But more fundamentally, Cumann na nGaedheal's political organization represented a certain understanding of politics that could not long hold sway in Ireland. The idea that the Dáil representatives (TD's) should play the key role in local organization – a policy, as we will see, that Fianna Fáil embraced fully – was often debated among Cumann na nGaedheal leaders; although it was considered and remained a controversial issue, in the end it was not effectively implemented. Warner Moss, in *Political Parties in the Irish Free State*, quotes a member of the party adamantly opposed to such "personalistic" interference by the constituency's representatives. His thinking, particularly his identification of Cumann na nGaedheal with the old Unionist Party, captures the frame of mind that informed Cumann na nGaedheal politics:

> We do not want to prevent anyone from writing to T.D.'s, but we do intend that if this organisation is going to be a true organisation and not a mere machine for putting people into the Dáil, this Association is going to run the country just as the old Unionists ran the country. If we are going to take it over, we have to do what the old Unionists in Ireland did when they ran it through the County Clubs. In every county in Ireland there was a county club and the County was run from that. Now we have clubs open to the people and no one is prevented from joining these clubs, and if the Cumann na nGaedheal organisation is going to be the ruler, it must dig itself in in the way that we propose.[48]

According to this view, Ireland had to accommodate to its increasingly democratic character, but the efficient, orderly, and proper way to accomplish this would be to institute an effective and rational political organization capable of organizing and containing popular expression. In a fashion, this scheme worked as intended, for populist inputs into the Free State were limited and contained and the structures of political rule became increasingly secure. But the accomplishment was achieved at a considerable price: Substantial segments of the population refused to identify with or participate in the political system.

The rise of Fianna Fáil meant the rise of an alternative form of party organization; the party and its organization challenged the ruling cultural assumptions about the relationship of the political system to the population and the appropriate form for democratic politics. Fianna Fáil's political organization reflected its interest in mobilizing a disaffected population. It used every conceivable mechanism to do this and, in the process, to both vitiate Cumann na nGaedheal's influence and vitalize the people. The ultimate aim was to develop in the population a deep and abiding identification with the party and its political program.

The formal structures of the two parties did not differ significantly; the difference lay in the extent to which the party's actual functioning deviated from the organization chart. For Cumann na nGaedheal there was a reasonably close correspondence between the two, whereas for Fianna Faíl formal organization, which emphasized the role of national leadership, was treated as a structure to work around. In fact, as Bruce Logan notes, the drafting of the organization plan for Fianna Fáil was an afterthought, occurring several months after the party's formation.[49] Even at the national level, the emphasis was constantly on cultivating local people to strengthen the party from below.

Reflecting its strong egalitarian, popular commitments, the party's first impulse was not to create a leadership aristocracy, divorced from the party by formal mechanisms, but to involve as many people as possible. By the summer of 1927, Fianna Fáil had approximately 1,000 local branches, a number no other political party could approach.[50] When a branch was organized, it was customary to send de Valéra to speak first to the local organizers and then to the public.[51] De Valéra's charismatic appeal enhanced local organizational efforts, generating a personal commitment with which Cumann na nGaedheal could not compete.

But the most significant difference between the two parties was the role that the TD played in the local branch. Fianna Fáil relied almost exclusively on the TD for leadership. The strong conviction of the party leaders that the TD had a vested interest in active local organization helped produce vital local branches. Fianna Fáil did not shirk from a conception of politics that was largely patrimonial and local. The TD, as I will describe, viewed his role largely as that of an ambassador for his constituency and was devoted to using his political clout to reward his constituents materially and otherwise. As a result, the selection of candidates for the Dáil was in local hands, certainly more than for Cumann na nGaedheal.[52]

Fianna Fáil's attention to its local membership, reflected in this unique pattern of political organization, corresponded to the egalitarian Gaelic-Romantic tradition. The rejection of an aristocracy of leadership, divorced from the people by a system of formal political organizations, embraced the more romantic notion of political life in which all shared in the decision-making process and focus was on a fair distribution of resources to all. Similarly, its local orientation reflected the provincialism inherent in the Gaelic-Romantic tradition, whereby politics was concerned not with the problem of relations between nations but rather with an improved life for all Irish men and women. Fianna Fáil's success in activating a previously demobilized population cannot be attributed only to its success in rewarding local constituents; it also depended on the party's conformity to the assumptions held by these people regarding the appropriate purposes of politics.

The party's localism, however, was not the only way it reflected Gaelic-Romantic sentiments. Its authoritarian and hierarchical relations – whereby strong national leaders implemented specific policies to serve an absolute, ideal image of the Irish nation – was also part of Fianna Fáil's appeal. Although the party largely gave free rein to the TD as it affected his local supporters, party discipline remained firm. TD's, once in the Dáil, were severely sanctioned – usually by expulsion from the party – if they deviated from party policy.

Party leaders saw themselves as having a mission – to shift the development of the nation away from that of a "mini-Britain" and toward the creation of an autonomous Irish Republic. Clearly, it was a more authoritarian conception of political rule than the Free State had experienced thus far: Fianna Faíl's political elite was absolutely confident in its purposes and therefore required little guidance from the rank-and-file concerning the appropriate aims of the party. Much more so than Cumann na nGaedheal leaders, the Fianna Fáil elite experienced politics as a "calling," viewing itself as entrusted with the transformation of Ireland.

These autocratic tendencies of de Valéra and other party elites were tempered by their dependence on a strong grass-roots following. In fact, as Bruce Logan notes, the localism of the party typically produced Fianna Fáil TD's that were not of "front bench caliber" and whose interest in national affairs was minimal.[53] Such a split between the national party elite and the rank-and-file TD's ensured a party leadership capable of pursuing its romantic vision of national affairs while rewarding its followers with TD's who, while falling in line behind national policy, were primarily concerned with their constituents' interests.

This combination of egalitarianism and authoritarianism captured the Gaelic-Romantic imagination. Fianna Fáil adopted a political form and style meaningful to a substantial sector of the public that had heretofore been incapable of identifying with the more distant, rationalized, and "purposeless" Cumann na nGaedheal Party. This explains, in large measure, the rapid success of the Fianna Fáil party: In creating a new type of political organization, it tapped a resonant chord in a substantial sector of the Irish population. And the remarkable loyalty that the party enjoyed in subsequent years (also perhaps the reason why Cumann na nGaedheal had to regroup after 1932 under a new name, Fine Gael) was a function of a particular "irrational" commitment to an authoritarian politics that provided personal payoffs to its supporters.

But, more importantly for our purposes, Fianna Fáil's success in forging a new kind of political organization and enlisting a loyal following promoted a stronger, more culturally integrated public. Political debate at its most general level consisted of disagreement over the purposes and ends of political policy: its sacredness or profaneness, its cosmopolitanism or localism, its formalism or its negotiated and personalistic character. But – and this is the important point – the debate involved almost all members of the political community and accepted the existing structures of political rule. No longer was it a question of whether the Free State had the right – legal, moral, or otherwise – to represent the whole Irish population, but rather which political vision – Fianna Fáil's or Cumann na nGaedheal's – would express and direct the nation. The emergence of a genuinely functioning party system, incorporating these contending cultural traditions, marked for the first time the success of the Free State in generating democratic stability.

8. The Uniqueness of Irish Democracy

Ireland's democratic achievement, as I have argued, was a result both of Cumann na nGaedheal's unflagging commitment to parliamentary structures, despite the political costs to the party, and of Fianna Fáil's strengthening of the public by including culturally disaffected members. The need for both strong institutions, buffered from the population, and cultural integration involved the creation of a uniquely Irish pattern of democracy. It was a pattern deeply beholden to parliamentary forms while simultaneously responsive to the understandings of politics that emerged through the Irish public. Fianna Fáil's success in broadening the social composition of the public required new patterns of relatedness between the political elite, the institutions of rule, and the public.

In every society where the social composition of the public has expanded, the character of democratic politics has been profoundly altered. When, for example, the working classes in England, France, and Germany gained political rights, party systems were transformed, political accountability was expanded, and the criteria for political decision making became more articulate and universalistic. Politics was no longer the preserve of an elite few, nor was the state in service solely to a relatively small, privileged group.

The expansion of the public in Ireland produced similarly dramatic shifts in the nature of politics and the extent of elite accountability. But because this occurred in the twentieth century rather than the nineteenth, and after the population had been substantially mobilized and politicized in the nationalist struggle, the meaning and consequence of a broader public were very different. Fianna Fáil's success in bringing into the Free State previously disaffected sectors promoted a recasting of democratic politics in a traditional form. Now the public understanding of the character of politics, the nature of legitimate authority, and the ultimate aims of the Free State came to correspond more closely to Gaelic-Romantic sentiments, which thrived in the rural and peripheral sectors. To be sure, those understandings represented some amalgam of the two traditions. But the success of Fianna Fáil – through both its political rhetoric and its organization – placed Irish-Enlightenment convictions on the defensive. In the 1932 election, for example, Cumann na nGaedheal leaders capitulated to Fianna Fáil initiatives on land annuities, arguing also that they should be retained by the Irish government and halved, rather than being passed on to the British.

As already mentioned, there was an additional change in the nature of politics as a result of the ascendance of Fianna Fáil. Political life no longer was so intensely committed to the propriety and decorum to which members of the Cumann na nGaedheal Party aspired. Increasingly it became the domain of contest and discord; Fianna Fáil TD's hardly conformed to a pattern of reasoned and respectable debate. Instead, political discourse, in the Dáil and elsewhere, was passionate and intense. The party's ambivalent relation to the Free State structures infused political life with a new vitality; indeed, Fianna Fáil expressed an ethic of volatility that made a reasonably secure political order appear gravely precarious. And in encouraging those groups who were ambivalent toward the Free State to enter that realm of public debate and discourse, the government's ability to contain antidemocratic sentiments was always open to some question.

Because Fianna Fáil ascended to power so quickly, however, the danger of volatility created by the party was partially mitigated. Entrusted, by 1932, with preserving the democratic structures while simultaneously engaged in quasi-Gaelic-Romantic political rhetoric, Fianna Fáil managed to respond to an explosive public while keeping the institutions intact. In fact, the party proved no less harsh in its treatment of dissidents; it, too, outlawed the IRA and enacted one public safety bill after another in defense of the political apparatus.

But the rise of Fianna Fáil produced other, more fundamental, and more consequential changes in the character of Irish democracy. Although these changes did not threaten the democratic institutions, they profoundly transformed the nature of political life. As a result of the more inclusive public, the character of political relationships was altered to correspond more closely to a Gaelic-Romantic view. Politics, as I have suggested, became substantially traditionalized, and in this process, the divergence between the Irish form of democracy and other Western democracies became more evident.

In recent years, many scholars of Irish society and politics have noted the "irony of Irish democracy" – how, for example, the structures of political rule closely paralleled those of Britain and other Western democracies, whereas the rules that governed political interactions between individuals and elites strongly diverged from those followed by these other stable orders.[1] Using different terminologies, they note the strength in Ireland of authoritarianism and personal loyalties, two features that typically mitigate against democratic stability. And yet, Irish democracy has accommodated itself to these relationships.

Democratic political structures ideal-typically promote a public sphere where the individual citizen stands in direct relation to political authority, unmediated by a hierarchical authority structure. Further, modern politics increasingly focuses on questions of individual rights owed and responsibilities due. Democratic structures, in short, ideal-typically promote a public sphere ever more individualistic and egalitarian, where politics becomes increasingly removed from ascriptive or even particularistic considerations. Solidarity is based upon new principles of political organization – that is, the solidarity of like-minded or like-situated citizens – and no longer upon premodern principles or attachments. Yet the presence of both authoritarianism and personalism in Irish democracy expresses, in one respect, the idiosyncratic nature of Irish political forms and, as I shall argue, its unique accommodation to its public. These features of Irish democracy imply neither a universalistic politics based upon the individual citizen nor the elimination of traditional solidarity. Irish democracy became a peculiar blend of universalistic and individualistic principles expressed in the institutions of parliamentary rule. Concomitantly, the public tolerated the survival of those more collectivist and particularistic attachments that preceded the birth of the new state.

Throughout this book, there have been many references to the political expression of authoritarianism. Although undoubtedly derivative, as Basil Chubb suggests, from "the attitude of the Church toward a society that is predominantly rural and partly peasant,"[2] its political expression assumed the form of an absolute and unquestioned vision of the new Ireland of which the elites possessed privileged insight. From the point of view of the rank-and-file, political authoritarianism entailed the popular acquiescence to that vision. It was expressed through an irrational commitment to absolutist leaders unaccompanied by an ethic of critical, individualized judgment concerning the purposes of politics. Authoritarianism was politics in service to an absolute ideal, for which the elite needed no guidance, but only acquiescence, for its implementation. Further, it promoted the popular conviction that political accountability extended no further than the elite's articulation of that vision.

The inability of the Cosgrave government to rid the nation of the IRA and the formation of other paramilitary organizations revealed the strength of authoritarian politics in Ireland – the presence of a revolutionary cadre and large groups who more or less unequivocally accepted the authority of that elite. Even after de Valéra's rise to power, the threat of new paramilitary organizations – including the fascist Blue Shirt movement that emerged from the Free State army – demonstrated the persistence of this political form.

Basil Chubb concluded rightly that these examples of paramilitary activities in the 1920s and early 1930s "are noteworthy only to illustrate how firmly democratic, rather than authoritarian, ideas have dominated Irish politics."[3] Yet the interesting feature of Irish politics is not the ultimate victory of democratic ideas over an authoritarian alternative. Rather, it is the fact that authoritarian political relations became institutionalized and accommodated within democracy. The inclusive public, incorporating these cultural understandings, insisted upon this development. Through the public, traditional beliefs and attachments endured and continued to influence modern institutions. To appreciate the role of the public in this capacity is to acknowledge the interpenetration of culture and politics; it is to perceive the substantial influence of preexisting convictions and beliefs on new institutions.

De Valéra and Fianna Fáil promoted this compromise between authoritarian political patterns and egalitarian democratic structures; as a result, authoritarian politics was allowed to attenuate the egalitarianism of the more narrowly inclusive Cosgrave public. Fianna Fáil's ascent to power, although demonstrating the victory of democratic institutions and ideas, did not eliminate these unequal, uncritical political relationships that had not previously been expressed in the Free State but, instead, brought them into the Free State.

The manner in which the party entered the government and the kinds of voters the party mobilized produced a powerful "cultural" politics and froze the development of the Irish political system. Political divisions – now within the Free State – became culturally derived; Gaelic-Romantic and Irish-Enlightenment convictions were now being fought over by the two major parties in the Dáil. Party loyalty remained extraordinarily stable over the many years of Fianna Fáil rule. That loyalty was largely a function of shared cultural sensibilities and less a result of the application of an impersonal, rational calculus of political accountability. Naturally, as in any competitive party system, the opposing parties adapted to the strategies of their competitors, thereby producing an inordinate emphasis on cultural politics. The Civil War, partition, and other culturally powerful indicators became always at least the subtext, if not the themes, of political debate. This, in sum, represents the democratic accommodation to political authoritarianism: the institutionalization of Gaelic-Romantic ideals and patterns of authority within Irish-Enlightenment structures.

Fianna Fáil distinguished itself from its political adversaries by insisting upon debate at this ideological level, always careful to specify the relation between policies and cultural commitments. This method is in marked contrast to more typical Western democratic patterns of party debate, which focus on the development of a coherent political program designed to benefit specific sectors of the population. This is the importance of the often noted characterization of the Irish party system as having been born during the Civil War, without social bases, and subsequently shaping the character of Irish politics.[4] The intensity of the cultural conflict prior to and during the Civil War – the polarized conceptions of Gaelic-Romantic and Irish-Enlightenment adherents – coupled with the forced, perhaps premature entry of Fiana Fáil into the Dáil produced an Irish politics incapable of evolving soon into a more modern party system. Instead of parties serving the interests of particular groups who shared a common identity or attachment based upon their relationship to the economy, for example, Fianna Fáil represented those sectors who, by virtue of their relation to the center, had a different cultural conception of the world. The Irish party system, while similarly promoting political integration and enabling discourse between sectors of the population, achieved this on the basis of traditional attachments to region, community, and land rather than on more individualistic premises.

The Irish party system, bound by democratic procedures, institutionalized in one political system individuals who occupied different cultural worlds – one provincial and inward-looking, the other cosmopolitan and outward-looking. Political contests were a struggle between culturally divergent ways of perceiving the world. Fianna Fáil's capacity to tap and mobilize Gaelic-Romantic sentiment produced this Gaelicization of Irish political life. Paul Sacks, in his book about contemporary political life in Donegal, captures the nature of the political difficulty posed by such integration:

> Modern political loyalties were largely overlays of older and more durable structures. Thus, the solidarities that emerged out of the national movement were traversed by deeper and more numerous divisions. To the extent that party followings emerged, they consisted of compromises with the substructure of political attachments. Thus they were largely personal and local in nature.[5]

The Character of Irish Democracy

In helping to institutionalize authoritarianism and its concomitant cultural world view, Fianna Fáil helped transform Irish political life in another way. As the preceding quote implies, the endurance of these more parochial loyalties in political life simultaneously promoted a deeply personal view of the world that had an impact on both local and national politics. Authoritarianism in Ireland goes hand in hand with (what might at first seem contradictory) a politics deeply infused with an ethos of personalism. And, as I shall describe, Irish democracy has depended on this curious combination.

This Irish penchant for perceiving political life as mediated through persons, rather than offices, and the conviction that political decisions and actions are a function of personal reciprocities once again contradicts the ideal-typical features of the democratic state. In the abstract, an ethos of personalism undermines the ability of the state to function in a universalistic manner. It undercuts the basis of democratic legitimacy whereby resources are allocated according to conceptions of individual need and equity. Instead, politics is viewed far more venally; the state serves those who possess influence and can demand the state's attention and resources.

The belief in the personalism of the state, one would think, would undermine the ruling elites' efforts to present themselves and the institutions of rule as serving public, not private, interests. Further, it would weaken their ability to present themselves as representing the collective will of the nation, not of employing the resources of the state to repay personal debts. Typically, when the public holds no higher view of the purposes of the state, the ability of the rulers to generate deep and abiding commitments to the political structure is severely limited. The result often is a rapid turnover of political elites; the belief in the corruption and corruptibility of political rulers commonly produces periods of intense political instability. New nations of the Third World have frequently suffered from this strain of personalism; linked to a profound cultural malintegration is the inability of the state to generate the belief that political rule is anything more (if, indeed it is) than the command of the state by one cultural group imposing its power on the entire society.

Irish democracy is notable and unique for its accommodation to a personalistic ethos within democratic institutions. Personalism remains strong in the Irish public, but so, too, does parliamentary rule. Fianna Fáil ushered in, as I have described, a politics sharply divergent from those patterns to which Cumann na nGaedheal aspired. It did so by both localizing and personalizing politics. Through its innovations in political organization, the party legitimated the Gaelic-Romantic conception of political life. This conception was captured by Paul Sacks:

> An Irishman sees his world around him as a vast network of personal relations. It is through this network and those of others, that he knows much about the world. . . . He perceives persons not primarily in their formal roles, as bureaucrats, lawyers, company directors, but in the first place as friends, friends of friends, relations of friends: persons who owe him or a close connection of his some favour. In other words, in his view, each person is, orally or otherwise, indebted to a number of persons.[6]

The centrality of the Fianna Fáil TD to the local party organization was the key feature in the institutionalization of personalism in the Irish democratic structure. In connecting his political success to the power of the local organization, the TD increasingly came to perceive his role as an ambassador to the Dáil, as the emissary of his constituents. In establishing this largely patrimonial relationship between the TD and his constituents, the character of national political life was altered, reflecting both the increasing strength of the local constituencies and personalism in national political life.

First and for obvious reasons, the TD increasingly was born, resided, and was prominent in the local district. Whereas the TDs in the early years of the Free State were disproportionately national figures well known for their role in the nationalist struggle or in the Civil War, the local figure – centrally located in the district but often unknown nationally – became more and more common in the Dáil.[7] When Fianna Fáil forged this pattern of representation, a competitive party system demanded that other parties follow suit. The increasingly local character of TD representatives came to be a feature of all parties, not just Fianna Fáil.

Second, the TD increasingly saw himself and was widely viewed not only as the constituents' ambassador to the national government and various bureaucracies but, more particularly, as the constituents' broker. The TD was the representative of the community vying for the resources, material and nonmaterial, of the state. As R. K. Carty writes, "Irish politicians are all competing brokers; their continuing public careers depend on their ability to establish a large enough personal network of political clients to assure electoral success."[8]

The TD served as the intermediary between the agents of local and central government and the local constituents; as a broker, his task was to use personal influence and a reservoir of debts owed to meet the interests of those who elected him. The TD's charge, as Basil Chubb

221

cleverly expressed it, was to "[go] about persecuting civil servants."[9] As the emissary of his constituents, the TD used his connections to reduce the impersonality and universality of government bureaucracies. Pitted against this elaborate system of government arrangements was the growth of an equally elaborate – more informal though no less structured – set of personalistic connections, whereby the bureaucracy increasingly functioned by bending its rules to respond to personal debts and obligations.

Although government institutions did accommodate to this brand of personalistic politics, it did not succumb entirely. This is the interesting problem of Irish democracy: How could personal politics flourish without destroying the legitimacy of the parliamentary institutions? Why did Irish politics not become popularly perceived as corrupt and unworthy of public support? Why wasn't it seen as serving private rather than public interests and depending exclusively on the capacity of the TD to broker successfully for its constituents?

It has been suggested that the patronage system in Ireland is compatible with traditional and Catholic conceptions of authority, and thereby received popular support. R. K. Carty, for example, cites Kenney, who, writing about patronage in Spain, concludes that "in a Catholic society there is a strong ideological basis for a system of patronage, for there is great similarity between the function of saints and mortal patrons."[10] Similarly, Paul Sacks asserts that the presence of machine politics in Donegal corresponds to more traditional notions of the nature of authority and the political process.[11] But, in fact, these explanations can only partially answer the question posed. By themselves, they fail to explain the peaceful coexistence of formal democratic structures opposed to personalism and the presence of broker–client relations. They do not, by themselves, explain how in Ireland democratic structures were able to accommodate to this personalistic ethos without sacrificing the universalistic principles of allocation and distribution.

A more complete and historically specific answer to the problem of accommodation begins with the recognition that personalism became institutionalized within an active and vital party system – a system that, by its very nature, confirmed and strengthened the democratic structures. Second, and paradoxically, personalism was accommodated because the same people who held to a personalistic understanding of political relationships also possessed a strong authoritarian strain.

Personalism emerged as a powerful force in national politics through Fianna Fáil. Because the party expressed this traditional understanding of political relationships, yet vied for political power through the Free State structures of party contest and elections, personal conceptions of politics became mediated through political discourse. The nature of political relationships, that is, the tension between personal and impersonal political relationships, became part of public debate.

As a way of organizing political life, personalism became expressed through the political rhetoric of Fianna Fáil, particularly in its concern for the welfare of the common man. Support for the party implied, in part, a preference for localism and brokerage relationships. Yet as part of public debate, the ethic's influence was neither total nor completely antithetical to the given institutions. Instead, the degree to which the state would move away from principles of complete impersonality in rule and universalism became the stuff of political and partisan contest. As a consequence, the ethic of personalism did not transcend partisan division or stand opposed to democracy, but instead was expressed within it.

As Carty and others have noted, despite the strength of machine politics in Ireland, it did not produce a crass struggle between unconstrained personal brokers. Had that occurred, it was questionable whether democratic institutions could survive. Instead, however, the strength of partisan attachments resulted in brokerage within intraparty competition.[12] Brokerage itself, in intensifying party conflict at the local level, reaffirmed the strength of the party system and thereby limited its antidemocratic potential. As Carty writes, "The local patron and machine boss is not free to take his support across party lines, nor do his political behaviour and/or his personal qualities have much of an impact on the partisan division of the vote. Voting decisions are basically structured by partisan divisions."[13]

The fact that the nature of political relationships became a public issue and did not remain a reason for Gaelic-Romantics to refuse to participate in national politics strengthened rather than weakened democratic institutions. And to the extent that, especially with the rise of Fianna Fáil to power, those understandings of political life increasingly gained sway, the state apparatus was able to demonstrate its responsiveness to previously unrepresented cultural alternatives. The movement toward a more personalistic politics, then, represented the remarkable ability of the political institutions to accommodate to the cultural beliefs of the citizens. This accommodation helps to explain the cultural uniqueness and the success of Irish democracy.

Ireland's authoritarian strain further explains the state's capacity to accommodate sentiments that might otherwise have weakened democratic forms. Popular support for a given political party, as I have previously described, stemmed increasingly from its ability to deliver resources to its constituents. But, in addition, party support resulted from the popular identification of the party with a nationalist vision of Ireland. These two dimensions together have rarely intersected in Irish politics, producing, in the words of Conor Cruise O'Brien, "a long and complex tradition of nationalist rhetoric, combining with material interest politics."[14] The special feature of Irish politics is that nationalist concerns and instrumental politics have largely remained separate orientations of the political community.

Fianna Fáil, for example, has enjoyed remarkable loyalty from its supporters over the years. This loyalty is reflected not only in voter constancy from election to election but also in a commitment that has spanned generations. For the Fianna Fáil supporter (like the Fine Gael supporter), voting consists of an expression of solidarity with a particular cultural orientation. Often expressed through the old Civil War divisions but, as I have argued, possessing far deeper roots, party support is an expression of solidarity with one's family over time and with a given cultural world view. Crossing party lines implies more than the rejection of particular policies adopted by the party; it means that one has abandoned the political and cultural convictions held by earlier family members. Despite personal disenchantment with a party policy or program, many Irish citizens simply cannot bring themselves to defect from their party.

At the same time, contest *within* the party for local control has often been intense and has produced a far more unstable intraparty system. Dissatisfaction with the party resulted in considerable in-house dissension, which was typically expressed through contests over local party control. This divisiveness within the party corresponded to the continued imperative of the TD and other local officials to respond to their constituents. Because the party official at the local level was subject to his constituents' evaluation, whereas the party at the national level was relatively immune to their dissatisfaction, democratic politics was able to accommodate the personalism of political life without jeopardizing national institutions. The division between loyalty and deference to the party at the national level, as an institution of solidary attachment, and rational interest assessments at the local level, enabling rapid turnovers in leadership, has produced this form of Irish democracy. It is a democratic form both authoritarian and participatory, personalistic and universalistic.

Irish democracy today has changed greatly since the 1930s. The foregoing account has not been intended as a portrait of the political system today. Irish society has experienced some remarkable transformations, especially in the last several decades, and the influence of the enduring democratic structures upon the polity has surely altered both cultural beliefs and their public expression. Nevertheless, the political events of the 1920s and early 1930s continue to have a powerful influence on contemporary Ireland – on the capacity of the state to defend itself against its detractors and to accommodate to changing public beliefs about the appropriate purposes of the state, the character of authority, and the nature of political relationships. I hope that this book has provided an understanding of the exceptional nature of the Irish democratic achievement.

Further, these chapters offer a framework through which to understand the sources of strain and conflict that make the preservation of democracy, in any nation and at any time, always a political accomplishment, one never taken for granted. The Irish achievement of democracy reveals the dual requisites for democratic order. Effective political institutions that maintain political order and deliver material goods to the population are not sufficient for the establishment of democratic stability. The achievement of a party system whereby diverse cultural world views and commitments are expressed and contested through normal politics is also essential in the construction of democracy.

Just as interest politics are always a feature of modern political systems – sometimes straining the institutional apparatus beyond its capacity – so, too, are cultural strains. At times, these tensions tax the institutions, sometimes sufficiently to raise the specter of political disorder. At these moments, cultural divisions threaten to overwhelm the capacity of political discourse to contain them. But the Irish case demonstrates the important role that political parties play. When the parties articulate with cultural orientations – as they must, to be effective – they serve as more than a means to promote their constituents' perceived interests. They are the mechanisms through which contending visions become articulated in national politics. Through parties, people find their identity in the national political system. Or, stated more broadly, democratic stability depends, as the case of Ireland illustrates, upon the presence of a public sphere where interest and cultural politics flourish, but where the institutions of political rule are presumed to be the legitimate arbiters of those contests. Yet, as the history of new nations of the twentieth century sadly reveals, the gap between understanding the requisites of democratic stability and its actual achievement is great indeed.

Notes

CHAPTER 1

1. In this respect, the treatment of the creation of political and social order in one nation corresponds more closely to the studies of the achievement of social and political stability in Western societies. H. Eckstein, *Division and Cohesion in Democracy, A Study of Norway* (Princeton, N.J.: Princeton University Press, 1966); S. M. Lipset, *The First New Nation* (New York: Basic Books, 1963); J. H. Plumb, *The Origins of Political Stability in England 1675–1725* (Boston: Houghton Mifflin, 1967).
2. See, for example, B. Moore, Jr., *Social Origins of Dictatorship and Democracy* (Boston: Beacon Press, 1966); T. Skocpol, *States and Social Revolution* (New York: Cambridge University Press, 1979).
3. See, for example, S. Huntington, *Political Order in Changing Societies* (New Haven, Conn.: Yale University Press, 1968). See also J. Prager, "Moral Integration and Political Inclusion: A Comparison of Durkheim's and Weber's Theories of Democracy," *Social Forces* 59 (June 1981):918–50.
4. C. Geertz, "The Integrative Revolution: Primordial Sentiments and Civil Politics in the New States," in *The Interpretation of Cultures* (New York: Basic Books, 1973); E. Shils, "Political Development in the New States," *Comparative Studies in Society and History* 2 (3, 1960):265–92; 2 (4, 1960):379–411; J. C. Alexander, "Core Solidarity, Ethnic Outgroup and Social Differentiation: A Multidimensional Model of Inclusion in Modern Societies," in J. Dofny, ed., *National and Ethnic Movements* (London: Sage, 1980), pp. 3–26.
5. S. N. Eisenstadt, *Revolution and the Transformation of Societies* (Glencoe, Ill.: Free Press, 1978), pp. 19–51.
6. E. Shils, "On the Comparative Study of New States," in C. Geertz, ed., *Old Societies, New States* (Glencoe, Ill.: Free Press, 1963), p. 21.
7. E. Durkheim, *Professional Ethics and Civic Morals*, (Glencoe, Ill.: Free Press, 1958), p. 79. See also Prager, "Moral Integration." Durkheim sees the democratic state as synonymous with modern political orders where authority derives from popular consent, not divine right. He insists that such political organization inexorably leads to the creation of a democratic morality whereby equality under the law promotes individuation and the ethic of individualism. Durkheim acknowledges, of course, the possibility of "pathological" forms of modern politics; indeed, his essay "Civic Morals" examines the ways in which the democratic state may be subverted by either radical populism or radical elitism. But Durkheim cannot envision the rise of the totalitarian state, a new twentieth-century form of rule whereby modern egalitarianism systematically subverts the process of individuation and the

226

ethic of individualism. See also Chapter 1, note 28, and Prager, "Totalitarian and Liberal Democracy: Two Types of Modern Political Orders," in J. Alexander, ed., *Neo-Functionalism* (Beverly Hills, Calif.: Sage, 1985).

8. Durkheim, *Professional Ethics*, p. 82.

9. See, for example, R. Miliband, *The State in Capitalist Society*, (New York: Basic Books, 1969); F. Parkin, *Class Inequality and Political Order* (London: Holt, Rinehart and Winston, 1971); N. Poulantzas, *Political Power and Social Classes* (London: New Left Books, 1973); J. Habermas, *Legitimation Crisis* (Boston: Beacon Press, 1975); C. Offe, "The Abolition of Market Control and the Problem of Legitimacy," *Kapitalistate* 1(1973):109–16; J. O'Connor, *The Fiscal Crisis of the State* (New York: St. Martin's Press, 1973). See also D. Gold, C. Lo, and E. Wright, "Recent Developments in Marxist Theories of the Capitalist State," *Monthly Review* 27 (October 1975):29–43; (November 1975):36–51.

10. See, for example, Huntington, *Political Order*, especially pp. 78–92. See also D. Beetham, *Max Weber and the Theory of Modern Politics* (London: Allen & Unwin, 1974). Weberian treatments of modern politics are discussed more fully in Prager, "Moral Integration." See M. Weber, *The City* (New York: Free Press, 1958); see also J. C. Alexander, *Theoretical Logic in Sociology*, Vol. III: *The Classical Attempt at Synthesis: Max Weber* (Berkeley and Los Angeles: University of California Press, 1983).

11. L. Pye, "Introduction: Political Culture and Political Development," in L. Pye and S. Verba, eds., *Political Culture and Political Development* (Princeton, N.J.: Princeton University Press, 1965), p. 8.

12. S. Verba, "Conclusion: Comparative Political Culture," in Pye and Verba, eds., *Political Culture*, p. 519.

13. See, for example, S. M. Lipset, *The First New Nation* (New York: Basic Books, 1963); R. Rose, "England: A Traditionally Modern Political Culture," in Pye and Verba, eds., *Political Culture*, pp. 83–129; S. Verba, "Germany: The Remaking of Political Culture," in ibid., pp. 130–70; Eckstein, *Division and Cohesion*; M. Kilson, Jr., *Political Change in a West African State* (Cambridge, Mass.: Harvard University Press, 1966).

14. See, in particular, L. Binder, J. Coleman, J. LaPalombara, L. Pye, S. Verba, and M. Weiner, *Crises and Sequences in Political Development* (Princeton, N.J.: Princeton University Press, 1971).

15. See, for example, D. Lerner, *The Passing of Traditional Society*, (New York: Free Press, 1964); W. Rostow, *The Stages of Economic Growth* (Cambridge: Cambridge University Press, 1961).

16. See, for example, S. M. Lipset, "Economic Development and Democracy," in *Political Man: The Social Bases of Politics* (New York: Anchor Books, 1963); P. Cutright, "National Political Development," *American Sociological Review* 28 (1963):253–64; P. Cutright, "Political Structure, Economic Development and National Security Programs," *American Sociological Review* 30 (1965):537–50; also G. Almond and S. Verba, *The Civic Culture* (Princeton, N.J.: Princeton University Press, 1963); A. Inkeles and D. H. Smith, *Becoming Modern: Individual Change in Six Developing Countries* (Cambridge, Mass.: Harvard University Press, 1974). For an overview of the literature on the conditions necessary for democracy, see J. Roland Pennock, *Democratic Political Theory* (Princeton, N.J.: Princeton University Press, 1979).

17. For an example of a sensitive statement about the nondeterminist character of political culture theory, see Verba, "Conclusion." For examples of a critique of the particularist/universalist dichotomy, see R. Bendix, "Tradition and Modernity Revisited," reprinted in *Nation-Building and Citizenship*

(Berkeley and Los Angeles: University of California Press, 1977), and S. N. Eisenstadt, "Social Change, Differentiation and Evolution," *American Sociological Review* 29 (1964):378–86, and "Social Transformation in Modernization," *American Sociological Review* 30 (1965):659–73. For a more recent elaboration of this critique, see S. N. Eisenstadt, *Revolution*.

18. For example, A. G. Frank, *Capitalism and Underdevelopment in Latin America* (New York: Monthly Review, 1967); A. Quijano, *Nationalism and Capitalism in Peru* (New York: Monthly Review, 1971); T. Dos Santos, "The Structure of Dependency," in K. T. Fann and D. Hodges, eds., *Readings in United States Imperialism* (Boston: Porter Sargent, 1971), pp. 225–36. See also T. McDaniel, "Class and Dependency in Latin American," *Berkeley Journal of Sociology* 21 (1967–8):51–88; and M. Hechter, *Internal Colonialism: The Celtic Fringe in British National Development, 1536–1966* (Berkeley and Los Angeles: University of California Press, 1975).

19. I. Wallerstein, *The Modern World-System* (New York: Academic Press, 1974); E. Wolf, *Europe and the People without History* (Berkeley and Los Angeles: University of California Press, 1982).

20. It is not true, however, that contemporary political and historical sociology has completely ignored the relation between culture and politics, although the recent influence of these works has not been decisive in reshaping the field. The sociological interest in culture and politics derives from the functionalist tradition; in this regard, Parsonian sociology has been the main inheritor of the Weberian and Durkheimian concern for the interpenetration of these two realms. In particular, S. N. Eisenstadt has brilliantly introduced into functional analysis the role of cultural orientations and symbolic articulation as analytically independent of institutional structure. Demonstrating in *Revolution and the Transformation of Societies* the former's contribution to patterns of change, Eisenstadt, in a formal way, advances our understanding of the interaction between culture and politics. The essays of Edward Shils, in particular in *Tradition* (Chicago: University of Chicago Press, 1981), focus on the centrality of cultural work for sociological analysis. See also Ben-David and T. N. Clark, eds., *Culture and its Creators* (Chicago: University of Chicago Press, 1977). More empirically, Michael Walzer's *The Revolution of the Saints* (Cambridge, Mass.: Harvard University Press, 1965) still remains an exemplar of sociological research on culture and politics. Craig Calhoun's work, *The Question of Class Struggle* (Chicago: University of Chicago, 1982), in many respects is also part of this tradition. Yet, the important point is that the current empirical work in sociology, when compared with the work of social historians and anthropologists, remains resolutely anticultural in orientation. Within sociology, the cultural realm, by and large, is denied an analytically independent status; therefore, the problem of assessing the importance of cultural patterns for other spheres of social life is largely ignored.

21. See, for example, W. H. Sewell, Jr., *Work and Revolution in France: The Language of Labor from the Old Regime to 1848* (Cambridge: Cambridge University Press, 1980). E. Berenson, *Populist Religion and Left-Wing Politics in France 1830–1862* (Princeton, N.J.: Princeton University Press, 1983); N. Z. Davis, *Society and Culture in Early Modern France* (Stanford, Calif.: Stanford University Press, 1965); W. Reddy, "The Batterers and the Informers' Eye: A Labor Dispute Under the French Second Empire," *History Workshop* 7 (Spring 1979):30–44; D. Cannadine, "Civic Ritual and the Colchester Oyster Feast," *Past and Present* 94 (February 1982):107–30; and T. Tackett, "The West in France in 1789: No Religious Factor in the Origins of the Counter-Revolution," *Journal of Modern History* 54 (December 1982):715–45. There is, in ad-

dition, a growing literature in Ireland concerning the intersection of culture and politics. See, for example, M. R. Beames, "The Ribbon Societies; Lower-Class Nationalism in Pre-Famine Ireland," *Past and Present* 97 (November 1982):128–43; N. Canny, "The Formation of the Irish Mind: Religion, Politics and Gaelic-Irish Literature 1580–1750," *Past and Present* 95 (May 1982):91–116; and T. Garvin, *The Evolution of Irish Nationalist Politics* (New York: Holmes and Meier, 1981).

22. M. J. Weiner, *English Culture and the Decline of the Industrial Spirit 1850–1980* (Cambridge: Cambridge University Press, 1981).

23. L. Hunt, *Politics, Culture and Class in the French Revolution* (Berkeley and Los Angeles, University of California Press, 1984).

24. William H. McNeill, *The Metamorphosis of Greece Since World War II* (Chicago: University of Chicago Press, 1978).

25. In this analysis, I employ the terms "values" and "norms," and distinguish between them in a specific way. By values, I mean those abstract agreements, often inchoate and unstated, of the general purposes, goals, and aspirations that unite the population in a common outlook and understanding and orient their action. Such a consensus implies a general agreement on what constitutes the good society. Norms, by contrast, are more concrete specifications of value commitments. They are judgments internalized by members of the community, institutionalized in the structures of various institutions, and typically codified in law (about the appropriateness of the normal, routine, day-to-day practices by which societal members interact). These judgments are made with reference to these more abstract values; the assessment implicitly concerns whether the patterns of social interaction, or social relations, promote and articulate the values for which social life is putatively organized. For further elaboration, see Chapter 2, especially note 5.

26. T. Parsons, *The System of Modern Societies* (Englewood Cliffs, N. J.: Prentice-Hall, 1971), p. 11.

27. David Easton, *A System Analysis of Political Life* (Chicago: University of Chicago Press, 1979), pp. 190–211. I am indebted to Charles Nixon for suggesting this formulation of the problem.

28. The meaning of democratic stability, which defines the central analytic problem of this work, presents an intellectual problem that defies easy definition. To treat the issue adequately would require substantial elaboration, but to do so here, in my view, would distract from the book's main concern in explaining a particular political outcome in the Irish Free State. I have written elsewhere about the theoretical issues that the concept raises; see my "Totalitarian and Liberal Democracy: Two Types of Modern Political Orders." The obvious questions that the concept of democratic stability pose are: How is it distinct from nondemocratic stability, and how is it different from the more general concept of political stability? "Democracy" refers to two distinct phenomena: First, it implies a political organization whose authority derives from the mandate of the people, that is, whose legitimacy depends upon the support of the people. In this sense, democratic stability characterizes many, perhaps most, contemporary states and is in contrast to premodern political organizations because of the now almost universal belief that power emanates from the people and not from the divine right of kings or from other forms of religious cosmology. Nearly all modern societies are politically organized, in this sense, as democracies. "Democracy," as I employ the term (and as Durkheim and Weber both mean it) also refers to the modern practice whereby institutions of the state and the ruling elite are constrained in their

actions by their commitment to the belief and the popular expectation that the citizen is protected from the state, that there is an institutionalized distinction between the state and society. Legitimacy here depends on the safeguarding of individual freedom and on the capacity of groups within civil society to organize against policies of the government. In this sense, modern political systems, all of which derive their authority from the people, are distinguished by their commitment to promoting a democratic morality, that is, an activist, individualist orientation to popular governance. Democracy, in this sense, is dependent upon the achievement of modern democratic forms of political organization but further requires the commitment to democratic individualism. My discussion of "democratic stability" in Ireland refers to this latter meaning of democracy; what is distinctive about the Irish accomplishment is not that institutions were constructed reflecting the view that political authority depended upon popular consent, but that the ruling elite was able to institutionalize a democratic morality while preserving the structures of rule.

29. For a further articulation of this position, see T. Garvin, "Nationalist Elites, Irish Voters and Irish Political Development: A Comparative Perspective," *Economic and Social Review* 8 (April 1977):161–84; also Garvin, *Nationalist Politics*.

30. It should be apparent that the aim of this work is not to "prove" that Ireland, for all intents and purposes, is a Third World nation (or that all Third World nations have identical characteristics) or that the lessons learned from the Irish case have direct and immediate relevance to order and disorder in other newly independent nations of the twentieth century. Nor is it my intention to lay bare the cultural "variable," thereby offering the key to explain all that has been unexplained about stability and instability in Ireland or other new nations. The point is more subtle and less ambitious. To the extent that this work is broader in intent than simply an examination of the Irish case, its purposes are conceptual and methodological. First, I suggest that, before any explanation can be offered, the Irish achievement needs to be understood from the point of view of the actors participating in Irish political history. This methodological approach to nation building, I suggest, is no less appropriate for the study of other new nations. Second, an appreciation of the political problems of nation building also requires a deeply intertwined conception of the cultural dimension of social life. It is surely true that despite some impressive similarities between Ireland and other new nations, there are significant differences: demographic ones, degrees of urbanization, ethnic and religious homogeneity, class structure, and so on. At the same time, and despite these differences, this attempt to understand the Irish accomplishment through an appreciation of the connection of culture and politics, it is hoped, will serve as a corrective to those who attempt to cast all social action as "structurally" derived.

31. J. H. Whyte, "Ireland: Politics without Social Bases," in R. Rose, ed., *Electoral Behavior: A Comparative Handbook* (New York: Free Press, 1974), pp. 619–51.

32. P. Bew, *Land and the National Question in Ireland 1858–1882* (Atlantic Highlands, N.J.: Humanities Press, 1979); see also the slightly different discussion by Hechter, *Internal Colonialism*.

33. Sean Cronin, *Irish Nationalism* (Dublin: Academy Press, 1981).

34. "Structural strain" theory, or ecological analysis, in the Irish case has been most systematically developed by E. Rumpf and A. C. Hepburn, *Nationalism and Socialism in Twentieth-Century Ireland* (Liverpool: Liverpool University Press, 1977), and by Tom Garvin. See, for example, Garvin's "Political Cleavages, Party Politics and Urbanisation in Ireland: The Case of the Periphery-

Dominated Centre," *European Journal of Political Research* 2 (1974):307–27. See also A. Orridge, "Explanations of Irish Nationalism: A Review and Some Suggestions," *Journal of Conflict Research* 1 (1972):29–57. Garvin's subsequent work, in particular, has been sensitive to the limitations of an explanation of political behavior based solely on factors that, by their very nature, ignore the voluntaristic and meaning-making process in social and political life. See his "The Destiny of the Soldiers: Tradition and Modernity in the Politics of de Valéra's Ireland," *Political Studies* (August 1978), pp. 328–47 and especially "Theory, Culture and Fianna Fáil: A Review," in M. Kelly, L. O'Dowd, and J. Wickham, eds., *Power, Conflict and Inequality* (Dublin: Turoe Press, 1982), pp. 171–85. See also R. K. Carty, *Party and Parish Pump: Electoral Politics in Ireland* (Ontario: Wilfred Laurier University Press, 1981).

35. On structural strain, see Neil Smelser, *Theory of Collective Behavior* (New York: Free Press, 1962), pp. 15–16.
36. Basil Chubb, *The Government and Politics of Ireland* (London: Oxford University Press, 1970), p. 45; Brian Farrell, "The Paradox of Irish Politics," in Farrell, ed., *The Irish Parliamentary Tradition* (Dublin: Gill & Macmillan, 1973), pp. 13–25.
37. Ronan Fanning, "Leadership and Transition from the Politics of Revolution to the Politics of Party: The Example of Ireland, 1914–1939," unpublished manuscript, p. 11.
38. G. Almond and S. Verba, "The Civic Culture and Democratic Stability," in Almond and Verba, eds., *The Civic Culture*, pp. 473–505.
39. For the classic sociological formulations of citizenship in modern orders, see T. H. Marshall, *Class, Citizenship and Social Development* (Chicago: University of Chicago Press, 1977), and Bendix, *Nation-Building*.
40. Almond and Verba, eds., *The Civic Culture*, pp. 161–179.
41. Ibid., pp. 493–96.
42. C. Geertz, "Thick Description: Toward an Interpretive Theory of Culture," in *Interpretation*, pp. 3–32.
43. R. Turner and L. Killian, *Collective Behavior*, 2nd ed. (Englewood Cliffs, N.J.: Prentice-Hall, 1972), p. 179.
44. The "public," as described in the text, refers broadly to what Durkheim identifies as "collective consciousness." See "Individualism and the Intellectuals," in R. N. Bellah, ed., *Emile Durkheim on Morality and Society*, (Chicago: University of Chicago Press, 1973), pp. 43–60; *Suicide* (Glencoe, Ill.: Free Press, 1951), especially pp. 306–25; and *The Division of Labor in Society* (New York: Free Press, 1933), book I, chap. V; to what Shils, *Comparative Study*, p. 21, describes as "moral consensus," and to what Parsons, *Modern Societies*, p. 11, characterizes as the societal community or the integrative subsystem of a society. Yet the public has a more specific derivation as well. Turner and Killian, *Collective Behavior*, J. Dewey, *The Public and its Problems* (Chicago: Henry Holt, 1927) and R. Park, *The Crowd and the Public* (Chicago: University of Chicago Press, 1972) before them, developed the concept of the public as an entity with influence over its members. It is to be distinguished from public opinion, commonly understood as the total of individual opinions. Turner and Killian's interest, in contrast to the one here, is in the emergence of various publics within a democratic community that focuses on specific issues and that expands and contracts as interest in those issues waxes and wanes. The present attention to a single public is not opposed to the notion of a multiplicity of publics, but simply asserts that a central feature of a national community is the emergence of an independent arena where such social understandings and meanings are forged. Within that

arena, various individuals and collectivities attend to specific concerns, that is, many publics are formed. Although Turner and Killian concentrate on the emergent, situationally specific character of public understandings, this approach also attends to the parameters – cultural and institutional – within which public discourse operates. Thus, although public expression is, indeed, forged through subjective debate, I hold that the content of the outcome is not entirely indeterminate: It represents some degree of accommodation between cultural values, beliefs, and sentiments and particular institutional exigencies. This point will be developed further in the text. It should also be noted that Talcott Parsons makes use of the concept of public in "Voting and the Equilibrium of the American Political System," in *Politics and Social Structure* (New York: Free Press, 1969), pp. 208–9. Although entirely congruent with the analysis presented here, this reference was discovered only after the central argument was developed.

45. I am indebted to Aaron Cicourel for this formulation of the public as a meta-concept.
46. Keith Michael Baker, "Ideological Origins of the French Revolution," in D. LaCapra and S. L. Kaplan, eds., *Modern European Intellectual History: Reappraisals and New Perspectives* (Ithaca, N.Y.: Cornell University Press, 1982), p. 203.
47. See J. R. Pole, *The Pursuit of Equality in American History* (Berkeley and Los Angeles: University of California Press, 1978); P. Colomy, "Stunted Differentiation: A Sociological Examination of Virginia's Political Elite, 1720–1850" (Ph.D. diss., UCLA, 1982).
48. Baker, "Ideological Origins," pp. 203–4.
49. C. Geertz, "Ideology as a Cultural System," *Interpretation*, pp. 218–19.

CHAPTER 2

1. Cited and discussed in W. K. Hancock, "Saorstát Éireann," in *Survey of British Commonwealth Affairs*, Vol. 1, 1918–1936, (London: Oxford University Press, 1937), p. 147.
2. Leo Kohn, *The Constitution of the Irish Free State* (London: Allen & Unwin, 1932), p. 56.
3. *Official Report of Debate on the Treaty*, Dáil Éireann (December 1922), p. 177.
4. See Brian Farrell, "The Paradox of Irish Politics," in Farrell, ed., *The Irish Parliamentary Tradition* (Dublin: Gill & Macmillan, 1973), pp. 16–17.
5. As the reader will discover in my discussion of the normative differences between the two traditions, I treat three distinct, although interrelated, aspects of normative commitments, each related to the general value orientations of these systems of meaning. First, norms address the question, who are the rightful members of the society? What categories of individuals can be rightfully included in or excluded from membership? These jurisdictional issues are explicitly addressed in legal documents, like the Constitution, and are defined and redefined with respect to the understanding of the purposes or goals of the society. When a society is normatively integrated, there is common agreement on the issue of jurisdiction. Second, normative judgments refer to the understood proper relationships between members of the society. They consist of "patterns of expectation" concerning the appropriate relationship of hierarchy to deference, the legitimacy of authority and its connection to egalitarianism, the role of the elite vis-à-vis the power of the masses, and the relationship of the individual to the collectivity. See Talcott Parsons, "Durkheim's Contribution to the Theory of

Integration of Social Systems," in K. Wolff, *Essays on Sociology and Philosophy* (New York: Harper & Row, 1964), pp. 118–53. These regulatory principles are also specified in law but operate informally, even unconsciously, as well. See Neil Smelser, *Theory of Collective Behavior* (New York, Free Press, 1962), p. 27. Finally, norms are a specification of the appropriate mechanisms by which social conflict is settled. They address the question, what legitimate mechanisms are available to seek redress of grievances or to implement change? For example, where authority in a social order is deemed legitimate, a pattern of conflict resolution will be promoted in which the wronged parties engage in moral appeal, political suasion, peaceful agitation, and so on. Moreover, it will result in those parties ultimately abiding by the procedural outcomes. However, when authority or hierarchy is deemed illegitimate, procedures for redress are antiauthoritarian and typically produce no respect for gradualist or moderate modes of reform.

6. F. S. L. Lyons, *Culture and Anarchy in Ireland, 1890–1939* (London: Oxford University Press, 1979). Lyons identifies three cultural traditions: the Anglo-Irish, the Gaelic-Irish, and the English. The analysis here broadly corresponds to Lyons's in that the Irish-Enlightenment tradition roughly parallels his Anglo-Irish, and the Gaelic-Romantic corresponds to his Gaelic-Irish. I rejected Lyons's terms because, despite his caution in using them, they too closely connote an attachment to specific groups in Irish society. Although cultural traditions are carried by specific individuals, I argue, they cannot be understood reductively as expressions of the interests of particular groups, such as the Anglo-Irish.

7. T. Garvin, *The Evolution of Irish Nationalist Politics* (New York: Holmes and Meier, 1981), passim.

8. *Census of Population, 1926*, Vol. 1 (Dublin: Stationary Office, 1928).

9. S. Clark, *Social Origins of the Irish Land War* (Princeton, N.J.: Princeton University Press, 1979), pp. 122–38.

10. Garvin, *Nationalist Politics*, pp. 54–5.

11. Joseph Lee, *The Modernisation of Irish Society, 1848–1918* (Dublin: Gill & Macmillan, 1973), pp. 2–35.

12. Ibid., p. 49; see also E. Larkin, "The Devotional Revolution in Ireland, 1850–75," *American Historical Review* 77 (June 1972):625–52.

13. M. Hechter, *Internal Colonialism: The Celtic Fringe in British National Development, 1536–1966* (Berkeley and Los Angeles: University of California Press, 1975).

14. Ibid., pp. 266–93, esp. pp. 292–3.

15. Ibid., p. 293.

16. Ibid.

17. E. Rumpf and A. C. Hepburn, *Nationalism and Socialism in Twentieth-Century Ireland* (Liverpool: Liverpool University Press, 1977).

18. Ibid., p. 68.

19. Ibid.

20. Ibid.

21. Ibid.; see also T. Garvin, "Nationalist Elites, Irish Voters, and Irish Political Development: A Comparative Perspective," *Economic and Social Review* 8 (April 1977):169.

22. Rumpf and Hepburn, *Nationalism and Socialism*, p. 68.

23. Max Weber, " 'Objectivity' in Social Science and Social Policy," in E. Shils and H. Finch, trans. and eds., *The Methodology of the Social Sciences* (New York: Free Press, 1949), p. 90; emphasis in the original.

24. Ibid., pp. 95–6.

25. Lyons, *Culture*, p. 67–8.
26. Weber, "Objectivity," p. 111; emphasis in the original.
27. Garvin, "Nationalist Elites," pp. 160–1, passim.
28. Cited in J. L. McCracken, "The United Irishmen," in T. D. Williams, ed., *Secret Societies in Ireland* (Dublin: Gill & Macmillan, 1973), p. 60.
29. For a summary description of the United Irishmen, see ibid., pp. 58–67.
30. Cited in Leo Kohn, *The Constitution of the Irish Free State* (London: Allen & Unwin, 1932), pp. 24–5.
31. T. Garvin, "Defenders, Ribbonmen and Others: Underground Political Networks in Pre-Famine Ireland," *Past and Present* 96 (August 1982):133–55.
32. Ibid.
33. For an excellent extended treatment of this Anglo-Irish interest in both creating an Irish literary revival and preventing its politicization, see N. Mansergh, *The Irish Question, 1840–1921* (Toronto: University of Toronto Press, 1975), pp. 271–387. See also Lyons, *Culture*, pp. 27–55. See also Farrell, "Paradox," p. 19, for a reconsideration of Thomas Davis, who has commonly been portrayed as a man of physical force. Farrell argues that Davis more appropriately should be seen as an advocate of the parliamentary tradition.
34. George Russell (AE), "On behalf of some Irishmen Not Followers of Tradition," *Collected Poems* (1928), cited in Mansergh, *Irish Question*, p. 287.
35. See, for example, Farrell, ed., *Parliamentary Tradition*.
36. Larkin, "Devotional Revolution."
37. Ibid., p. 639.
38. See E. R. Norman, *The Catholic Church and Ireland in the Age of Rebellion, 1859–1873*, (London: Longmans, 1965).
39. B. Solow, "A New Look at the Irish Land Question," *The Economic and Social Review* 12 (July 1981):301–14.
40. Lyons, *Culture*, p. 82.
41. T. D. Williams, "The Irish Republican Brotherhood," in Williams, ed., *Secret Societies*, p. 146.
42. Mansergh, *Irish Question*, p. 60.
43. Norman, *Catholic Church*, pp. 86–134. See also McCartney, "The Churches and Secret Societies, in Williams, ed., *Secret Societies*, pp. 68–78.
44. See, for example, Sean Cronin, *Irish Nationalism* (Dublin: Academy Press, 1981), pp. 62, 79.
45. Quoted in J. Curran, *The Birth of the Irish Free State, 1921–23* (University, Ala.: University of Alabama Press, 1980), pp. 17–18.
46. See ibid., p. 18.
47. F. S. L. Lyons, *Ireland Since the Famine* (London: Fontana, 1972), pp. 402–3.
48. Ibid., p. 402.
49. Quoted in Dorothy Macardle, *The Irish Republic* (London: Victor Gollanz, 1937).
50. Lyons, *Famine*, pp. 400–4.
51. *Official Report of Debate on the Treaty* (Dublin: Dáil Éireann, January 6, 1922), p. 272.
52. *Official Report of Debate on the Treaty* (Dublin: Dáil Éireann, January 7, 1922), p. 344.
53. Ibid., p. 338.
54. Cited in Carlton Younger, *Ireland's Civil War* (London: Frederich Muller, 1968), p. 203.
55. *Official Report of Debate on the Treaty* (Dublin: Dáil Éireann, January 7, 1922), p. 340.

56. This relationship between the army and the civilian government will be the subject of Chapter 4.
57. Peadar O'Donnell, *There Will Be Another Day* (Dublin: Dolman Press, 1963), p. 22.
58. *The Constructive Work of Dáil Éireann* (Dublin: Dáil Éireann, 1920), p. 12.
59. *Official Report of Debate on the Treaty* (Dublin: Dáil Éireann, December 7, 1922), p. 330.
60. *Official Report of Debate on the Treaty* (Dublin: Dáil Éireann, December 17, 1922), p. 230.
61. Ibid., p. 245; emphasis mine.
62. *Official Report of Debate on the Treaty* (Dublin: Dáil Éireann, January 7, 1922), p. 332.
63. *Official Report of Debate on the Treaty* (Dublin: Dáil Éireann, December 14, 1921), p. 125.
64. Cited in Younger, *Civil War*, p. 476; emphasis mine.
65. Cited in Leon O'Broin, *Michael Collins* (Dublin: Gill and Macmillan, 1980), p. 88.
66. Cited in ibid., p. 111.
67. *Official Report of Debate on the Treaty* (Dublin: Dáil Éireann, December 19, 1922), p. 32.
68. Ibid., p. 32.
69. Cited in O'Broin, *Collins*, pp. 136–7; emphasis mine.
70. Ibid., p. 133.
71. Recall the Sinn Féin Constitution of 1917; referred to in Curran, *Birth*, pp. 17–18.
72. *Official Report of Debate on the Treaty* (Dublin: Dáil Éireann, January 6, 1922), p. 272.
73. Younger, *Civil War*, p. 124.
74. Éamon de Valéra, "Fianna Fáil and Its Economic Policy" (Dublin: Fianna Fáil, 1928), p. 12.
75. T. Ryle Dwyer, *Éamon de Valéra* (Dublin: Gill & Macmillan, 1980), p. 56.
76. *Official Report of Debate on the Treaty* (Dublin: Dáil Éireann, January 6, 1922), p. 274.
77. *Census of Population*, 1926, Vol. III, part 1. At the same time, as one anonymous reviewer pointed out, the presence of a single large religious group in a nation has typically interfered with or slowed the process of political modernization. The capacity of the political apparatus to promote certain political interests, irrespective of the interests of the religious organization, enhances the resources of the modern state and promotes stability. Yet in the Irish case, political institutions were not entirely differentiated from the church, because of its omnipresence in the society, and, therefore, their ability to act independently was curtailed. Although religious homogeneity probably inhibited some forms of polarization, it also inhibited the process of differentiation. Thus, one should be wary of concluding that political stability in Ireland was simply a function of the absence of religious divisions in the nation.
78. Horace Plunkett, *Ireland in the New Century* (London: J. Murray, 1904), pp. 94–5, cited in David Schmitt, *The Irony of Irish Democracy* (Lexington, Mass.: Lexington Books, 1973), p. 48. Given the significance of Roman Catholicism in Irish life, it is important to warn the reader that in the following analysis of Irish politics, there will be little specific attention to the role played by the church in the political developments of the 1920s. The evidence suggests

that, during this decade, the church did not intervene with a heavy hand to obtain results opposed by the new government. Rather, as J. H. Whyte concludes in *Church and State in Modern Ireland 1923–1970* (Dublin: Gill & Macmillan, 1971), p. 373, the church's role in the state policy was "unobtrusive." One should not conclude that the church refrained from political intervention in secular affairs as a matter of policy or principle; rather, in this decade, the political actions of the new government were compatible with church interests, enabling the church to stand essentially as a silent witness to political developments.

CHAPTER 3

1. Gianfranco Poggi, *The Development of the Modern State* (Stanford, Calif.: Stanford University Press, 1978), pp. 104–7.
2. Carl Friedrich, *Transcendent Justice: The Religious Dimension of Constitutionalism* (Durham, N.C.: Duke University Press, 1964), p. 66.
3. Albert O. Hirschman, *Exit, Voice, and Loyalty* (Cambridge, Mass.: Harvard University Press, 1970).
4. Max Lerner, "Constitution and Court as Symbols," *Yale Law Journal* 46 (June 1937):1305.
5. Carl Friedrich, *Constitutional Government and Democracy: Theory and Practice in Europe and America* (Boston: Little, Brown, 1941), p. 535.
6. Reinhard Bendix, *Kings or People? Power and the Mandate to Rule* (Berkeley and Los Angeles: University of California Press, 1980).
7. Friedrich, *Justice*, p. 161.
8. The most comprehensive account of the drafting of the Free State Constitution is found in D. H. Akenson and J. F. Fallin, "The Irish Civil War and the Drafting of the Free State Constitution," *Eire-Ireland* 5 (no. 1, 2, and 4) (Spring, Summer, Winter 1970):10–26, 42–93, 28–70. Unless otherwise stated most of the historical narrative is largely taken from Akenson and Fallin. As they note, because of the Constitution's failure to prevent civil war, most of the materials relating to the drafting process have been suppressed. The authors base their account on the relatively small body of material that is now available, especially from British sources. See also J. Curran, *The Birth of the Irish Free State, 1921–23* (University, Ala.: University of Alabama Press, 1980), chap. 14.
9. Akenson and Fallin, "Drafting," no. 1, 20–1.
10. The Collins–de Valéra pact, referred to earlier, was an outgrowth of this initial agreement. When Collins realized in mid-May that more time was needed to draft a Constitution and, it was hoped, to avert civil war, he negotiated an extension with de Valéra. Again, as I describe later in the text, he held out the promise of a republican Constitution free of reference to the Anglo-Irish Treaty.
11. Akenson and Fallin, "Drafting," no. 1, 22.
12. Hugh Kennedy, "Character and Sources of the Constitution of the Irish Free State," *American Bar Association Journal* 14 (August–September 1928):442, cited in Akenson and Fallin, "Drafting," no. 1, 23.
13. Three drafts were actually prepared. The third draft will not be discussed because it was written by only two members of the committee and was not taken seriously by the committee as a whole. This third draft, authored primarily by Alfred O'Rahilly, combined religious conservatism and a fundamental rejection of the British party system. O'Rahilly convinced only James Murnaghan to support that version and, as Akenson and Fallin note,

it was largely ignored. "It may not be totally irrelevant," Akenson and Fallin write, "to note that both the men were university professors." Akenson and Fallin, "Drafting," no. 2, 48.

14. Ibid., 88.
15. Ibid., 46.
16. Leo Kohn, *The Constitution of the Irish Free State* (London: Allen & Unwin, 1932), pp. 80–120.
17. Ibid., pp. 103–11.
18. Akenson and Fallin, "Drafting," no. 4, 80–2.
19. Ibid., no. 4, 37.
20. Ibid., 38.
21. Darrell Figgis stated later that Collins blamed the Republicans for the British rejection of the Constitution. Collins felt that had the Constitution been submitted before the anti-Treaty outcry had peaked, the British would have confirmed it. See Curran, *Birth*, p. 204.
22. Akenson and Fallin, "Drafting," no. 4, 59–60, attribute principally political motives to Griffith's actions and conclude that, in all likelihood, he played a strong role in this capitulation. They cite evidence that the British government believed that an open split between Griffith and Collins was imminent. Collins's ambivalence toward the Irish-Enlightenment tradition and Griffith's complete embrace of it increases our understanding of the political differences between the two men.
23. From the perspective of British Commonwealth affairs, granting to the Free State coequal membership represented a considerable concession to national sovereignty. Ireland was the first British possession granted coequal status, yet when compared to what the Free State had hoped to achieve, coequality was clearly below Irish aspirations.
24. *The Sunday Times*, cited in Dorothy Macardle, *The Irish Republic* (London: Victor Gollancz, 1937), p. 754.
25. Kohn, *Constitution*, pp. 80–1.
26. Dáil Debates, 1/358, September 18, 1922.
27. Dáil Debates, 1/477, September 20, 1922.

CHAPTER 4

1. M. R. D. Foot, "Revolt, Rebellion, Revolution, Civil War: The Irish Experience," in Elliot-Bateman, Ellis, T. Bowden, eds., *Revolt to Revolution* (Manchester: Manchester University Press, 1974), p. 184.
2. F. S. L. Lyons, *Ireland Since the Famine* (London: Fontana, 1973), pp. 467–8.
3. James Meenan, *The Irish Economy Since 1922* (Liverpool: Liverpool University Press, 1970), p. 35.
4. Lyons, *Famine*, p. 484.
5. Dáil Debates, 6/1894–5, March 11, 1924. The following discussion of the army mutiny is derived principally from parliamentary debates and newspaper reports of the events. There has been only spotty treatment of the mutiny in Irish historiography and little analysis of the surrounding events. For the exception, see Frank Munger, *Legitimacy of Opposition: The Change of Government in Ireland in 1932* (Beverly Hills, Calif.: Sage, 1975); see also Ronan Fanning, *The Irish Department of Finance 1922–1958*, (Dublin: Institute of Public Administration, 1978), pp. 116–19. The analysis here would have been aided had the minutes from the party councils been available for public review, but they remain secret documents. The papers of Richard Mulcahy and the cabinet minutes have been utilized. Because the dispute developed into a

conflict between three different factions within the government, the parliamentary papers are remarkably revealing. Each faction used Dáil deliberations to selectively reveal information designed to harm the opposition. Each such revelation, separated from the political motivation for its release, was useful in reconstructing the sequence of events of the mutiny and the meaning behind the government's response.

6. Dáil Debates, 6/1896, March 11, 1924.
7. A further motivation for demobilization of the army is suggested by Darrell Figgis in the Dáil Debates, 3/1600, June 7, 1923. One condition of the Anglo-Irish Treaty was that the Free State army should not exceed a certain proportion of the total Irish population, thus requiring a substantial reduction in the size of the army following the end of the Civil War. Yet, when later charges were made that the demobilization scheme was British inspired, the government adamantly denied this. The veracity of this argument is largely irrelevant, for during the course of the mutiny, it was not a charge popularly leveled against the Government.
8. *The Irish Times*, March 8, 1924, p. 7.
9. Mulcahy Papers, University College Dublin (UCD), P7/B/188. In June 19, 1923, notes on demobilization plans, Mulcahy listed various ways of giving preference to ex-army men for employment: (1) arrangements to be made with government offices that all vacancies for temporary clerks, porters, and so on be filled by ex-army men; (2) preference in government contracts be given to employers who employ 10% ex-Army men; (3) encouragement of public bodies to hire 10 percent ex-army men and that 50 percent of all new employees under the proposed new Road scheme be ex-army men.
10. Kevin Nowlan, "Dáil Éireann and the Army: Unity and Division (1919–1921)," Desmond Williams, ed., *The Irish Struggle, 1916–1926* (London: Routledge & Kegan Paul, 1966), pp. 67–8; see also Lyons, *Famine*, p. 411.
11. Memo by Richard Mulcahy, Mulcahy Papers, UCD, P7/B/195, January 17, 1924.
12. Memo by Richard Mulcahy, Mulcahy Papers, UCD, P7/B/195, January 11, 1924.
13. "Interview with old IRA," Mulcahy Papers, UCD, P7/B/196, June 25, 1923.
14. Dáil Debates, 7/3123–24, June 26, 1924.
15. Dáil Debates, 7/3128, June 26, 1924.
16. Dáil Debates, 7/3126, June 26, 1924.
17. "Letter Received by the Minister for Defense," Mulcahy Papers, UCD, P7/B/195, January 19, 1924.
18. "Secret Report on IRA Organisation," Mulcahy Papers, UCD, P7/B/196, January 4, 1924.
19. "Secret Report on IRA Organisation," Mulcahy Papers, UCD, P7/B/196, January 4, 1924. For a chronicle of the events leading up to the army mutiny, see "Chairman's Reservation to Report of Army Inquiry Committee," Mulcahy Papers, UCD, P24/208E.
20. "Memos," Mulcahy Papers, UCD, P7/B/195, January 24, 1924.
21. *The Irish Times*, March 10, 1924, p. 5.
22. Dáil Debates, 6/2311, March 26, 1924.
23. *The Irish Times*, March 11, 1924, p. 5.
24. Dáil Debates, 6/1989, March 12, 1924.
25. Dáil Debates, 6/1896, March 12, 1924.
26. *The Irish Times*, March 12, 1924, p. 7.
27. Dáil Debates, 6/1982, March 12, 1924.
28. Dáil Debates, 6/1984–85, March 12, 1924.

29. Dáil Debates, 6/2213, March 19, 1924.
30. "Lessons of the Irish Crisis," *The Manchester Guardian*, March 14, 1924, in Mulcahy Papers, UCD, P7/B/196.
31. Dáil Debates, 6/2367, March 26, 1924.
32. Ibid.
33. *The Irish Times*, March 19, 1924, p. 5.
34. Dáil Debates, 7/3143–4, June 26, 1924.
35. Cited in *The Sunday Times* (London), March 23, 1924, in Mulcahy Papers, UCD, P7/B/196.
36. Ibid.
37. Dáil Debates, 6/2211, March 19, 1924.
38. Dáil Debates, 6/2243, March 20, 1924.
39. Dáil Debates, 6/2215, March 19, 1924.
40. Dáil Debates, 6/2217, March 19, 1924.
41. Saorstát Éireann, "Report of the Army Inquiry Committee," June 1924, paragraph 2.
42. Ibid., paragraph 15.
43. Ibid., paragraph 16.
44. Ibid., paragraph 24. See also "Chairman's Reservation to Report of Army Inquiry Committee," UCD, P24/208E, a document far more critical of Mulcahy and his policies.
45. *The Leader*, March 29, 1924, p. 177.
46. Dáil Debates, 6/2225, March 19, 1924.
47. Dáil Debates, 6/2225–6, March 19, 1924.
48. Dáil Debates, 7/3110, June 26, 1924.
49. In a report Mulcahy received on the IRA organization in January 1924, it was stated that "the IRA bunch are quite convinced also that it is now only a matter of time until the President will resign, and McGrath has so convinced them of the amount of support he is receiving from various members of the Government Party in the Dáil that his crowd are beginning to see visions of him as President in the near future." "Secret Report of the IRA Organisation," Mulcahy Papers, UCD, P7&B/196, January 4, 1924.
50. *The Irish Times*, March 24, 1924, p. 5.
51. Ibid.
52. Ibid.
53. See McGrath's statement and the debate on "no-victimisation," Dáil Debates, 6/2367–2433 passim, March 26, 1924.
54. *The Irish Times*, March 31, 1924, p.5.
55. Dáil Debates, 6/1988–89, March 12, 1924.
56. Dáil Debates, 6/2246, March 20, 1924.
57. Munger, *Legitimacy*, p. 32.
58. See Maurice Manning, *The Blueshirts* (Dublin: Gill & Macmillan, 1970). Interestingly, the Army Comrades Association was led, for most of its life, by General Eoin O'Duffy, inspector general and general officer of the armed forces during the army mutiny.
59. Dáil Debates, 6/1988, March 12, 1924.
60. *The Irish Times*, March 13, 1924, p. 6.

CHAPTER 5

1. *The Irish Times*, April 28, 1923, p. 7.
2. Ibid., p. 8.
3. Ronan Fanning, "Leadership and Transition from the Politics of Revolution

to the Politics of Party: The Example of Ireland 1914–1939," unpublished manuscript, p. 11.

4. *The Statesman*, December 6, 1924, p. 30.
5. Ibid.
6. *The Irish Times*, September 1, 1923, p. 7.
7. Dáil Debates, 4/36, September 20, 1923.
8. Arthur Mitchell, *Labour in Irish Politics, 1890–1930* (Dublin: Irish University Press, 1974), p. 192.
9. Basil Chubb, "Cabinet Government in Ireland," *Political Studies* 3 (1955):272.
10. *The Statesman*, December 6, 1924, p. 39.
11. Peter Pyne, "The Third Sinn Féin Party: 1923–1926," *Economic and Social Review* 1 (no. 2, January 1970):248.
12. *The Leader*, February 23, 1924, p. 54.
13. Article XII of the Articles of Agreement for a Treaty between Great Britain and Ireland, December 6, 1921; reprinted in *Report of the Irish Boundary Commission, 1925* (Shannon: Irish University Press, 1969), p. 3.
14. For primary accounts of the Treaty negotiations, see especially Thomas Jones, *Whitehall Diary*, Vol. III, 1918–1925, Keith Middlemass, ed. (London: Oxford University Press, 1971), pp. 155–64, 180–94, 220–46, and passim. For secondary treatments, see especially Frank Pakenham (Lord Longford), *Peace by Ordeal, The Negotiations of the Anglo-Irish Treaty, 1921* (London: Jonathan Cope, 1935); see also F. S. L. Lyons, *Ireland since the Famine* (London: Fontana, 1973), pp. 433–8.
15. Pakenham, *Peace*, pp. 187, 222, seq. pp. 262, 267–9.
16. Maureen Wall, "Partition: The Ulster Question (1916–1926)," Desmond Williams, ed., *The Irish Struggle, 1916–1926* (London: Routledge & Kegan Paul, 1966), p. 87.
17. Document Number 2, reprinted in Dorothy Macardle, *The Irish Republic* (London: Victor Gollancz, 1937), pp. 996–1000.
18. Cited in Wall, "Partition," p. 87.
19. "The engagements to which the Irish Signatories attach the greatest importance are those implicit in Article 12." Memorandum signed by Lionel Curtis on "Commitments of the late Government in respect of the Irish Treaty," November 12, 1922 (P.R.O. London, Cab. 27/157); cited in Geoffrey J. Hand, "MacNeill and the Boundary Commission," in F. X. Martin and F. J. Byrne, eds., *The Scholar Revolutionary: Eoin MacNeill, 1867–1945, and the Making of the New Ireland* (Shannon: Irish University Press, 1973), p. 202.
20. Local county governments in Northern Ireland tended to be dominated by Irish nationalists. Nationalists had had a majority on several local councils; proportional representation, as a voting system, strengthened nationalist influence in local Northern Irish politics. Patrick Buckland, *Irish Unionism: Ulster Unionism and the Origins of Northern Ireland, 1886–1922* (Dublin: Gill & Macmillan, 1973), p. 151.
21. Jones, *Diary*, p. 223 (June 26, 1923). It was, in fact, the formation of the Boundary Bureau that succeeded for a time in convincing the Irish press to cease its campaign against the government about the Boundary. Ibid.
22. *The Leader*, September 29, 1923.
23. For a summary of these statements, see North-Eastern Boundary Bureau, Index to Boundary Commission Dates and Conferences, May 1921 to December 1925, Dublin, State Paper Office, S1801P.
24. T. Jones, *Diary*, p. 224 (March 19, 1924).
25. Ibid., p. 228 (March 30, 1924).

26. Hand, "Boundary Commission," p. 204.
27. Ibid., p. 205.
28. Cited in W. Allison Phillips, *The Revolution in Ireland, 1906–1923*, 2nd ed. (London: Longmans, 1926), Appendix F, p. 326.
29. Dáil Debates, 8/2502, October 15, 1924.
30. Hand, "Boundary Commission," p. 222.
31. Ibid., p. 226; see also Jones, *Diary*, p. 223 (July 31, 1924).
32. *Irish Statesman*, September 13, 1924.
33. Dáil Debates, 8/2539, October 15, 1924.
34. Government leaders were concerned, even during the Civil War, about the persecution of Catholics in the North. There was also increasing agitation by the Northern nationalists after the Civil War in anticipation of reunification. See Jones, *Diary*, p. 220. These concerns were real, not merely symbolic, and motivated the new government to end partition. Although it is impossible to assign a relative valence to real as opposed to symbolic concerns, the former do not seem to have been as powerful in dictating political action as the latter.
35. Jones, *Diary*, pp. 239–40 (November 29, 1925). The Boundary Commission Report was not made public (until 1965), and for reasons that I will describe in this section, the award never was enacted. Had it been made, however, a summary of the transfers would have been as follows: To the Irish Free State, 183,290 acres and 31,319 persons, of whom 27,843 were Roman Catholics and 3,476 of other denominations. To Northern Ireland, 29,243 acres and 7,594 persons, of whom 2,764 were Roman Catholics and 4,830 of other denominations. *Boundary Commission Report*, p. 146.
36. *The Irish Times*, November 21, 1925, p. 7.
37. Dáil Debates, 13/623–4, November 19, 1925.
38. Interview in Limerick, *The Irish Times*, November 24, 1925, p. 8.
39. *The Irish Times*, November 23, 1925, pp. 5–6.
40. Dáil Debates, 13/802–4, November 24, 1925.
41. Jones, *Diary*, p. 241 (November 29, 1925).
42. *The Irish Times*, November 30, 1925, p. 5.
43. *The Irish Times*, December 3, 1925, p. 7.
44. Speech by de Valéra, *The Irish Times*, November 30, 1925, p. 6.
45. *The Irish Times*, December 1, 1925, p. 5.
46. Dáil Debates, 13/810, November 24, 1925.
47. Dáil Debates, 13/1171, 1185, December 2, 1925.
48. *The Irish Times*, December 2, 1925, p. 8.
49. *The Irish Times*, November 30, 1925, p. 5.
50. *The Irish Times*, December 5, 1925, p. 7.
51. Dáil Debates, 13/1157, December 7, 1925.
52. Dáil Debates, 13/1392, December 7, 1925.
53. *The Irish Times*, December 12, 1925, p. 7.
54. Dáil Debates, 13/1304–5, December 7, 1925.
55. Dáil Debates, 13/1355, December 7, 1925.
56. Dáil Debates, 13/1283–6, December 7, 1925.
57. Dáil Debates, 13/1475, December 8, 1925.
58. See Mitchell, *Labour*, p. 238.
59. *The Irish Times*, December 9, 1925, p. 8.
60. *The Irish Times*, December 14, 1925, p. 5.
61. Dáil Debates, 13/1389, December 7, 1925.
62. Dáil Debates, 13/1957–58, December 15, 1925.
63. *The Irish Times*, December 16, 1925, p. 7.

CHAPTER 6

1. Cited in Bowyer Bell, *The Secret Army* (London: Sphere Books, 1972), pp. 70–1.
2. Peadar O'Donnell, *There Will Be Another Day* (Dublin: Dolman Press, 1963).
3. Ibid., p. 19.
4. Cohan, *The Irish Political Elite* (Dublin: Gill & Macmillan, 1972); see also T. Garvin, "Political Cleavages, Party Politics and Urbanisation in Ireland: The Case of the Periphery-Dominated Centre," *European Journal of Political Research* 2 (1974):307–27; Garvin, "Center, Periphery and Fianna Fáil: A Rejoinder to Carty," unpublished manuscript.
5. "The Constructive Work of Dáil Eireann," No. 1 (Dublin: Dáil Eireann, 1920), p. 12. Art O'Connor was to become president of the Republic after Éamon de Valéra resigned the position, left Sinn Féin, and formed Fianna Fáil.
6. O'Donnell, *Another Day*, p. 35.
7. *The Irish Times*, March 10, 1926, p. 7.
8. F. S. L. Lyons, *Ireland since the Famine* (London: Fontana, 1973), p. 494.
9. *The Irish Times*, March 10, 1926, p. 7.
10. *The Irish Times*, March 12, 1926, p. 7.
11. *The Irish Times*, May 13, 1926, p. 7.
12. J. L. McCracken, *Representative Government in Ireland* (London: Oxford University Press, 1958), p. 104.
13. *The Round Table*, "Ireland: Events in the Free State," June 1926, p. 253.
14. Dáil Debates, 20/826–42, July 26, 1927.
15. *The Irish Times*, July 12, 1927, p. 7.
16. Cited in Pakenham and O'Neil, *Éamon de Valéra* (London: Hutchinson, 1970), p. 253.
17. *The Irish Times*, July 23, 1927, p. 8.
18. Dáil Debates, 20/1252, August 1, 1927.
19. Dáil Debates, 20/1362–3, August 3, 1927.
20. Dáil Debates, 20/959, July 27, 1927.
21. Dáil Debates, 20/973, July 27, 1927.
22. Dáil Debates, 20/1603, August 4, 1927.
23. Dáil Debates, 20/995, July 27, 1927.
24. Dáil Debates, 20/986, July 27, 1927.
25. Dáil Debates, 20/1004, July 27, 1927.
26. Dáil Debates, 20/1107, July 28, 1927.
27. Dáil Debates, 20/1053–4, July 28, 1927.
28. *The Irish Times*, August 11, 1927, p. 7.
29. D. O'Sullivan, *The Irish Free State and Its Senate* (London: Faber & Faber, 1940), p. 219.
30. *The Irish Times*, August 15, 1927, p. 7.
31. Dáil Debates, 22/1615–16, March 21, 1928.
32. Dáil Debates, 28/1398–1400, March 14, 1929.
33. Maurice Manning, *Irish Political Parties* (Dublin: Gill & Macmillan. 1972), p. 13.
34. Garvin, "Political Cleavages," 309.
35. Lyons, *Famine*, p. 496.
36. Dáil Debates, 24/704, June 15, 1928.
37. Dáil Debates, 24/934, June 28, 1928.
38. Dáil Debates, 24/1390, June 26, 1928.
39. Dáil Debates, 24/1758, June 28, 1928.

CHAPTER 7

1. For a discussion of the concept of inclusion applied in a different context, see T. Parsons, "Full Citizenship for the Negro American," *Daedalus* 94 (Fall 1965):1009–54.
2. T. Parsons, "Voting and the Equilibrium of the American Political System, in *Politics and Social Structure* (New York: Free Press, 1969).
3. T. Garvin, "Nationalist Elites, Irish Voters and Irish Political Development: A Comparative Perspective," *Economic and Social Review* 8 (April 1977):161.
4. Peadar O'Donnell, *There Will Be Another Day* (Dublin: Dolman Press, 1963).
5. For an account of this uneasy relationship of Fianna Fáil both to Republicans and to the Free State government, see Lyons, *Famine*, pp. 502–3.
6. Garvin, "Nationalist Elites," 169.
7. Ibid.
8. Ibid.
9. Ibid.
10. See W. Moss, *Political Parties in the Irish Free State* (New York: AMS Press, 1968), p. 19.
11. See Garvin, "Nationalist Elites," 170.
12. T. Garvin, "Continuity and Change in Irish Electoral Politics, 1923–1969," *Administration* 3(1971):357–72; B. Chubb, "Going About Persecuting Civil Servants: The Role of the Irish Parliamentary Representative," *Political Studies* 11 (no. 3) (October 1963):272–86.
13. Moss, *Political Parties*, p. 136.
14. T. Garvin, "Political Cleavages," Party Politics and Urbanisation in Ireland: The Case of the Periphery-Dominated Centre," *European Journal of Political Research* 2 (1974):309.
15. See Garvin, "Nationalist Elites," 178.
16. Ibid., 179.
17. E. Rumpf and A. C. Hepburn, *Nationalism and Socialism in Twentieth-Century Ireland* (Liverpool: Liverpool University Press, 1977), p. 81.
18. See Arthur Mitchell, *Labour in Irish Politics, 1890–1930* (Dublin: Irish University Press, 1974), pp. 192–216.
19. See Frank Munger, *Legitimacy of Opposition: The Change of Government in Ireland in 1932* (Beverley Hills, Calif.: Sage, 1975).
20. Garvin, "Theory, Culture and Fianna Fáil: A Review," in M. Kelly, L. O'Dowd, and J. Wickham, eds., *Power, Conflict, and Inequality* (Dublin: Turoe Press, 1982), p. 172.
21. Ibid., passim.
22. Garvin, "Nationalist Elites," p. 173.
23. Garvin, "Political Cleavages," p. 309.
24. Garvin, "The Destiny of Soldiers: Tradition and Modernity in the Politics of De Valéra's Ireland," *Political Studies* 26 (no. 3, 1978):333; also, Garvin, "Centre, Periphery and Fianna Fáil: A Rejoinder to Carty," unpublished manuscript.
25. Garvin, "Political Cleavages."
26. Garvin, in "Theory," makes this point as well. He argues that political culture has been mistakenly viewed "as part of the rational environment of politics." It is treated as "a true independent variable which causes but is not itself caused, which persists despite anyone's wish, and is 'natural' and independent of conscious human agency" (p. 177). Cultural analysis requires an examination of how it is embedded in various institutional practices.

27. Seán Lemass, "The Need of Sinn Féin: A Fighting Policy," *An Poblacht* (Dublin, 1926), cited in Bruce Logan, "Parliamentary Democracy in Ireland" (Ph.D. diss., University of Chicago, 1978), p. 448.
28. Sean Lemass, "The Will to Win," *An Poblacht*, cited in Logan, "Democracy," p. 448.
29. Peter Pyne, "The Third Sinn Féin Party: 1923–1926," *Economics and Social Review* 1 (no. 1, October 1969):47.
30. See William T. Cosgrave, *To the People of Ireland* (Dublin: Cumann na nGaedheal, 1923) and *Cumann na nGaedheal: To the Electors of North Dublin* (Dublin: Gaelic Press, 1923), cited in Logan, "Democracy," p. 375.
31. *The Irish Times*, May 23, 1927, p. 7.
32. William Cosgrave, "Policy of the Cumann na nGaedheal Party" (Dublin: National Library, 1927, Pamphlets Irish History I 94109 P11), pp. 15–16.
33. Moss, *Political Parties*, pp. 181–2.
34. *The Irish Times*, May 11, 1927, p. 7.
35. *The Irish Times*, August 28, 1927, p. 5.
36. "A New Alignment? Organisation Born of Activity," *An Poblacht* cited in Logan, "Democracy," p. 466.
37. Ibid.
38. Handbill, in O'Brien Paper, LOP111, item No. 19; cited in Logan, "Democracy," p. 468.
39. Published as "Fianna Fáil and its Economic Policy" (Dublin: Fianna Fáil, 1928), I94109 Pamphlet 1, Irish History, pp. 2–3.
40. See de Valéra, "Address to Ard-Feis, 14 November 1926," cited in Logan, "Democracy," p. 467.
41. See "Fianna Fáil and Its Economic Policy," p. 12.
42. Speech by de Valéra, *The Irish Times*, November 26, 1926, p. 5.
43. Moss, *Political Parties*, p. 184.
44. See Garvin, "Theory," for a comparison of this traditionalization of Irish politics with problems faced by other new nations; see also, more generally, Samuel Huntington, *Political Order in Changing Societies* (New Haven, Conn.: Yale University Press, 1968).
45. For expanded treatments of this, see, in particular, Clifford Geertz, "Ideology as a Cultural System," in *The Interpretation of Culture* (New York: Basic Books, 1973), and even more to the point his *Negara: The Theatre State in Nineteenth-Century Bali* (Princeton, N.J.: Princeton University Press, 1980).
46. Memorandum, n.d. in Mulcahy Papers, "Cumann na nGaedheal – 1924," Appendix 1, Cumann na nGaedheal, Annual Convention Report, 1926, p. 3; cited in Logan, "Democracy," p. 396. Note: Little research has been done on the political organization of the two contending parties of the 1920s. Moss, *Political Parties*, discussed this topic, but that work was originally published in 1933. The only recent research has been that of Logan, "Democracy." The following discussion relies especially on Logan's research; although individual citations will be provided, his important contribution to the subsequent discussion on political organization should be noted here.
47. Logan, "Democracy," p. 394.
48. Moss, *Political Parties*, pp. 80–1.
49. Logan, "Democracy," p. 458.
50. Ibid., p. 457.
51. Ibid., p. 456.
52. Ibid., p. 460.
53. Ibid.

CHAPTER 8

1. See, in particular, David Schmitt, *The Irony of Irish Democracy* (Lexington, Mass.: Lexington Books, 1973); Basil Chubb, *The Government and Politics of Ireland*, 2nd ed. (Stanford, Calif.: Stanford University Press, 1982); T. Garvin, "Theory, Culture and Fianna Fáil: A Review," in *Power, Conflict and Inequality* (Dublin: Turoe Press, 1982). R. Kenneth Carty, *Party and Parish Pump: Electoral Politics in Ireland* (Ontario: Wilfrid Laurier University Press, 1981); Mart Bax, *Harpstrings and Confessions: Machine-Style Politics in the Irish Republic* (Assem: Von Gorcum, 1976); Paul Sacks, *The Donegal Mafia: An Irish Political Machine* (New Haven, Conn.: Yale University Press, 1976). J. Raven and C. T. Whelan, "Irish Adults' Perceptions of Their Civic Institutions and Their Own Role in Relation to Them," in J. Raven et. al., eds., *Political Culture in Ireland: The Views of Two Generations* (Dublin: Institute of Public Administration, 1976).
2. Chubb, *Government and Politics*, p. 55.
3. Ibid., p. 20.
4. J. H. Whyte, "Ireland: Politics without Social Bases," in R. Rose, ed., *Electoral Behavior: A Comparative Handbook* (New York: Free Press, 1974).
5. Sacks, *Mafia*, p. 61.
6. Ibid., p. 184.
7. T. Garvin, "Continuity and Change in Irish Electoral Politics 1923–1969," *Administration* 3 (1971):361.
8. Carty, *Parish Pump*, p. 129.
9. Basil Chubb, "Going About Persecuting Civil Servants: The Role of the Irish Parliamentary Representatives," *Political Studies* 11 (October 1963):272–86.
10. Kenny, cited in Carty, *Parish Pump*, p. 142.
11. Sacks, *Mafia*, p. 61.
12. Carty, *Parish Pump*, p. 138; Bax, *Harpstrings*, p. 50.
13. Carty, *Parish Pump*, p. 140.
14. Cited in Sacks, *Mafia*, p. 4.

References

BOOKS AND ARTICLES

Akenson, D. W., and J. F. Fallin. "The Irish Civil War and the Drafting of the Free State Constitution," *Eire-Ireland* 5 (1, 2, and 4) (Spring, Summer, Winter 1970):10–26, 42–93, 28–70.

Alexander, Jeffrey C. "Core Solidarity, Ethnic Outgroup and Social Differentiation: A Multidimensional Model of Inclusion in Modern Societies," in Jacques Dofny, ed., *National and Ethnic Movements*, London: Sage Publications in World Sociology, 1980, pp. 3–26.

———.*Theoretical Logic in Sociology*, Vol. III, *The Classical Attempt at Synthesis: Max Weber*. Berkeley and Los Angeles: University of California Press, 1983.

Almond, Gabriel, and Sidney E. Verba. *The Civic Culture*. Princeton, N.J.: Princeton University Press, 1963.

Baker, Keith M. "Ideological Origins of the French Revolution," in D. LaCapra and S. C. Kaplan, eds., *Modern European Intellectual History: Reappraisal and New Perspectives*, Ithaca, N.Y.: Cornell University Press, pp. 197–219.

Bax, Mart. *Harpstrings and Confessions: Machine-Style Politics in the Irish Republic*. Assen: Van Gorcum, 1976.

Beames, M. R. "The Ribbon Societies: Lower-Class Nationalism in Pre-Famine Ireland." *Past and Present* 97 (November 1982):128–43.

Beetham, David. *Max Weber and the Theory of Modern Politics*. London: Allen & Unwin, 1974.

Bell, Bowyer. *The Secret Army*. London: Sphere Books, 1972.

Ben-David, and T. N. Clark, eds. *Culture and Its Creators*. Chicago: University of Chicago Press, 1977.

Bendix, Reinhard. "Tradition and Modernity Revisited" in *Nation Building and Citizenship*. Berkeley and Los Angeles: University of California Press, 1977, pp. 361–434.

———. *Nation-Building and Citizenship*. Berkeley and Los Angeles: University of California Press, 1977. Originally published in 1964.

———. *Kings or People? Power and the Mandate to Rule*. Berkeley and Los Angeles: University of California Press, 1980.

Berenson, Edward. *Populist Religion and Left-Wing Politics in France, 1830–1862*. Princeton, N.J.: Princeton University Press, 1984.

Bew, Paul. *Land and the National Question in Ireland 1858–1882*. Atlantic Highlands, N.J.: Humanities Press, 1979.

Binder, Leonard, J. Coleman, J. La Palombara, L. Pye, S. Verba, and M. Weiner. *Crises and Sequences in Political Development*. Princeton, N.J.: Princeton University Press, 1971.

References

Buckland, Patrick. *Irish Unionism: Ulster Unionism and the Origins of Northern Ireland, 1886–1922*. Dublin: Gill & Macmillan, 1973.

Calhoun, Craig. *The Question of Class Struggle*. Chicago: University of Chicago Press, 1982.

Cannadine, David. "Civic Ritual and the Colchester Oyster Feast," *Past and Present* 94 (February 1982):107–30.

Canny, Nicholas. "The Formation of the Irish Mind: Religion, Politics and Gaelic-Irish Literature 1580–1750," *Past and Present* 95 (May 1982):91–116.

Carty, R. Kenneth. *Party and Parish Pump: Electoral Politics in Ireland*. Ontario: Wilfrid Laurier University Press, 1981.

Chubb, Basil. "Cabinet Government in Ireland," *Political Studies* 3 (October 1955):256–74.

———. "Going About Persecuting Civil Servants: The Role of the Irish Parliamentary Representatives," *Political Studies* 11 (October 1963):272–86.

———. *The Government and Politics of Ireland*. London: Oxford University Press, 1970.

———. *The Government and Politics of Ireland*, 2nd ed. Stanford, Calif.: Stanford University Press, 1982.

Clark, Samuel. *Social Origins of the Irish Land War*. Princeton, N.J.: Princeton University Press, 1979.

Cohan, Al. *The Irish Political Elite*. Dublin: Gill & Macmillan, 1972.

Colomy, Paul. "Stunted Differentiation: A Sociological Examination of Virginia's Political Elite, 1720–1850." Ph.D. dissertation, UCLA, 1982.

Cosgrave, William T. "Cumann na nGaedheal: To the Electors of North Dublin." Dublin: Gaelic Press, 1923.

———. "To the People of Ireland." Dublin: Cumann na nGaedheal, 1923.

———. "Policy of the Cumann na nGaedheal Party." Dublin: National Library Pamphlets, 1927. Irish History I 94109 P11.

Cronin, Sean. *Irish Nationalism*. Dublin: Academy Press, 1981.

Curran, J. M. *The Birth of the Irish Free State, 1921–1923*. University, Ala.: University of Alabama Press, 1980.

Cutright, Phillip. "National Political Development," *American Sociological Review* 28 (1963):253–64.

———. "Political Structure, Economic Development and National Security Programs." *American Sociological Review* 30(1965):537–50.

Davis, Natalie Z. *Society and Culture in Early Modern France*. Stanford, Calif.: Stanford University Press, 1965.

De Valéra, Éamon, "Fianna Fáil and Its Economic Policy." Dublin: Fianna Fáil, 1928.

Dewey, James. *The Public and Its Problems*. Chicago: Henry Holt, 1927.

Dos Santos, T. "The Structure of Dependency," in K. T. Fann and Donald Hodges, eds., *Readings in United States Imperialism*. Boston: Porter Sargent Publishers, 1971, pp. 225–236.

Durkheim, Emile, *The Division of Labor in Society*. New York: Free Press, 1933.

———. *Suicide*. Glencoe, Ill.: Free Press, 1951.

———. *Professional Ethics and Civic Morals*. Glencoe, Ill.: Free Press, 1958.

———. "Individualism and the Intellectuals," in Robert N. Bellah, ed., *Emile Durkheim on Morality and Society*. Chicago: University of Chicago Press, 1973, pp. 43–60.

Dwyer, T. Ryle. *Éamon de Valéra*. Dublin: Gill & Macmillan, 1980.

Easton, David. *A Systems Analysis of Political Life*. Chicago: University of Chicago Press, 1979.

Eckstein, Harry. *Division and Cohesion in Democracy, A Study of Norway*. Princeton, N.J.: Princeton University Press, 1966.

References

———. "A Theory of Stable Democracy," in *Division and Cohesion in Democracy, A Study of Norway*. Princeton, N.J.: Princeton University Press, 1966, Appendix A.

———. "On the 'Science' of the State," *Daedalus* 108 (Fall 1979):1–20.

Eisenstadt, S. N. "Social Change, Differentiation and Evolution," *American Sociological Review* 29 (1964):378–86.

———. "Social Transformation in Modernization," *American Sociological Review* 30 (1965):659–73.

———. *Revolution and the Transformation of Societies*. Glencoe, Ill.: Free Press, 1978.

Fanning, Ronan. "Leadership and Transition from the Politics of Revolution to the Politics of Party: The Example of Ireland, 1914–1939." Paper presented at the XIVth International Congress of Historical Sciences, 1975.

———. *The Irish Department of Finance, 1922–1958*. Dublin: Institute of Public Administration, 1978.

Farrel, Brian. "The Paradox of Irish Politics," in Farrell, ed., *The Irish Parliamentary Tradition*. Dublin: Gill & Macmillan, 1973, pp. 13–25.

Foot, M. R. D. "Revolt, Rebellion, Revolution, Civil War: The Irish Experience," in Elliot Bateman, J. Ellis, and T. Bowden, eds., *Revolt to Revolution*. Manchester: Manchester University Press, 1974, pp. 161–85.

Frank, André Gunder. *Capitalism and Underdevelopment in Latin America*. New York: Monthly Review Press, 1967.

Friedrich, Carl. *Constitutional Government and Democracy: Theory and Practice in Europe and America*. Boston: Little, Brown, 1941.

———. *Transcendent Justice: The Religious Dimension of Constitutionalism*. Durham, N.C.: Duke University Press, 1964.

Garvin, Tom. "Continuity and Change in Irish Electoral Politics 1923–1969," *Administration* 3 (1971):359–72.

———. "Political Cleavages, Party Politics and Urbanisation in Ireland: The Case of the Periphery-Dominated Centre," *European Journal of Political Research* 2 (December 1974):307–27.

———. "Centre, Periphery and Fianna Fáil: A Rejoinder to Carty," unpublished manuscript.

———. "Nationalist Elites, Irish Voters and Irish Political Development: A Comparative Perspective," *Economic and Social Review* 8 (April 1977):161–84.

———. "The Destiny of the Soldiers: Tradition and Modernity in the Politics of De Valéra's Ireland," *Political Studies* 26 (August 1978):328–47.

———. *The Evolution of Irish Nationalist Politics*. New York: Holmes & Meier, 1981.

———. "Defenders, Ribbonmen and Others: Underground Political Networks in Pre-Famine Ireland," *Past and Present* 96 (August 1982):133–55.

———. "Theory, Culture and Fianna Fáil: A Review," in M. Kelly, L. O'Dowd, and J. Wickham, eds., *Power, Conflict and Inequality*. Dublin: Turoe Press, 1982, pp. 171–85.

Geertz, Clifford, "After the Revolution: The Fate of Nationalism in the New States," in *The Interpretation of Cultures*. New York: Basic Books, 1973, pp. 234–54.

———. "Ideology as a Cultural System," in *The Interpretation of Cultures*. New York: Basic Books, 1973, pp. 193–233.

———. "The Integrative Revolution: Primordial Sentiments and Civil Politics in the New States," in *The Interpretation of Cultures*. New York: Basic Books, 1973, pp. 255–310.

References

———. "The Politics of Meaning," in *The Interpretation of Cultures*. New York: Basic Books, 1973, pp. 311–326.

———. "Thick Description: Toward an Interpretive Theory of Culture," in *The Interpretation of Cultures*. New York: Basic Books, 1973, pp. 3–32.

———. *Negara: The Theatre State in Nineteenth Century Bali*. Princeton, N.J.: Princeton University Press, 1980.

Gold, David, Clarence Lo, and Erik Wright. "Recent Developments in Marxist Theories of the Capitalist State," *Monthly Review* 27 (October–November 1975):29–43, 36–51.

Habermas, Jürgen. *Legitimation Crisis*. Boston: Beacon Press, 1975.

Hancock, W. K. "Saorstát Éireann," in *Survey of British Commonwealth Affairs*, Vol. 1, *1918–1936*. London: Oxford University Press, 1937, pp. 92–165.

Hand, Geoffrey J. "MacNeil and the Boundary Commission," in F. X. Martin and F. J. Byrne, eds., *The Scholar Revolutionary: Eoin MacNeill, 1867–1945, and the Making of the New Ireland*. Shannon: Irish University Press, 1973, pp. 199–275.

Hechter, Michael. *Internal Colonialism: The Celtic Fringe in British National Development, 1536–1966*. Berkeley and Los Angeles: University of California Press, 1975.

Hirschman, Albert. *Exit, Voice and Loyalty*. Cambridge, Mass.: Harvard University Press, 1970.

Hunt, Lynn. *Politics, Culture and Class in the French Revolution*. Berkeley and Los Angeles: University of California Press, 1984.

Huntington, Samuel. *Political Order in Changing Societies*. New Haven, Conn.: Yale University Press, 1968.

Inkeles, Alex, and David H. Smith. *Becoming Modern: Individual Change in Six Developing Countries*. Cambridge, Mass.: Harvard University Press, 1974.

Jones, Thomas. *Whitehall Diary*, Vol. III, *1918–1925*, K. Middleman, ed. London: Oxford University Press, 1971.

Kennedy, Hugh. "Character and Sources of the Constitution of the Irish Free State," *American Bar Association Journal* 14 (August–September 1928):437–45.

Kilson, Martin, Jr. *Political Change in a West African State*. Cambridge, Mass.: Harvard University Press, 1966.

Kohn, Leo. *The Constitution of the Irish Free State*. London: Allen & Unwin, 1932.

Larkin, Emmet. "The Devotional Revolution in Ireland, 1850–1875," *American Historical Review* 77 (June 1972):625–52.

Lee, Joseph. *The Modernisation of Irish Society, 1848–1918*. Dublin: Gill & Macmillan, 1973.

Lemass, Seán. "The Need of Sinn Féin: A Fighting Policy," *An Poblacht* (Dublin): January 22, 1926.

———. "The Will to Win," *An Poblacht* (Dublin): February 5, 1926.

Lerner, Daniel. *The Passing of Traditional Society*. New York: Free Press, 1964.

Lerner, Max. "Constitution and Court as Symbols," *Yale Law Journal* 46 (June 1937):1290–1319.

Lipset, Seymour Martin. "Economic Development and Democracy," in *Political Man: The Social Bases of Politics*. New York: Anchor Books, 1963, pp. 45–76.

———. *The First New Nation*. New York: Basic Books, 1963.

———. "Social Conflict, Legitimacy and Democracy," in *Political Man: The Social Bases of Politics*. New York: Anchor Books, 1963, pp. 77–96.

Logan, Bruce. "Parliamentary Democracy in Ireland." Ph.D. dissertation, University of Chicago, 1978.

Lyons, F. S. L. *Ireland Since the Famine*. London: Fontana, 1972.

References

———. *Culture and Anarchy in Ireland, 1890–1939*. London: Oxford University Press, 1979.

Macardle, Dorothy. *The Irish Republic*. London: Victor Gollancz, 1937.

McCartney, Donal. "The Churches and Secret Societies," in T. D. Williams, ed., *Secret Societies in Ireland*. Dublin: Gill & Macmillan, 1973, pp. 68–78.

McCracken, J. L. *Representative Government in Ireland*. London: Oxford University Press, 1958.

———. "The United Irishmen," in T. D. Williams, ed., *Secret Societies in Ireland*. Dublin: Gill & Macmillan, 1973, pp. 58–67.

McDaniel, Tim. "Class and Dependency in Latin America," *Berkeley Journal of Sociology* 21 (1976–7):51–88.

McNeill, William H. *The Metamorphosis of Greece Since World War II*. Chicago: University of Chicago Press, 1978.

Manning, Maurice. *The Blueshirts*. Dublin: Gill & Macmillan, 1970.

———. *Irish Political Parties*. Dublin: Gill & Macmillan, 1972.

Mansergh, Nicholas. *The Irish Question, 1840–1921*. Toronto: University of Toronto Press, 1975.

Marshall, T. H. *Class, Citizenship and Social Development*. Chicago: University of Chicago Press, 1977.

Meenan, James. *The Irish Economy Since 1922*. Liverpool: Liverpool University Press, 1970.

Miliband, Ralph. *The State in Capitalist Society*. New York: Basic Books, 1969.

Mitchell, Arthur. *Labour in Irish Politics, 1890–1930*. Dublin: Irish University Press, 1974.

Moore, Barrington, Jr. *Social Origins of Dictatorship and Democracy*. Boston: Beacon Press, 1966.

Moss, Warner. *Political Parties in the Irish Free State*. New York: AMS Press, 1968. Originally published, New York: Columbia University Press, 1933.

Munger, Frank. *Legitimacy of Opposition: The Change of Government in Ireland in 1932*. Beverly Hills, Calif.: Sage, 1975.

Norman, E. R. *The Catholic Church and Ireland in the Age of Rebellion, 1859–1873*. London: Longmans, 1965.

Nowlan, Kevin. "Dáil Éireann and the Army: Unity and Division (1919–1921)," in Desmond Williams, ed., *The Irish Struggle, 1916–1926*. London: Routledge & Kegan Paul, 1966, pp. 67–78.

O'Broin, Leon. *Michael Collins*. Dublin: Gill & Macmillan, 1980.

O'Connor, James. *The Fiscal Crisis of the State*. New York: St. Martin's Press, 1973.

O'Donnell, Peadar. *There Will Be Another Day*. Dublin: Dolman Press, 1963.

Offe, Claus. "The Abolition of Market Control and the Problem of Legitimacy," *Kapitalistate* 1 (1973):109–16.

Orridge, A. "Explanations of Irish Nationalism: A Review and Some Suggestions," *Journal of the Conflict Research Society* 1 (1972):29–57.

O'Sullivan, D. *The Irish Free State and Its Senate*. London: Faber & Faber, 1940.

Pakenham, Frank (Earl of Longford). *Peace by Ordeal*. London: Jonathan Cape, 1935.

Pakenham, Frank (Earl of Longford), and T. P. O'Neil, *Éamon De Valéra*. London: Hutchinson, 1970.

Park, Robert. *The Crowd and the Public*. Chicago: University of Chicago Press, 1972.

Parkin, Frank. *Class Inequality and Political Order*. London: Holt, Rinehart and Winston, 1971.

References

Parsons, Talcott. "Durkheim's Contribution to the Theory of Integration of Social Systems," in Kurt H. Wolff, ed., *Essays in Sociology and Philosophy*. New York: Harper & Row, 1964, pp. 118–53.

———. "Full Citizenship for the Negro American," *Daedalus* 94 (Fall 1965):1009–54.

———. "Voting and the Equilibrium of the American Political System," in *Politics and Social Structure*. New York: Free Press, 1969, pp. 204–40.

———. *The System of Modern Societies*. Englewood Cliffs, N.J.: Prentice-Hall, 1971.

Pennock, J. Roland. *Democratic Political Theory*. Princeton, N.J.: Princeton University Press, 1979.

Phillips, W. Allison. *The Revolution in Ireland, 1906–1923*, 2nd ed. London: Longmans, 1926.

Plumb, J. H. *The Origins of Political Stability in England, 1675–1725*. Boston: Houghton Mifflin, 1967.

Plunkett, Horace. *Ireland in the New Century*. London: J. Murray, 1904.

Poggi, Gianfranco. *The Development of the Modern State*. Stanford, Calif.: Stanford University Press, 1978.

Pole, J. R. *The Pursuit of Equality in American History*. Berkeley and Los Angeles: University of California Press, 1978.

Poulantzas, Nicos. *Political Power and Social Classes*. London: New Left Books, 1973.

Prager, Jeffrey. "Democratic Stability in Ireland: Strategies of Crisis Resolution in the Irish Free State, 1922–1932." Ph.D. dissertation, University of California, Berkeley, 1978.

———. "Moral Integration and Political Inclusion: A Comparison of Durkheim's and Weber's Theories of Democracy," *Social Forces* 59 (June 1981):918–50.

———. "Totalitarian and Liberal Democracy: Two Types of Modern Political Orders," in J. Alexander, ed., *Neo-Functionalism*, Beverly Hills, Calif.: Sage, 1985.

Pye, Lucian. "Introduction: Political Culture and Political Development," in L. Pye and S. Verba, eds., *Political Culture and Political Development*. Princeton, N.J.: Princeton University Press, 1965, pp. 1–26.

Pyne, Peter. "The Third Sinn Féin Party: I. Narrative Account," *Economic and Social Review* 1 (October 1969):29–50.

———. "The Third Sinn Féin Party: 1923–1926," *Economic and Social Review* 1 (January 1970):229–58.

Quijano, Anibal. *Nationalism and Capitalism in Peru*. New York: Monthly Review Press, 1971.

Raven, John, and C. T. Whelan. "Irish Adults' Perceptions of Their Civic Institutions and Their Own Role in Relation to Them," in J. Raven et. al., eds., *Political Culture in Ireland: The Views of Two Generations*. Dublin: Institute of Public Administration, 1976.

Reddy, William. "The Batterers and the Informer's Eye: A Labor Dispute under the French Second Empire," *History Workshop* 7 (Spring 1979):30–44.

Rose, Richard. "England: The Traditionally Modern Political Culture," in L. Pye and S. Verba, eds., *Political Culture and Political Development*. Princeton, N.J.: Princeton University Press, 1965, pp. 83–129.

Rostow, Walt W. *The Stages of Economic Growth*. Cambridge: Cambridge University Press, 1961.

Rumpf, E., and A. C. Hepburn. *Nationalism and Socialism in Twentieth-Century Ireland*. Liverpool: Liverpool University Press, 1977.

Russell, George William. "On behalf of some Irishmen not Followers of Tradition," in *Collected Poems by A. E.* London: Macmillan, 1928.

251

References

Sacks, Paul M. *The Donegal Mafia: An Irish Political Machine*. New Haven, Conn.: Yale University Press, 1976.

Schmitt, David. *The Irony of Irish Democracy*. Lexington, Mass: Lexington Books, 1973.

Sewell, William H., Jr. *Work and Revolution in France: The Language of Labor from the Old Regime to 1848*. Cambridge: Cambridge University Press, 1980.

Shils, Edward. "Political Development in the New States," *Comparative Studies in Society and History* 2(3, 1960):265–92; 2(4, 1960):379–411.

———. "On the Comparative Study of New States," in Clifford Geertz, ed., *Old Societies, New States*. Glencoe, Ill.: Free Press, 1963, pp. 1–26.

———. *Tradition*. Chicago: University of Chicago Press, 1981.

Skocpol, Theda. *States and Social Revolution*. Cambridge: Cambridge University Press, 1979.

Smelser, Neil J. *Theory of Collective Behavior*. New York: Free Press, 1962.

———. "Toward a Theory of Modernization," in *Essays in Sociological Explanation*. Englewood Cliffs, N.J.: Prentice-Hall, 1968, pp. 125–46.

Solow, Barbara. "A New Look at the Irish Land Question?" *The Economic and Social Review* 12 (July 1981):301–14.

Tackett, Timothy. "The West in France in 1789: No Religious Factor in the Origins of the Counter-Revolution," *Journal of Modern History* 54 (December 1982): 715–45.

Turner, Ralph H., and Lewis M. Killian. *Collective Behavior*, 2nd ed. Englewood Cliffs, N.J.: Prentice-Hall, 1972.

Verba, Sidney. "Conclusion: Comparative Political Culture," in L. Pye and S. Verba, eds., *Political Culture and Political Development*. Princeton, N.J.: Princeton University Press, 1965, pp. 512–60.

———. "Germany: The Remaking of Political Culture," in L. Pye and S. Verba, eds., *Political Culture and Political Development*. Princeton, N.J.: Princeton University Press, 1965, pp. 130–70.

Wall, Maureen. "Partition: The Ulster Question (1916–1926)," in Desmond Williams, ed., *The Irish Struggle, 1916–1926*. London: Routledge & Kegan Paul, 1966, pp. 79–94.

Wallerstein, Immanuel. *The Modern World System*. New York: Academic Press, 1974.

Walzer, Michael. *The Revolution of the Saints*. Cambridge, Mass.: Harvard University Press, 1965.

Weber, Max. " 'Objectivity' in Social Science and Social Policy," in E. Shils and Henry Finch, trans. and eds., *The Methodology of the Social Sciences*. New York: Free Press, 1949, pp. 49–112.

———. *The City*. New York: Free Press, 1958.

Weiner, Martin. "Political Integration and Political Development," *Annals of the American Academy of Political and Social Sciences* 358 (March 1965): 52–64.

Whyte, J. H. *Church and State in Modern Ireland 1923–1970*. Dublin: Gill & Macmillan, 1971.

———. "Ireland: Politics without Social Bases," in R. Rose, ed. *Electoral Behavior: A Comparative Handbook*. New York: Free Press, 1974, pp. 619–51.

Wolf, Eric. *Europe and the People without History*. Berkeley and Los Angeles: University of California Press, 1982.

Wiener, Martin J. *English Culture and the Decline of the Industrial Spirit 1850–1980*. Cambridge: Cambridge University Press, 1981.

Williams, T. D. "The Irish Republican Brotherhood," in Williams, ed., *Secret Societies in Ireland*. Dublin: Gill & Macmillan, 1973, pp. 138–49.

Younger, Carlton. *Ireland's Civil War*. London: Frederick Muller, 1968.

References

OFFICIAL RECORDS

Cabinet Papers, 1922–8
Dáil Éireann Files, State Paper Office, Dublin Castle, Dublin.

PRIVATE PAPERS

Ernest Blythe Papers, University College Archives, Dublin
Richard Mulcahy Papers, University College Archives, Dublin

OFFICIAL PUBLICATIONS

The Constructive Work of Dáil Éireann, Dáil Éireann. Dublin, 1920.
(Official Record) Minutes of Proceedings of the First Parliament of the Republic
    of Ireland, 1919–21. Dublin: Stationery Office.
(Official Report) Dáil Éireann: August 1921 and February–June 1922. Dublin:
    Stationery Office.
Private Sessions of [the] Second Dáil, 1921–2 (August–September 1921 and De-
    cember 1921–January 1922). Dublin: Stationery Office.
(Official Report) Debate on the Treaty between Great Britain and Ireland, De-
    cember 1921–January 1922). Dublin: Stationery Office.
The Census of Ireland, 1926. Dublin: Stationery Office.
Report of the Irish Boundary Commission, 1925. Shannon: Irish University Press,
    1969.

NEWSPAPER AND PERIODICALS

The Irish Times (Dublin), 1921–32
The Leader (Dublin), 1921–9
The Manchester Guardian (Manchester), 1922–32
The Round Table (London), 1922–32
The Statesman (Dublin), 1922–29
The Sunday Times (London), 1922–32

Index

Akenson, D. H., 73, 82, 85–86
Almond, Gabriel, 19
Anglicanism, 43–44
Anglo-Irish Treaty, 16, 27–30, 50, 75, 87–
    88, 103, 124, 140–41, 143, 145–46, 162;
    and anti-Treatyites, 29–30, 51, 53, 82,
    86, 103, 134, 139, 142–43; Article V of,
    152; Article XII of, 141–45, 147–48, 151;
    Articles of Agreement, 27–28, 88; and
    Confirmation of Amending Agreement
    Bill, 151–52, 154; and Document No. 2,
    63, 142; and moral conflict, 51, 53, 75;
    and opposition from the West, 34–35;
    and pro-Treatyites, 29, 51, 53–54, 75,
    103, 134. See also Great Britain
Anglo-Irish War, 14
army, 54, 57, 61, 63, 97, 100–4, 106, 111,
    115, 117, 119, 127, 129; and civilian con-
    trol, 54, 63, 102, 107, 111, 126; and de-
    mobilization, 97, 101–2, 104, 106–7, 127,
    238; and relationship to Free State gov-
    ernment, 101–3, 105–7, 111–12, 117,
    126–27, 129
Army Comrades Association, 127, 239
Army Council, 103, 106–7, 117–20, 126–27
Army Inquiry Committee, 121, 123, 126,
    128
army mutiny (1924), 97, 100–1, 106–31,
    135, 149, 237–38; and dismissal of Army
    Council, 107, 119, 123, 125; and govern-
    ment's response, 107–30; and "Old
    IRA," 103–7, 114, 124–25
authoritarianism, 217–20, 223
authority, political, 23, 38, 41, 53, 68, 76,
    79, 98, 109–10, 126, 128–29

Baker, Keith Michael, 23–24
Baxter, Patrick F., 174
Beaslái, Piérás, 29
Black and Tan campaign, 34, 56
Blue Shirts, 218
Blythe, Ernest, 133
Boland, Harry, 60

Boundary Commission, 132, 141–50, 152–
    53, 157–58, 161, 241; and East Donegal,
    147; and Monoghan County Council,
    147. See also Northern Ireland, and
    partition
British Commonwealth of Nations, 27–28,
    63, 88
Brugha, Cathal, 49, 52, 55–58, 60
Byrne, J. J., 172

Carty, R. K., 221–23
Catholic Church (in Ireland), 42–43, 65,
    192, 217, 235–36; as anti-Anglican, 43–
    45; and devotional revolution, 42; and
    disestablishment of Church of Ireland,
    43–44; and education, 43–44; and land
    reform, 43; traditionalism of, 42–43
Catholicism, 194–205
Catholics, 38, 40–42, 55, 65, 142–44, 191,
    241
Chubb, Basil, 217–18, 221–22
Churchill, Winston, 59
Church of Ireland, 43
Citizen's Army, 102
citizenship, 23, 41, 69, 84
civic culture, 20, 23, 25
Civil Service Regulation Act (1923), see
    Government of Irish Free State
Civil War, 14–17, 26–27, 30–31, 50, 54, 64,
    96, 101, 126, 131–32, 134, 167, 188, 190–
    91, 198; casualties, 96; and weak public,
    26, 30, 58, 185
Clann Éireann, 165
Collins, Michael, 58–64, 71–73, 75–76, 78,
    83–87, 96, 100, 103, 142, 192, 237
Collins-de Valéra Pact, 62–63, 73, 86, 236
Comhairle na Poblachta (Central Council
    of the Republic), 188–89
Constitution (Amendment No. 17) Bill
    (1931), see Government of Irish Free
    State
constitutionalism, 68–71, 80, 132

Index

Constitution Bill (1927), *see* Government of Irish Free State

Constitution Drafting Committee, 71–73, 75–78, 80, 87; and Document No. 39, 77–79, 81, 83

Constitution of Ireland Bill (1922), *see* Government of Irish Free State

Constitution of Irish Free State, 66–67, 71–77, 83, 87, 89–90, 97, 109, 123, 140, 156, 168–72; and analysis of preamble, 73–75, 78–79; and initiative, 84–85, 169, 171, 180; and referendum, 84–85, 156–57, 168–69, 171, 180–81

Cooper, Major Bryan, 151

Cosgrave, William, 96–97, 99–101, 108–16, 121, 126, 128–30, 133, 143–53, 156–57, 160, 166, 169, 171, 173–74, 176, 178–79, 181, 187, 192, 217

Council of Ireland, 152, 154

Craig, Sir James, 144

cultural analysis: in study of new nations, 10, 19, 67; interconnectedness of culture and politics in, 218–25, 228, 230

cultural orientations: achieved status of, 23; antinomies in, 15–16, 20, 26, 63–64, 67, 73–76, 91, 114; and cosmopolitan-provincial split, 190–95, 219; distinguished from ideology, 25; relationship to institutional structures, 5–6, 19, 24, 26, 35, 64, 66, 91, 95, 198; relationship to political elites, 26, 95; synthesis of antinomies in, 26, 37, 58, 74–75, 197–98, 208, 214, 217–19. *See also* Gaelic-Romantic tradition; Irish-Enlightenment tradition

Cumann na nGaedheal, 12, 116, 122, 124–25, 133–40, 149–50, 154–56, 158–59, 161, 165–67, 169, 173–75, 178–81, 185, 189–90, 192–95, 197, 199–212, 215–16, 220; and constituency, 192; objectives of, 133; and power politics, 135, 137, 139–40, 168–70; and tension between state power and symbolic issues, 132, 136, 139, 155, 158

Dáil Éireann (Republican, 1919–1921), 48–49, 52, 54, 84, 162; and Democratic Program, 49, 84

Dáil Éireann (Free State Parliament, 1922–1937), 28–29, 53, 56, 82, 96, 108–10, 120–23, 128–29, 147, 150–1, 154, 156, 169, 175–77, 221; and allegiance to British Crown, 28, 30, 82, 139, 154, 168–69, 171, 175–76; and army mutiny, 109–113, 120–23, 126, 128

Dalton, Colonel Charles, 100–1, 110–11, 114–15

Davis, Thomas, 39

Defense Forces Act (1923), *see* Government of Irish Free State

democracy, 67, 71, 215–16, 223–25

Democratic Program (1919), *see* Dáil Éireann (Republican, 1919–1921)

democratic stability, 11–13, 15–16, 26, 91, 98–99, 157, 173, 195, 209, 214, 225, 229–30

de Valéra, Éamon, 47–49, 52, 58–59, 61–64, 71–72, 85–86, 96, 142, 150, 156, 163–66, 174, 177–80, 187, 195, 197, 199, 201, 204–6, 213, 218

Document No. 2, *see* Anglo-Irish Treaty

Document No. 39, *see* Constitution Drafting Committee

Douglas, James, 78

Durkheim, Emile, 6–8, 226; political sociology of, 7–8

Easter Rising, 29, 48

Easton, David, 11

ecological analysis, 17, 230–31

egalitarianism, 38, 45–46, 77, 212–13, 217–18

Electoral Amendment Bill (1927), *see* Government of Irish Free State

elites, political: elite-mass differences, 190–91; and relationship to the people, 81, 190–91; role in forging solidary nation, 10, 24, 31, 64, 71, 81, 132, 191–92

Etchingham, Seán, 55, 60

extern ministers, 82–83, 86

Fallin, J. F., 73, 82, 85–86

Fanning, Ronan, 15, 134

farmers, 191–92, 207

Feetham, Richard, 146

Fenian rising, 47

Fianna Fáil (Soldiers of Destiny), 12, 95, 164–67, 173–81, 185–87, 189, 192, 195–201, 203–13, 215–16, 218–24; ambivalent relationship to Dáil, 175–78, 189, 216; entry into Dáil, 175–79; and inclusion of peripheral sectors into Irish politics, 197–200, 204, 208–9, 213, 215

Figgis, Darrell, 72–73, 75, 78

Fine Gael, 213, 224. *See also* Cumann na nGaedheal

Fischer, Joseph, 146

Fitzgerald, Desmond, 181

Flinn, Hugo, 180

Four Courts (Dublin), 61

Friedrich, Carl, 68, 70

Gaelic-Romantic tradition, 16–18, 31, 33, 36–37, 42–44, 46–48, 50–52, 55–56, 63–64, 73–80, 82–83, 128, 162, 192, 194, 196–99, 205, 208–9, 212, 215, 218–19, 221, 233; and Catholic Church, 42–44,

47, 56, 77; and decentralized political authority, 77, 79; and the family, 32, 42, 207; peasant in, 43, 45, 55; and Republicanism, 44–46; and traditionalism, 42–44; and violence, 45–47. *See also* cultural orientations, antinomies in

Garda Siorchanna (Civic Guard), 99, 108, 163, 171

Garvin, Tom, 31, 37, 39, 188, 190, 192, 195–96

Geertz, Clifford, 5, 20, 25

General Army Convention, 161–64

George, Lloyd, 37, 59, 86, 145

Government of Ireland Act (Partition) (1920), *see* Great Britain

Government of Irish Free State: administrative and political leadership, 98–99; and Civil Service Regulation Act (1923), 99; and compromise pattern of crisis resolution, 112–20, 124–29, 149–52, 154, 156–57; and Constitution (Amendment No. 17) Bill (1931), 179; and Constitution Bill (1927–8), 168–69, 171–74, 180; and Constitution of Ireland Bill (1920), 90; and Defense Forces Act (1923), 108, 118; and Electoral Amendment Bill (1927), 168, 172–73, 175; and Executive Council, 107–9, 112–16, 118–19, 121–23, 125, 128, 148, 169, 171–72, 179–80; and Intoxicating Liquor Act (1927), 179; and Juries Protection Act (1929), 189; and party rule, 129–30; and Public Safety Bill (1923), 98; and Public Safety Bill (1924), 98; and Public Safety Bill (1926), 163; and Public Safety Bill (1927), 168, 173, 176; and removal of initiative and referendum, 168, 171–72; and Treaty (Confirmation of Amending Agreement) Bill (1925), 154, 156–57. *See also* Irish Free State (Saorstát Éireann)

Great Britain, 10, 27–29, 47, 81, 83, 140–41, 143, 145–46, 150–52, 154, 161–62, 204–5, 215; Constitution of, 83; and Government of Ireland Act (Partition) (1920), 140; House of Commons, 29; House of Lords, 81; and Irish Draft Constitution, 86–87; and Judicial Committee of the Privy Council, 146; and monarchy, 87, 89, 91; and parliamentary system, 83, 85

Griffith, Arthur, 39, 49, 52–54, 57–58, 72–73, 85, 87, 96

Hand, Geoffrey, 145

Hechter, Michael, 33–34

Hepburn, A. C., 34–35

Hewart, Sir Gordon, 87

Hirschman, Albert, 69

Hogan, Patrick K., 172

ideal type, 35–37, 217, 220

inclusion, political, 186–87, 191, 197–200, 204, 208–9, 213, 215

individualism, 41, 53, 127–29

initiative, *see* Constitution of Irish Free State

intelligentsia, 39–40

interpretation: of meaning of political action, 21–22, 35, 37, 68, 74–75

Intoxicating Liquor Act (1927), *see* Government of Irish Free State

Ireland: and devotional revolution, 33, 42; and the economy, 96, 102–3; and emigration, 32; and ethnic homogeneity, 65; and famine of 1848, 32; and literacy, 32; and modernization, 31–32, 39; and parliamentary tradition, 15, 40–42, 52–55; and physical force tradition, 14–15, 46–50, 57; and population decline, 32; and religious homogeneity, 65; and revival of Irish language and literature, 39; socio-geographical correlates of political action, 34; and traditions of violence and parliamentarianism, 14–16

Irish-Enlightenment tradition, 16–17, 31, 33, 36–37, 39, 48–54, 57, 61–62, 72–79, 128, 192, 194, 196–99, 201–3, 207–10, 216, 218–19, 233; and centralized state, 76–77; and cosmopolitanism, 37, 192, 194; and democratic individualism, 41, 53, 128; and independence, 37–38, 40, 44, 48, 61; and Ireland as a moral community, 41; and nonsectarianism, 38, 41; and parliamentarianism, 38, 40–41, 48; and Protestant ascendancy, 38. *See also* cultural orientations, antinomies in

Irish Free State (Saorstát Éireann): Anglo-Irish elite in, 39, 42; and anti-British rule, 40–41, 65; and centralization of authority, 109–10, 126, 128–30, 135–38, 140; and cultural antinomies, 16–17, 21–22, 30, 47, 51, 63–64, 67, 73–79, 91, 169; and democratic stability, 11–12, 15–16, 26, 91, 98–99, 157, 173, 195, 209, 214, 225; and dominion status, 27–29, 40, 87–88; and independence from Great Britain, 16–17, 28–29, 33, 37, 40, 49, 52–53, 141–43; and newly-independent nations, 13, 65; voting patterns in, 22, 136, 190, 196

Irish Press, 179

Irish Republican Army (IRA), 34–35, 52, 55–58, 96, 102–3, 105, 161–63, 166, 168, 187–90, 194, 216–17

Irish Republican Army Organization in Free State Army, *see* Army mutiny, and "Old IRA"

Irish Republican Brotherhood (IRB), 44, 48, 50, 59–60, 102–3, 105–6, 112, 114,

Index

Irish Republican Brotherhood (IRB) (*cont.*)
120–21, 192, 208; and Free State Army,
102–3, 105–6, 112, 114, 120–21
Irish Times, 108, 129, 149, 153, 170
Irish Volunteers, 102
Irish White Cross, 72

Johnson, Thomas, 109, 126, 128, 136, 148,
151, 154–55, 170
Jones, Thomas, 144
Juries Protections Act (1929), *see* Government of Irish Free State

Kohn, Leo, 28, 89

Labour Party, 126, 136–37, 144, 148, 154–
56, 161, 170, 174, 192–95, 207; and constituency, 193
land reform, 43, 45
land tenure, 43
Larkin, Emmet, 42
Leader, 122, 139
Lemass, Seán, 177, 200
Lerner, Max, 70
Logan, Bruce, 211, 213
Lynch, Liam, 57
Lyons, F. S. L., 31, 37, 48, 99, 164, 179

McCullough, Denis, 147–48
McGilligan, Patrick, 151
McGrath, Joseph, 106–8, 110–22, 124–26,
165
MacNeill, Eoin, 144, 146, 148–49
MacSwiney, Mary, 56, 60
Magennis, William, 153, 156, 165
Manchester Guardian, 113
Mansergh, Nicholas, 45–46
mass media, 20–22
Mitchell, Arthur, 136–37
modernization theory, 3–4, 9
Morning Post, 147, 157
Morrissey, Daniel, 153
Moss, Warner, 210
Mulcahy, General Richard, 97, 99, 102–8,
111–26, 149, 170
Munger, Frank, 127
Murnaghan, James, 236

National Defense Association, 127
nationalism, Irish, 12, 14, 16–17, 29, 34–
35, 37–38, 75, 104, 136, 140–41, 143, 201,
204–5, 208
national identity, 11, 69
National Party, 124–25, 165
norms, 13, 16, 31, 38, 40–41, 45, 51–52,
55, 58, 64, 68, 80, 97, 131–32, 229, 232–
33
North-Eastern Boundary Bureau, 144
Northern Ireland, 11, 28, 132, 139–41, 143,

147, 151–52, 154, 161; and partition,
140–45, 154

O'Brien, Conor Cruise, 224
O'Connel, T. J., 146
O'Connor, Art, 162
O'Donnell, Peadar, 54, 161–63, 188
O'Duffy, General Eoin, 108–9, 117–18
O'Higgins, Kevin, 90, 97, 99, 111–12, 118–
20, 122, 149, 151, 153, 160, 166–67, 171–
72, 175, 179
O'Rahilly, Alfred, 236
O'Sullivan, Donal, 177
O'Sullivan, John M., 170–71

parliamentarianism, 54–55, 63, 161, 163,
165, 197
Parsons, Talcott, 10, 186
partition, 140–45, 154
party system, 97, 132, 135, 219, 223
patronage system, 222
Pearse, Padraig, 49
peasants, 32, 45; and land annuity agitation, 162, 191, 207, 216. *See also* Gaelic-Romantic tradition, peasant in
personalism, 217, 220–24
Plunkett, Horace, 65
political culture, 8–10, 19–20, 22, 24
population census, 32
primordialism, 5, 42, 44, 76, 79
Protestants, 38, 41, 77, 136, 141, 193
Provisional Government, 30, 37, 52–55,
58, 67, 71, 77, 126
public, 20–24, 30, 66, 76, 98, 121–22, 130,
157, 171, 185–89, 195, 197–98, 200, 208–
9, 213, 218, 220, 231–32; as central feature of modern solidary community, 22,
24, 76; and changing political vocabulary, 24, 198; and civil society, 26; and
constraints on extremist politics, 186,
188; and emergent order of meanings,
22–23; its expansion in Ireland, 208–9,
215–16; and Irish Civil War, 26, 30–31;
in Irish politics, 21–22, 109, 130, 185–89,
195, 197–98, 200, 208–9, 213, 218, 220;
and political elites, 24–25; and popular
legitimacy, 22–26; and relationship to
state, 26
Public Safety Bill (1923), *see* Government
of Irish Free State
Public Safety Bill (1924), *see* Government
of Irish Free State
Public Safety Bill (1926), *see* Government
of Irish Free State
Public Safety Bill (1927), *see* Government
of Irish Free State
Pyne, Peter, 138

Index

Redmond, Captain William (Willie) Archer, 172
Referendum, *see* Constitution of Irish Free State
Republican Dáil, *see* Dáil Éireann (Republican 1919–1921)
Republican idealism, 54–56, 59, 200
Republicanism, 44–46, 48, 57, 90, 139–40, 164–67, 197; and Catholicism, 45, 56; and violence, 46, 47, 49, 57
Republicans, 61, 63, 65, 71, 89, 96, 98, 113, 125, 135, 139, 144, 150, 154–56, 161, 163–67, 170, 174, 176, 178, 188–93, 201
Ribbonism, 39
Round Table, 166
Rumpf, E., 34–35

Sacks, Paul, 219, 221–22
Saor Eire, 163
Seanad (Senate), 81, 84
secret societies, 38, 46, 49, 121. *See also* Irish Republican Brotherhood; United Irishmen
Shils, Edward, 6
Sinn Féin, 35, 47–49, 73, 86, 96, 134–40, 155, 161–64, 166, 168, 176, 187–88, 190–91, 194, 200–1, 204; and constituency, 191; and opposition to Cumann na nGaedheal, 137–39
Sinn Féin Ard Feis, 62, 73, 164
Sinn Féin Constitution (1917), 47, 52
social solidarity, 4–8, 15
Solow, Barbara, 43
Statesman, 137
structural analysis, 3–4, 33–34. *See also* ecological analysis
symbols, 31, 52, 57–58, 66, 68–70, 87, 89, 129–30, 132, 136, 139–44, 149, 155, 167,

194; of law and order, 167; monarchical, 87, 89–91; national, 69

Third World, 12, 220, 230
Thrift, William E., 152
Tobin, Major-General Liam, 100–1, 108, 110–11, 114–15
Tone, Wolfe, 38–39, 47, 84, 189
traditionalism, 6
Treaty (Confirmation of Amending Agreement) Bill (1925), *see* Government of Irish Free State

Ulster, 11, 142
Ulster Special Constabulary, 61
Unionists, 77, 192, 207; Northern, 144, 146; Southern, 83, 85, 87
United Irishmen, 38
universalism, 5, 17, 19, 31, 77

value conflicts, 131, 134. *See also* cultural orientations, antinomies in
values, 16, 26, 30–31, 38–41, 44–45, 47, 51–52, 55, 58, 64, 68–69, 80, 97, 131–32, 229
Verba, Sidney, 8, 19
verstehen, 36
violence, 46–47, 50, 160, 188–89, 193
voter turnout, 136, 196

Wall, Maureen, 142
Weber, Max, 35–37
Whyte, John, 14
Wilson, Sir Henry, 61
world systems analysis, 8

Yeats, W. B., 37, 39
Younger, Carlton, 63
Young Ireland Movement, 39